S0-AGY-616

DISCARDED

CAMBRIDGE STUDIES IN EARLY MODERN HISTORY

Editors

J. H. ELLIOTT   OLWEN HUFTON
H. G. KOENIGSBERGER

Richelieu and Olivares

CAMBRIDGE STUDIES IN EARLY
MODERN HISTORY

*Edited by Professor J. H. Elliott, The Institute for Advanced Study, Princeton, Professor
Olwen Hufton, University of Reading and Professor H. G. Koenigsberger, King's College,
London*

The idea of an 'early modern' period of European history from the fifteenth to the late
eighteenth century is now widely accepted among historians. The purpose of the
Cambridge Studies in Early Modern History is to publish monographs and studies which
will illuminate the character of the period as a whole, and in particular focus attention on a
dominant theme within it, the interplay of continuity and change as they are represented
by the continuity of medieval ideas, political and social organization, and by the impact of
new ideas, new methods and new demands on the traditional structures.

Richelieu
and
Olivares

J. H. ELLIOTT

The Institute for Advanced Study, Princeton

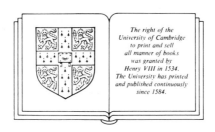

The right of the
University of Cambridge
to print and sell
all manner of books
was granted by
Henry VIII in 1534.
The University has printed
and published continuously
since 1584.

CAMBRIDGE UNIVERSITY PRESS

Cambridge

London   New York   New Rochelle

Melbourne   Sydney

Published by the Press Syndicate of the University of Cambridge
The Pitt Building, Trumpington Street, Cambridge CB2 IRP
32 East 57th Street, New York, NY 10022, USA
296 Beaconsfield Parade, Middle Park, Melbourne 3206, Australia

© Cambridge University Press 1984

First published 1984

Printed in Great Britain at the University Press, Cambridge

Library of Congress catalogue card number: 83-20929

British Library Cataloguing in Publication Data
Elliott, J.H.
Richelieu and Olivares.—(Cambridge Studies in
early modern history)
1. Richelieu Armand du Plessis, *duc de*
2. Olivares, Gaspar de Guzmán, *conde.-duque de*
I. Title
944'.032'0924   DC123.9.RS

ISBN 0 521 26205 4 hard covers
ISBN 0 521 27857 0 paperback

SE

ECC/USF Learning Resources
8099 College Parkway, S.W.
Fort Myers, Florida 33907-5164

Contents

Illustrations

Acknowledgements

My principal debt is to the Electors to the George Macaulay Trevelyan Lectureship for the invitation which encouraged me to attempt this essay in comparative history. It was a special pleasure to be invited to give these lectures, established in honour of a man who gave me much kindness during my years at Trinity College and whom I recall with admiration and gratitude. In preparing the lectures and subsequently revising them for publication, I drew on the advice and expertise of many friends. Richard Bonney, Marc Fumaroli and Orest Ranum all read the lectures before delivery, and gave an errant hispanist the benefit of their knowledge of seventeenth-century France. If the final text fails to incorporate some of their valuable suggestions, this is because the view from south of the Pyrenees occasionally offers an alternative perspective. I am also grateful for advice on French matters to Ralph Giesey and Russell Major, and to René and Suzanne Pillorget, splendid travelling companions on a memorable tour of Richelieu's native Poitou. Once again the perceptive comments of my colleague Felix Gilbert helped me to improve the text at several points, and I am grateful, too, to Helmut Koenigsberger and to Richard Ollard for their encouragement and help. Peggy Van Sant again typed and retyped my drafts with characteristic patience and skill. Finally my thanks go to William Davies of the Cambridge University Press for his wise advice and support, and to Elizabeth O'Beirne-Ranelagh for the tact and efficiency with which she edited the typescript.

Princeton
1 June 1983

Abbreviations

Archives and libraries

AAE	Archives des Affaires Etrangères, Paris
ADM	Archivo del Duque de Medinaceli, Seville
AGR	Archives Générales du Royaume, Brussels
AGS	Archivo General de Simancas
AHN	Archivo Histórico Nacional, Madrid
ASF	Archivio di Stato, Florence
ASV	Archivio di Stato, Venice
AV	Archivio Segreto Vaticano
BAV	Biblioteca Apostolica Vaticana
BL	British Library, London
BNM	Biblioteca Nacional, Madrid
BNP	Bibliothèque Nationale, Paris
PRO	Public Record Office, London
RAH	Real Academia de la Historia, Madrid

Other abbreviations

Avenel	*Lettres, instructions diplomatiques et papiers d'état du Cardinal de Richelieu*, ed. D.L.M. Avenel, 8 vols. (Paris, 1853–77).
Grillon	*Les Papiers de Richelieu. Section politique intérieure. Correspondance politique et papiers d'état*, ed. Pierre Grillon (Paris, 1975–).
MC	John H. Elliott and José F. de la Peña, *Memoriales y Cartas del Conde Duque de Olivares*, 2 vols. (Madrid, 1978–80).
TP	Richelieu, *Testament Politique*, ed. Louis André (Paris, 1947).

Introduction

It is perhaps not inappropriate that a book which started life as a series of lectures in commemoration of George Macaulay Trevelyan, the historian of Garibaldi, should begin by recalling an episode from that great nineteenth-century Italian historical novel, Manzoni's *The Betrothed*. The date is 1628, the year of the outbreak of the war of the Mantuan Succession; the place, the castle of the local baron, Don Rodrigo, near Lecco on the shores of Lake Como. The mayor is sitting at table with Don Rodrigo and his cousin and partner in crime, Count Attilio, and the company is discussing the international situation. The mayor, claiming inside knowledge, brushes aside the possibility of a compromise between France and Spain over Mantua, and is soon in full flood, expatiating with more enthusiasm than expertise on the political skills of the principal minister of the King of Spain, the Count–Duke of Olivares. The Count–Duke, he says, has eyes for everything. 'I'm sorry for the Cardinal [Richelieu] ... wanting to try his strength against a man like Count–Duke Olivares. I'd like to come back in two hundred years time and see what posterity says about his presumptuous ideas . . . The Count–Duke, gentlemen, is an old fox . . . who can shake anybody off his trail'; the mayor would have gone on for ever in this vein if Don Rodrigo had not had a sudden burst of inspiration. 'My dear mayor and gentlemen all. Pray silence for a toast to the Count–Duke – and you shall tell me whether the wine is worthy of the man.'[1]

Manzoni's recourse to historical irony is no doubt a shade too facile. Unlike the mayor in 1628, he and his readers knew the end of the story; and for the nineteenth century, as for the twentieth, what was Olivares in comparison with Richelieu? In all probability, little more than a name, or at best a collage of images preserved for posterity by the genius of

[1] Alessandro Manzoni, *The Betrothed*, ch. 5, trans. Bruce Penman (Harmondsworth, 1972), p. 104.

I

Velázquez: a corpulent form, a glowering face, swirling mustachios, an imperiously pointing baton. But if Manzoni allowed himself the licence of the novelist, his historical instinct, as so often, was sound, as the juxtaposition of his fictionalized conversation of 1628 with an authentic text of 1635 makes clear. In that year, Mathieu de Morgues, a former collaborator of Richelieu and now a bitter opponent, published another in his series of vitriolic anti-Richelieu tracts. In it he accused Richelieu's paid hacks of pandering to his hatred of Olivares. 'It is true that the Cardinal prides himself on appearing a clever man; but the outcome will show who managed better the welfare and reputation of his prince, and less jeopardized his own.'[2] The outcome did indeed show just this, although not quite in the way that Morgues had anticipated.

To the men of the 1620s and 1630s the rivalry of Richelieu and Olivares personified that of France and the House of Austria, and any reverse suffered by one side or the other was liable to be represented as a failure of statesmanship.[3] The Count–Duke's fall in January 1643, a few weeks after the death of Richelieu, gave his enemies in Madrid an opportunity to compare the records of the two ministers. Richelieu, they alleged, came to power in a France torn with schism and ravaged by rebellion, and at his death left it pacified and the arbiter of Europe. Olivares, on the other hand, had inherited a powerful and peaceful Spain, and had left it in a deplorable state with not an inch of territory won.[4]

Olivares, disgraced and banished from Madrid, produced a vigorous tract in his own defence, entitled the *Nicandro*,[5] but the world has remained unimpressed by his arguments. In historiography, as in life, winners tend to take all. As a loser, the Count–Duke was condemned first to obloquy and then to virtual oblivion. In 1717 a French writer, Guillaume de Valdory, published a two-volume work, *Anecdotes du ministère du Cardinal de Richelieu*, compiled from the famous *Mercurio* of Vittorio Siri. He followed this five years later with *Anecdotes du ministère du Comte Duc d'Olivarés*, and used its preface to attempt an itemized comparison of the two ministers.

The Count–Duke of Olivares, loved by his king, dies in disgrace. Cardinal Richelieu maintains his authority to the day of his death . . . The Count–Duke is

[2] Mathieu de Morgues, 'Jugement sur . . . les diverses pièces', *Recueil de pièces pour la defense de la Reyne Mère* (Antwerp, 1643), p. 33.
[3] ASF, Mediceo, filza 4963, despatch from Bernardo Monanni, 14 Nov. 1637, reporting criticisms of Olivares.
[4] Andrés de Mena, 'Cargos contra el Conde Duque', in *MC*, II, doc. XXa, p. 243.
[5] *MC*, II, doc. XXb.

no sooner disgraced than he is abhorred, and everything done during his ministry is changed. Cardinal Richelieu, although dead, succeeds in perpetuating his maxims ... The Spaniards scorn and condemn in the disgraced Count–Duke what they had praised and approved while he was in favour. The French praise and approve in Cardinal Richelieu, after he is dead, what they had failed to approve while he was alive. Finally, the Spaniards look on the ministry of the Count–Duke as the fatal moment when their Monarchy began to fall into decline; and the French look on that of Cardinal Richelieu as the happy moment when theirs began to rise to the great power which it has subsequently attained.[6]

Valdory's pithy verdicts have in general been allowed to stand. Although Olivares was too substantial a figure ever to be entirely forgotten, even a rapid glance at the literature devoted to the two ministers over the past two hundred years is enough to establish the high price of failure. The nineteenth-century statesman, Cánovas del Castillo, paid Olivares sympathetic attention,[7] but most Spanish historians have treated him as little more than a national disaster, worthy at best of summary dismissal. He has so far been the subject of only one biography – that published in 1936 by the noted Spanish physician, Gregorio Marañón, who was more concerned with his personality than his policies.[8]

Richelieu, on the other hand, has received extensive biographical treatment, which includes the six volumes of Hanotaux and La Force[9] and the three of Carl Burckhardt, visibly influenced by the events of the Second World War and its aftermath.[10] Similarly, there are valuable monographs on the Cardinal's ideas and policies, and on the institutions through which he governed France.[11] For Olivares and his Spain there is nothing comparable; and there is a similar disparity in the publication of contemporary documents. Richelieu's papers and correspondence – well

---

[6] *Anecdotes du ministère du comte duc d'Olivarés, tirées et traduites de l'Italien de Mercurio Siry, par Monsieur de Valdory* (Paris, 1722), preface (no page numbers).

[7] Especially in his *Estudios del reinado de Felipe IV*, 2 vols. (Madrid, 1888).

[8] *El Conde–Duque de Olivares. La pasión de mandar* (Madrid, 1936; 3rd, revised, edn, 1952). I hope to complete soon a study of Olivares' political career.

[9] Gabriel Hanotaux and Duc de La Force, *Histoire du Cardinal de Richelieu*, 6 vols. (Paris, 1893–1947).

[10] Carl J. Burckhardt, *Richelieu*, 4 vols. (Munich, 1933–67); Eng. trans., *Richelieu and his Age*, 3 vols. (London, 1940–71).

[11] For the Cardinal's ideas, see especially Henri Hauser, *La Pensée et l'action économiques du Cardinal de Richelieu* (Paris, 1944); Etienne Thuau, *Raison d'état et pensée politique à l'époque de Richelieu* (Paris, 1966); William F. Church, *Richelieu and Reason of State* (Princeton, 1972); Jörg Wollenberg, *Richelieu* (Bielefeld, 1977). For government and institutions, Roland Mousnier, *Les Institutions de la France sous la monarchie absolue*, I (Paris, 1974); Orest Ranum, *Richelieu and the Councillors of Louis XIII* (Oxford, 1963); Richard Bonney, *Political Change in France under Richelieu and Mazarin, 1624–1661* (Oxford, 1978).

over 3,000 pieces – were published by Avenel in eight massive volumes between 1853 and 1877,[12] and five volumes have so far appeared of a new edition of his domestic letters and papers.[13] Against this, it is only recently that a selection of Olivares' major state papers has finally found its way into print.[14]

Chance has played its part in this disparity of treatment. In the survival of documentation, as in so much else, Richelieu proved luckier than his rival. Both ministers characteristically insisted that the royal archives should house all papers dealing with affairs of state; but, no less characteristically, both of them sought to ensure that their own papers should remain in the hands of their families. The Richelieu papers eventually entered the royal archives in 1705, by which time many had been dispersed or lost; and in the nineteenth century they were subjected to the kind of rational reorganization which is the delight of archivists and the bane of historians.[15] But at least the Cardinal's papers survive in large quantities. The same cannot be said of those of the Count–Duke. The Olivares archive, along with that of his nephew and successor, Don Luis de Haro, seems largely to have been destroyed by fire in the Duke of Alba's Madrid palace in 1795 and 1796. While Spain's great national archive at Simancas contains a substantial body of conciliar documentation of the Olivares years, and letters from the Count–Duke continue to turn up in public and private archives inside and outside the Iberian peninsula, the surviving material is heavily weighted towards foreign, as distinct from domestic, policy, and much of it is fragmentary.[16]

The historian of Richelieu is fortunate, too, in being able to supplement his state papers and correspondence with a large body of additional material. Even if the Cardinal's memoirs[17] and his *Testament Politique*[18] were in large part the work of others, they can safely be taken as an expression of his own ideas and of the self-image which he wished to transmit to posterity. The Count–Duke's apologia, by contrast, is limited

---

[12] *Lettres, instructions diplomatiques et papiers d'état du Cardinal de Richelieu*, 8 vols. (Paris, 1853–77).
[13] *Les Papiers de Richelieu. Section politique intérieure. Correspondance politique et papiers d'état*, ed. Pierre Grillon, (Paris, 1975–).
[14] John H. Elliott and José F. de la Peña, *Memoriales y Cartas del Conde Duque de Olivares*, 2 vols. (Madrid, 1978–80).
[15] See Fritz Dickmann, 'Rechtsgedanke und Machtpolitik bei Richelieu', *Historische Zeitschrift*, 196 (1963), p. 267.
[16] For the history of Olivares' papers, see *MC*, 1, pp. xxvi–xxxi.
[17] *Mémoires du Cardinal de Richelieu*, ed. Société de l'Histoire de France, 10 vols. (Paris, 1907–31).
[18] Ed. Louis André (Paris, 1947).

to the *Nicandro*, an important but brief *pièce d'occasion*.[19] Richelieu was
also the author, as Olivares was not, of a number of published works.
Besides his religious writings, he also provided, if not the text, at least the
somewhat faltering inspiration for three plays written for performance at
the Palais Cardinal.[20]

The relative quantity and accessibility of Richelieu material in
comparison with that of Olivares goes some way towards explaining their
contrasting historiographical fortunes. Yet enough Olivares material has
survived to make possible the kind of decoding of ideas and intentions
that has been practised for Richelieu, even if the results are likely to be
more fragmentary and less finely drawn. The fact that this has not until
now been attempted is to be ascribed less to problems of documentation
than to the preferences and priorities of generations of historians,
Spanish and non-Spanish, who have chosen to devote their energies to
achievement rather than failure, to periods of greatness rather than
periods of decline. While this predilection is perfectly understandable, a
survey of the standard histories of the Europe of the Thirty Years' War
would suggest that the relative allocation of space to the France of
Richelieu and to the Spain of Olivares has seriously distorted contemporary realities. It is unlikely that we shall get the full measure of this
period until we pay as much attention to Spain as to France, and can
think ourselves back into the frame of mind of Manzoni's mayor of
Lecco, to whom it never occurred that Olivares would not win.

For too long those two great rivals of early seventeenth-century
Europe, France and Spain, have been treated as isolated and stereotyped
entities, one destined for greatness, the other for decline. The stereotypes
are tending to dissolve in the light of recent research: Spain turns out to
have possessed unexpected reserves of strength, and France to have been
afflicted by weaknesses which in certain circumstances might well have
proved disastrous. In this sense, the two countries are beginning to look
rather less different than they looked a generation ago. The time has
therefore come to place them in closer juxtaposition, to look at some of
their characteristics – those which they shared and those in which they

[19] For the text of the *Nicandro*, and a short introduction on the circumstances of its appearance, see
MC, II, doc. XX.
[20] For Richelieu as a writer, see Maximin Deloche, *Autour de la plume du Cardinal de Richelieu* (Paris,
1920). For his efforts as a dramatist, Léopold Lacour, *Richelieu dramaturge et ses collaborateurs*
(Paris, 1925).

differed – and follow their fortunes in tandem during those two critical decades, the 1620s and 1630s, which were to redraw the map of Europe.

In the present state of our knowledge, this can most effectively be done through a close comparison of the two ministers who sought to shape their destinies. Even Richelieu, a figure studied almost to excess, may begin to look a little different if we study him alongside Olivares, who, for contemporaries, as for posterity, was something of a puzzle. 'His name', wrote the French poet Vincent Voiture, who met him in Madrid in 1632, 'is known to all Europe, but his person to very few.'[21] Over the best part of two decades Richelieu and Olivares – the Cardinal–Duke and the Count–Duke – devoted themselves body and soul to the service of their monarchs. They shared many of the same problems; they came up with many of the same answers; and in the end they reached the conclusion that the world was too small to contain them both. In following their contrasting fortunes, we can hope to get to know them both a little better, and perhaps in the process enlarge our understanding of seventeenth-century statecraft and the seventeenth-century state.

In undertaking this attempt at comparative history, I should make clear that I hold no special brief for the defence of Olivares, whose record of defeat is plain for all to read. My only anxiety is to ensure that he should be given equal time. I am aware, too, that comparative history is a branch of historical writing more eulogized than practised, for reasons which will be painfully obvious to anyone who has made the attempt. It has recently been remarked that 'comparative history does not really exist yet as an established field within history or even as a well-defined method of studying history'.[22] I must confess to having failed to evolve a method. The technical difficulties are considerable, and not least among them is the problem of keeping two outsize personalities within a single field of vision. I have dealt with this as best I can, but I am afraid that this book is bound to have something of the character of a historiographical Wimbledon, as it switches from Richelieu to Olivares, and then back again to Richelieu. I can only hope that this will not leave the reader with a permanent crick in the neck. If, as is not improbable, a comparative historical approach is always likely to promise more than it can deliver, this is not to my mind an adequate reason for forgoing the attempt. At the

---

[21] *Les Oeuvres de M. de Voiture* (Paris, 1691), II, p. 254.
[22] George M. Frederickson, 'Comparative History', in *The Past Before Us*, ed. Michael Kammen (Ithaca–London, 1980), p. 459.

very least it may provide a new perspective on familiar figures and events. I should like to think, too, that it confirms the validity of a characteristically lapidary judgement delivered by G.M. Trevelyan in a footnote to his *Clio, A Muse*: 'The lives of rival statesmen . . . are often the quickest route to the several points of view that composed the life of an epoch.'[23] These words may serve as a text for this book.

[23] (London, 1913), p. 50, n. 1.

Statesmen and rivals

Those two great antagonists, Richelieu and Olivares, were almost exact contemporaries. There was a mere two years' difference between them – Richelieu was born in 1585, Olivares in 1587 – and they lived to almost the same age: Richelieu died at fifty-seven, Olivares at fifty-eight. They were both third sons of noble fathers employed in the royal service, a social category which contained far too many superfluous members on both sides of the Pyrenees. The Counts of Olivares, as members of the Andalusian titled aristocracy, no doubt had the social edge over the du Plessis, country gentry from Poitou, but both families nurtured a deep sense of grievance, born of the disparity between their actual standing and that to which they thought themselves entitled.[1]

The Counts of Olivares, members of a junior branch of the ducal family of Medina Sidonia, believed that they had been cheated out of the ducal title and estates. In compensation, they sought to establish their own branch of the family as rivals to the Dukes of Medina Sidonia by systematically pursuing careers in the royal service. Olivares' grand-father, the first count, married the daughter of Lope Conchillos, secretary to Ferdinand the Catholic and the Emperor Charles V. The modest family origins of the grandmother, and her notorious Jewish ancestry, would return to haunt the grandson. Olivares' father, the second count, made his name as a worthy sparring partner of the irascible Pope Sixtus V during his period as Spanish ambassador in Rome; and it was in Rome that Olivares himself was born in 1587. Subsequently his father served as viceroy of Sicily and Naples, before returning in 1600 to Madrid, where he was placed in charge of the crown's finances and given a seat on the supreme governing council of the Spanish Monarchy, the Council of State. In spite of these achievements he died in 1607 a disappointed man,

---

[1] For the family background and early years of the two men, see especially Henri Carré, *La Jeunesse et la marche au pouvoir de Richelieu, 1585–1624* (Paris, 1944), and Marañón, *Olivares*.

having failed to realize his supreme ambition of becoming a grandee.

The cadet branch of the du Plessis family, to which Richelieu belonged, also used marriages and court connections to advance its position in the world, although it did this with less apparent system, and certainly less success, than the Counts of Olivares. But Richelieu's father, a morose figure, was appointed Grand Provost of France by Henry III, and was one of his most trusted confidants. In spite of Henry's assassination, François du Plessis might well have succeeded in establishing the family fortunes if he had not died a year later, in 1590, at the age of only thirty-one. As it was, he left large debts, neglected estates, and a remarkable wife, Suzanne de La Porte, the daughter of a lawyer and granddaughter of an apothecary – origins as modest as those of Olivares' grandmother.

The awareness of a certain social inferiority in the recent family line is likely to have sharpened the almost obsessive preoccupation with the gradations of rank displayed by both Richelieu and Olivares, and to have reinforced their determination to make the world accept their own high estimate of the status of their families. But Richelieu suffered from the additional disadvantage of poverty. Olivares was brought up as befitted the son – even the younger son – of a viceroy; Richelieu was one of the five children of a widow living in acutely straitened circumstances, and when he wrote, as he did in the *Testament Politique*, of the necessities to which the provincial nobility of France were reduced, he wrote from the heart.[2]

As younger sons, both Gaspar de Guzmán and Armand du Plessis would in any event have had to make their own way in life, even if with the assistance of relatives at court. Ironically, the first was intended for an ecclesiastical, and the second for a lay, career, but in the event it was Olivares who remained the layman and Richelieu who took orders. Family requirements in both instances forced a change of plan. The Count of Olivares sent his son to Salamanca University in 1601 to study canon and civil law in preparation for a career in the church. Given his family connections he would probably in due course have become a cardinal, and the rivalry of the two great Catholic powers of Europe might have been personified in two princes of the church, Cardinals Guzmán and Richelieu. But the accidental death of his surviving elder brother left him as future head of the family and made it essential that he

---

[2] *TP*, part 1, ch. 3.

should marry and perpetuate the line. Leaving the university, where he had been elected rector by his fellow students, he joined his father at court, and succeeded him in 1607 as third Count of Olivares. He married a cousin who bore him three children, of whom only one, a daughter, María, survived infancy to become heiress presumptive to the title and estates.

Armand du Plessis' early training went in exactly the opposite direction. From the Collège de Navarre in Paris, to which he was sent at the age of nine, he moved on to Pluvinel's famous academy to be trained in the martial and courtly arts. It was the sudden decision of his brother, Alphonse, to become a Carthusian monk instead of accepting nomination to the family bishopric of Luçon which persuaded him and his family that he should abandon his plans for a military career and take orders instead. ' I will accept', he said, ' for the good of the church and the glory of our name.'[3] He returned to the Collège de Navarre to study theology and philosophy, which he did with an assiduity that Olivares had not displayed at Salamanca. In 1606, through the influence of his elder brother at court, he was duly nominated Bishop of Luçon, but, being still under the canonical age, had to go to Rome to seek a dispensation. Here, not yet twenty-three years old, he was ordained after making a considerable personal impact on Paul V, and was consecrated a bishop the same day. He was accepted as a Fellow of the Sorbonne, passed his examinations with brilliant success, and in December 1608 made his formal entry into his diocese – the first time in thirty years that it had set eyes on its bishop.

During his years in the poverty-stricken diocese of Luçon, from 1608 to 1616, Richelieu gained first-hand experience at local level of the two great problems afflicting France at the national level – the weakness of royal authority and the semi-autonomy of the Huguenots. Poitou, with its long seaboard, had been a rich province in the early sixteenth century, but had been badly hit by the Wars of Religion. Disorder was endemic, and Richelieu's own family was no stranger to the local feuds that had torn Poitou apart. On the orders of the Cardinal's grandmother his father had assassinated the local seigneur who killed his brother in front of the village church at Braye. The province was also bitterly divided by religious animosities. The Huguenots were a powerful minority in

---

[3] Carré, *La Jeunesse*, p. 19.

Poitou, and well enough entrenched in their eleven *places de sûreté* to cherish hopes of building a state within the state when the authority of the crown collapsed following the assassination of Henry IV in 1610.[4]

As an administrator and a cleric Richelieu moulded himself to the image of the Counter-Reformation bishop. He came into close contact with leading personalities in the Catholic reform movement, for whom Poitiers was an important centre; he published a manual for confessors; and he set out to reform his troubled diocese. He also developed during these years a highly effective style of pulpit oratory. As one of the promising young clerics singled out for special attention by that influential figure, Cardinal du Perron, he was chosen to speak for the clerical estate at the meeting of the Estates General at Poitiers in 1614, and made an eloquent plea for prayer, example and persuasion as the only proper weapons to be used against the Huguenots. Even if he was speaking on this occasion for his order rather than for himself, it would be surprising if this plea for toleration did not reflect a personal conviction born of the experience of running a diocese with a large Huguenot minority.[5]

While Richelieu was administering his Poitevin diocese, Olivares was back in Seville, attempting to set his house in order after running up enormous debts at court. Although born in Rome he was a son of Andalusia, just as Richelieu, although born in Paris, was very much a son of Poitou. Andalusia, whose fortunes for the past century had been tied to the New World of America, was still basking in the rather febrile prosperity brought by the riches of the Indies; but in the very years when Olivares was living the life of a munificent noble in that most opulent of cities, Seville, the American trade on which its prosperity depended was beginning to falter. The problems of Seville were those of shrinking resources and declining prosperity – the very problems which, on a national scale, would dominate Olivares' ministerial career when he moved to Madrid.

Unlike Richelieu, however, Olivares does not seem to have gained any serious administrative experience during those years of provincial life. He had inherited from his father the post of governor of the royal palace in Seville, but the duties were largely honorific. But he may be said to have completed in Seville the education which he had neglected in

---

[4] For Poitou in the age of Richelieu, see P. Boissonnade, *Histoire de Poitou* (Paris, 1915), chs. 8 and 9.
[5] Cf. Deloche, *Autour de la plume*, p. 97.

Salamanca. Early seventeenth-century Seville was a city which prided itself on its literary and artistic life, and Olivares became the companion and patron of poets and men of letters. He also at this time laid the foundations of what was to become one of the most splendid private libraries in all of seventeenth-century Europe.

Richelieu and Olivares were not the kind of men to be content with the constraints of provincial life. Each had his eyes firmly fixed on the court. But while awaiting their chance, they were both carefully building up a local power-base and forming a network of clients and agents for future use. The effects were to be seen when they came to power. Richelieu would be surrounded in Paris by Poitevins or men whose acquaintance he had made in Poitou: the Bouthilliers; Father Joseph; Théophraste Renaudot, the future founder of the *Gazette*; mariners like Razilly, who would advise him on naval and colonial affairs; and Poitevin relatives like the La Portes, who would be appointed to high military and administrative office.[6] The Poitevin connection in the Paris of Richelieu would be parallelled by the Andalusian connection in the Madrid of Olivares – in the first place his relatives, like the Haros and Don Diego Mexía, but also court and government officials, like Juan de Fonseca and Francisco de Calatayud, and that most illustrious of all Sevillians, the future court painter, Diego Velázquez.

Oddly enough it was the same event – the Franco-Spanish marriage alliance of 1615 – that gave each man his opportunity. Olivares' Seville years came to an end in 1614 when he was appointed to a court post as gentleman of the chamber to the heir to the throne, Prince Philip, who acquired a household of his own in anticipation of his marriage to Elizabeth, the sister of Louis XIII.[7] Louis himself was to marry Philip's sister, Anne, and the French court stopped at Poitiers on its journey to the frontier for the exchange of brides. Here the Bishop of Luçon met the Regent, Marie de Médicis, who needed an almoner, and their meeting produced the desired result. Once attached to the Queen Regent's household Richelieu slipped into the role of adviser, and a year later, in November 1616, her advocacy secured him ministerial office, as secretary of state. His tenure of office was abruptly terminated five months later by

[6] Boissonnade, *Poitou*, p. 224.
[7] Luis Cabrera de Córdoba, *Relaciones de las cosas sucedidas en la corte de España desde 1599 hasta 1614* (Madrid, 1857), pp. 545–6.

the assassination of his patron, Concini, but its attainment marked the beginning of his ministerial career. He was now thirty-one.

In 1615–16, then, both men finally broke into the magic circle of the court. For each of them, this was only the first step on the winding staircase that led to high office. It would take Olivares six more years, and Richelieu eight, to rise to the top, and both suffered dispiriting setbacks on the tortuous climb. These long, hard and emotionally exhausting years of waiting, scheming and waiting may be said to have completed their education in the only school of politics that counted – that of the court. The disappointments and humiliations of those years tested them to the limit, and confirmed what their enemies already suspected: that they were men of extreme ambition and fixity of purpose.

The two men, now moving into their thirties and on the threshold of power, presented an obvious contrast in personality and appearance: Olivares short, heavily set, robust-looking, and already tending to corpulence; Richelieu thin, pale, angular, with his high cheekbones and sharp pointed nose. Dr Gregorio Marañón, whose 1936 biography of Olivares makes him a pioneer in the now fashionable field of psycho-history, used these physical differences as the basis for an ingenious essay in posthumous psychoanalysis. Himself professionally interested in the correspondence between personality and physique, he was much influenced by the German psychologist Ernst Kretschmer, whose pioneering work on *Physique and Character* was published in 1925.[8] Kretschmer had found that the majority of his schizophrenic patients were tall, thin and pale, while the majority of his manic-depressive patients were round, florid and stocky. On the strength of this he built up a classification of two distinctive physical and personality types – the pyknic type with a cycloid temperament, and the asthenic type with a schizoid temperament. Mirabeau, one of nature's pyknics, was the prototype of the cyclothymic personality; Robespierre, physically as-thenic, of the schizothymic personality.

Marañón made this convenient classification his own. Morphologi-cally, Olivares – short, stocky and plump – was obviously a pyknic; and the distinguishing personality traits of the pyknic are a flamboyant dynamism, an untiring energy, a propensity for grandiose designs, and

---

[8] Eng. trans., 1936; 2nd edn, New York, 1970.

1 Diego de Velázquez, *Count–Duke of Olivares.*

2 Philippe de Champaigne, *Cardinal Richelieu.*

moods of extravagant elation alternating with profound depression. Richelieu, thin and angular, was no less clearly an asthenic – reserved, austere, idealistic, inflexibly severe.[9]

Kretschmer's thesis has failed to stand the test of time, not least because his classifications contain too many ambiguities. Nor is there any good reason to assume that human beings are quite such prisoners of their biological organism as he tried to suggest. It is true that Olivares reveals some of the characteristics of Kretschmer's cyclothymic personality. Moments of euphoria were succeeded by dark periods of discouragement, and both moods may indeed have run to extremes. It is true, too, that he displayed a penchant for grandiose designs, that he would indulge in long tirades, and bang the table in outbursts of fury, although he could also be affable, smooth, and indeed ingratiating in private conversation. But perhaps more impressive than the fluctuation of mood is the degree to which he succeeded in mastering his obviously powerful emotions. Contemporaries were impressed by his display of supreme self-control at the most terrible moment of his life, when his daughter died in childbirth in 1626 and all his hopes of succession were extinguished.

Now if we turn to Richelieu, what sort of man do we see? A man who, like Olivares, showed a marked propensity for grandiose designs. One who, certainly, could present an ice-cold exterior to the world. But one who also suffered from the most acute hypersensibility; who, like Olivares, was prone to sudden, terrifying outbursts of temper; who burst into tears with embarrassing ease; and whose nervous system was so highly strung that at moments of depression he would physically collapse. Mathieu de Morgues, a hostile witness but one who knew him well, describes him as a man of choleric and melancholy humour. 'He is unhappy in his happiness, in that good fortune, any more than evil fortune, does not bring him peace of mind . . . He is never at rest, because he is always suspended between fear and hope . . . He loses his temper with people, with events, with fortune, with himself.'[10]

Such contemporary accounts, which seem to suggest some striking similarities of temperament, prompt the obvious reflection that during their years of power both Richelieu and Olivares were working to the limits of their endurance, endlessly waiting for news which, more often

[9] Marañón, *Olivares*, pp. 63–4.
[10] Morgues, 'La Très Humble . . . remonstrance' (1631), *Recueil*, pp. 13 and 16. For Richelieu's character, see especially Louis Batiffol, *Richelieu et le roi Louis XIII* (Paris, 1934), ch. 2.

than not, was bad. It would be surprising if they did not succumb at times to acute depression. Circumstances, then, were hardly conducive to equanimity of mind. But beyond circumstance, there may also have been an element of design. Both men had a well-developed sense of theatre. Were the outbursts of fury invariably spontaneous and uncontrolled? Richelieu is not to be entirely disbelieved when he wrote to the Archbishop of Bordeaux: 'My rages are all inspired by reason.'[11] As for his tears, Marie de Médicis once remarked that 'he cries when he wants'.[12] Both ministers punctuated their careers with offers or threats of resignation. To some extent these coincide with moments of physical and mental prostration, but they can also be seen as calculated moves to reinforce their position at times of political crisis.

Yet when all this is conceded, contemporaries understandably felt that they were in the presence of two personalities who were not as other men. The Duke of Modena, whose qualifications for judgement are not entirely clear, was awestruck when he met Olivares in 1638. 'I simply cannot believe', he wrote, 'that there is any other man in the world like the Count. His head is worth more than that of ten men together . . .'[13] Richelieu's admirers stood similarly in awe of his genius. At the same time, their detractors also detected in the two men something out of the ordinary, and spoke darkly of mental and physical abnormality, the latter apparently of an epileptic character. There was certainly a strain of madness in the du Plessis family. If Richelieu's elder brother, Alphonse, thought at times that he was God, he was at least in good company; but his sister, Mme de Brézé, who dared not sit down because she thought she was made of glass,[14] might have stepped straight out of a Cervantes short story. Curious stories were in circulation about the Cardinal's strange behaviour in the privacy of his household,[15] and at moments of crisis he was alleged to howl and foam at the mouth. Olivares was also considered by his enemies to be not entirely sound in mind, and was said to have suffered periods of severe mental disturbance in his youth. It was

---

[11] Batiffol, *Richelieu et Louis XIII*, p. 59.

[12] *Ibid.*, p. 24.

[13] Quoted by Manuel Fernández Alvarez, 'El fracaso de la hegemonía española en Europa', *Historia de España Ramón Menéndez Pidal*, xxv (Madrid, 1982), p. 746.

[14] Philippe Erlanger, 'Le Roi et son ministre', in *Richelieu*, Collection Génies et Réalités, Hachette (Paris, 1972), p. 155.

[15] See the letter of Charlotte-Elizabeth of Bavaria, cited in Marc Pierret, *Richelieu ou la déraison d'état* (Paris, 1972), p. 73, where he is described as acting on occasion under the delusion that he was a horse.

observed, too, that he was liable to make sudden involuntary movements of his head, hands and legs.[16] His mental state in his final years in office remains an open question, but there is no doubt that his mind was gone at the time of his death in 1645.[17]

Both men were notorious hypochondriacs – Olivares joked about it when he thanked his brother-in-law for a letter 'as full of hypochondria as if it were one of my own'[18] – and both were periodically prostrated by what seem to have been excruciating migraine headaches. Both were insomniacs, and indeed Richelieu did much of his writing and dictating during the long night watches.[19] Olivares certainly looked the more robust of the two, at least until the cares of office took their toll, and he was a first-class horseman in his earlier years. But as the years passed he grew obese, in spite of a frugal style of life, and suffered increasingly from a variety of ailments, including gout. Richelieu's health was from the beginning precarious. His constitution was notoriously delicate, he was laid low by recurring illnesses, and he was permanently flanked by a bevy of doctors who bled and purged him remorselessly. Not surprisingly his letters are full of medical analogies. 'France's malady', he wrote in 1628, 'was one of those which the doctors call complicated.'[20] His own lent itself to the same diagnosis.

Yet for all their mental and bodily afflictions, both men showed an extraordinary capacity for overcoming their crises through a supreme effort of the will. Differences in physique and temperament pale into insignificance beside the obsessive determination which they both displayed to be the absolute masters of themselves and the world. One of the Venetian ambassadors described Olivares as a man with 'the ambition to dominate'.[21] Richelieu, according to Morgues, 'is everything, does everything, has everything'.[22] Both were driven forward by what Morgues, speaking of Richelieu, calls a 'déréglée ambition',[23] but there was something more at work here than ambition, powerful as it was.

The two men had a number of interests and characteristics in common.

[16] ASF, Mediceo, filza 4963, Monanni's despatch, 14 Nov. 1637.
[17] Marañón, *Olivares*, pp. 398–9.
[18] AGS, Estado, legajo 2713, Olivares to Monterrey, 30 Oct. 1629.
[19] A. Aubery, *Histoire du Cardinal Duc de Richelieu* (Paris, 1660), p. 595.
[20] Grillon, III, p. 204.
[21] N. Barozzi and G. Berchet, *Relazioni degli stati europei. Serie 1. Spagna* (Venice, 1856), II, p. 15.
[22] Morgues, 'Jugement sur la préface', *Recueil*, p. 20.
[23] 'La très humble . . . remonstrance', *Recueil*, p. 49.

In particular both were passionate book-collectors, who would go to almost any lengths to secure some coveted volume for their libraries. Richelieu also collected paintings and antique sculptures, but any inclinations that Olivares may have had in this direction seem to have been channelled into acquiring works for the great royal collection of Philip IV.[24] Nor is it known if Olivares shared Richelieu's enthusiasm for music.[25] Both men initially had a liking for pomp and circumstance, which Richelieu indulged to the full once he attained supreme power, partly but not entirely because he considered them proper to a person of his rank, and to his status as a prince of the church. Olivares, on the other hand, abandoned the splendid life-style of his early years in Seville soon after reaching high office, and by the end of the 1620s had come to adopt a regime of almost spartan austerity. He maintained a personal household, however, which was about the same size as that of the Cardinal, whose taste for magnificence was accompanied by a well-developed parsimony. There were 166 servants in Olivares' household, 180 in Richelieu's. Olivares' stables, on the other hand, had only 32 horses and mules, to Richelieu's 140.[26] Since – unlike Richelieu – he lived in the royal palace, he travelled much less.

The ministers shared, too, a compulsive addiction to architectural planning and building, although again this expressed itself in different ways. Where his own needs were concerned, Olivares confined himself to building in the 1630s a modest one-storey house adjoining a convent in Loeches, an insignificant town in the arid Castilian countryside, some twenty miles from Madrid. All his formidable energies as an architect *manqué* went into devising, building, and furnishing the great pleasure palace of the Buen Retiro which he constructed for Philip IV on the outskirts of the capital, and into arranging the planting and irrigation of its magnificent gardens.[27] Richelieu, on the other hand, built for himself on a massive scale, remodelling his châteaux at Limours and Rueil, and

---

[24] See Jonathan Brown and J. H. Elliott, *A Palace for a King. The Buen Retiro and the Court of Philip IV* (New Haven–London, 1980), ch. 5.

[25] For Richelieu and the musicians in his household, see Maximin Deloche, *La Maison du Cardinal de Richelieu* (Paris, 1912), ch. 11.

[26] Deloche, *La Maison*, p. 485; Marañón, *Olivares*, appendix VIII. The list of Olivares' servants unfortunately bears no date, and it is not clear whether it relates to the period before or after he took up residence in the palace, where he may have relied on the palace staff to attend to most of his needs. He continued to keep up, however, a fully staffed town house in the Calle de la Cruzada (see Marañón, *Olivares*, p. 263).

[27] For the Buen Retiro, see Brown and Elliott, *A Palace*.

constructing the Palais Cardinal in Paris and an enormous château at Richelieu in Poitou, where he created from nothing a new and obstinately lifeless town which was laid out in accordance with the most rational principles of seventeenth-century urban design.[28] It was one of the ironies of Richelieu's career that the burden of work and poor health prevented him from seeing the results of his town planning, or visiting the château he had built and furnished at such vast expense.

Another shared characteristic was the hankering of the two men for a military life. 'My greatest wish is not to die without first having been a soldier, something I have aspired to all my life', Olivares wrote to a friend in 1630.[29] The nearest he came to realizing his ambition was in 1642 when he accompanied the king as his lieutenant-general to the front in Aragon.[30] Four years earlier, when the French attacked Spain's northern fortress of Fuenterrabía, he had to content himself with directing relief operations at long distance from Madrid. Richelieu on the other hand succeeded three times in his ministerial career in getting close to the sound and smell of battle. At the siege of La Rochelle, clad in a bizarre costume, half ecclesiastical and half military, which he presumably considered appropriate garb for a prelate who was also the king's lieutenant-general,[31] he exercised a general control over strategy and on occasions assumed personal command of military operations; and in 1629 and again in 1630 he crossed with the French invading armies into Italy, sharing the hardships of the soldiers on their passage through the Alps.

If cravings for military command and architectural assertion were characteristic of the aristocratic ethos in Early Modern Europe, they also hint at a predisposition in favour of order, discipline and control. Both men were driven by a consuming determination to impose order on an unruly world. With the generality of mankind governed by the passions, it was, according to Richelieu, 'necessary to have a masculine virtue and do everything by reason'.[32] 'Women, and the majority of men', observed Olivares, 'are generally more easily persuaded to do things through severity and fear than through entreaties and love.'[33]

---

[28] See René Crozet, *La Vie artistique en France au XVIIe siècle* (Paris, 1954), pp. 90–4, and Louis Batiffol, *Autour de Richelieu* (Paris, 1937), ch. 4. For Richelieu on architects and architecture see in particular *TP*, pp. 236 and 279.

[29] ADM, legajo 79, Olivares to Marquis of Aytona, 16 Dec. 1630.

[30] See his strange letter of response to his appointment in *MC*, II, doc. XVIII.

[31] D.P. O'Connell, *Richelieu* (London, 1968), p. 166.

[32] *TP*, p. 276.

[33] BL, Add. Ms. 14,000, fo. 732, draft *voto* of Olivares, 15 Oct. 1626.

These authoritarian instincts may well have profound psychological origins, but their sources remain elusive. If they are not to be found in a presumed relationship between physique and temperament, perhaps they can be traced to childhood experience. But here again the evidence is baffling. Like so many of their contemporaries, both children were brought up in one-parent households. Olivares lost his mother, the 'holy countess' as Sixtus V called her, at the age of seven, and was brought up by a severe father, who never remarried. Richelieu, by contrast, lost his father at the age of five, and his childhood years were overshadowed by the presence of two domineering women, his mother and grandmother.[34]

Throughout his life Richelieu clearly held a great attraction for women, and his enemies spread many stories about his relationships with them, for none of which, however, strong supporting evidence exists. He himself warned in his *Testament Politique* that there was nothing more dangerous for a man in public life than attachment to women[35] – the not unnatural reaction of a man who was forced to invest a vast amount of time and emotional energy in unravelling the intrigues of politically minded women in high places, like the Queen Mother, Madame du Fargis, and the Duchess of Chevreuse. He had learnt at heavy cost, he wrote, 'how difficult it is to turn away women from resolutions taken under the influence of passion',[36] that word which for him was synonymous with disorder and misrule. Olivares shared these sentiments, which were a commonplace of the times. Unlike Richelieu he does not seem to have held many charms for members of the opposite sex. In his early years he led the conventionally promiscuous life of a young Spanish noble, and fathered a son who was eventually legitimized; but after the death of his daughter in 1626 he became a model of marital fidelity, and seems to have found increasing consolation in the company and support of his austere and rather forbidding wife.

The shadowy world of psycho-history seems unlikely in this instance to yield up many secrets. The authoritarianism of both men was rooted in an underlying pessimism about human nature that derived from their religion. 'We are men and bound to go astray', as Olivares observed.[37] Profoundly imbued with the sense of original sin, both he and Richelieu were sceptical about the prospects for the mass of mankind unless it was

---

[34] For an attempt to assess the psychological consequences, see Pierret, *Richelieu ou la déraison*.
[35] See Batiffol, *Richelieu et Louis XIII*, p. 51.
[36] Avenel, IV, p. 55.
[37] *MC*, II, p. 206, Olivares to Chumacero, 22 Oct. 1641.

subjected to rigorous discipline and control. But within the confines of a strict orthodoxy this did not preclude them from adopting a relatively tolerant form of Counter-Reformation Catholicism, characterized by intellectual curiosity and overtones of humanism. Both of them had been trained for an ecclesiastical career, and even if Olivares abandoned it, he seems to have maintained an active interest in theological problems. His library included by special dispensation a section of books on the Index, among them the works of Erasmus. He had a licence to own and study the works of rabbis on the Old Testament; and, at least according to his enemies, he made a practice of reading the Koran.[38]

Richelieu, as a professional churchman, presumably had a more extensive acquaintance than his rival with the finer points of theology. In his double capacity as a theologian and a pastor of souls he owed a deep debt to Spanish Counter-Reformation Catholicism, sharing with St François de Sales a particular admiration for the works of Fray Luis de Granada.[39] Granada's writings drew on a wide variety of spiritual traditions and sources, not the least of them being Erasmus' *Enchiridion*.[40] May we perhaps see some remnants of the Erasmian tradition in Richelieu's insistence on spiritual wisdom, his concern for practical piety, and his distaste for extremes, which led him to deplore the extravagances on the one hand of the *dévots* who advocated the extirpation of Protestantism by force, and on the other of the Jansenists?[41]

By temperament and vocation Richelieu was always the dialectical theologian, anxious to convert through argument and persuasion. Indeed, his career is incomprehensible unless it is appreciated that the *homme d'état* was also an *homme d'église*,[42] profoundly influenced by his experiences in his diocese of Luçon, where he faced the double challenge of converting the Protestants and reinvigorating Catholic life through the

---

[38] Charges of reading the Koran in AHN, Inquisición, legajo 494, no. 38, fos. 70–3, *Nacimiento, vida y costumbres de Don Gaspar de Guzmán, Conde–Duque de Olivares*. The copy of the catalogue of the Olivares library preserved in the Vatican Library (Barb. Lat. Ms. 3098) contains a section listing the prohibited books. I am indebted to Professor Antonio Domínguez Ortiz for the reference to the licence given by the Inquisitor General on 19 Jan. 1624 to study rabbinical works (AHN, Inquisición, libro 592, fo. 404).

[39] Deloche, *Autour de la plume*, pp. 32–6.

[40] Marcel Bataillon, *Erasmo y España* (Mexico, 1950), II, p. 197.

[41] Cf. Erich Hassinger, 'Das politische Testament Richelieus', *Historische Zeitschrift*, 173 (1952), p. 492.

[42] See J. Orcibal, 'Richelieu, homme d'église, homme d'état', *Revue d'Histoire de l'église de France*, 34 (1948), pp. 94–101.

imposition of discipline, order and reform. His contemporaries, bemused by the apparent secularism of so many of his policies, tended to question, like later generations, the genuineness of his religious commitment. But with him, as with Olivares, it seems to have deepened with the passage of the years.

There are indications in 1636 of some form of religious crisis, when the conjunction of threatened national calamity and personal despair came near to overwhelming the Cardinal. Where Olivares had Jesuit confessors, Richelieu had Capuchins; and it was his friend and confidant, the Capuchin Father Joseph, who rallied his spirits at this critical moment.[43] Father Joseph's mystical sense of the overshadowing presence of a supernatural power helped revive Richelieu's confidence in himself and his mission, and apparently brought new fervour to his devotions. In the early 1630s he had taken vigorous measures, at the instigation of Father Joseph, against the upsurge of Illuminism in France; but in his later years he listened sympathetically to reports of miracles and divine revelations, which he came to see as precious indications of the intervention of Providence in the affairs of men.[44]

Olivares, for his part, always seems to have been guarded in his response to reports of supernatural revelations, which were so characteristic a feature of Spanish religious life in his age.[45] But his own religious life, which was conventional enough in his early years, underwent a profound transformation when his daughter died in 1626. The sudden dramatic extinction of his line brought home to him, as nothing else could have done, the vanity of human planning and the emptiness of human hopes. From now on, although he fought hard against despair, he seems to have been afflicted by an underlying melancholy, and was much preoccupied by thoughts of sin and death. It was now that he turned his back for ever on the ostentation of his early life and became almost fanatically punctilious in the observance of his religious exercises, confessing and taking communion daily, and spending long hours in a devotion bordering on ecstasy before his favourite images. 'Salvation', he wrote, 'is all that counts.' Everything else, he concluded, was 'vanity and madness'.[46]

[43] Gustave Fagniez, *Le Père Joseph et Richelieu* (Paris, 1891–4), II, pp. 309–10.
[44] *Ibid.*, p. 62, and pp. 310–12.
[45] See *MC*, II, p. 272, n. 52.
[46] BL, Egerton MS. 2053, fo. 34, Olivares to Duke of Carpiñano, 20 Oct. 1628. For the impact of his daughter's death, see Marañón, *Olivares*, pp. 78–9.

The strong streak of credulity in both men extended to a willingness to patronize the experiments of alchemists, although Olivares, unlike Richelieu, had no use for astrology.[47] But the credulity coexisted with a humanist rationalism inculcated by education and reading. The two of them, as proud possessors of splendid libraries, lived their lives surrounded by books. Their library catalogues still have to be systematically studied, but they suggest similar tastes; a strong interest in ancient and modern history, and in theology, philosophy and medicine.[48] While it is one thing to collect books and another to read them, the evidence of a contemporary indicates that Richelieu at least was a 'devourer of books'.[49] Olivares, for his part, enjoyed the company and discourse of scholars and is said to have had a general acquaintance with all the sciences.[50] Both men prided themselves on their erudition, and Richelieu read Greek, Latin, Italian and Spanish,[51] but it is not clear whether Olivares, in addition to Latin and Italian, had any French.

Classical wisdom provided them with the indispensable navigational aids for charting their voyage through the turbulent political waters of the 1620s and 1630s. Their critics accused them of having read their classical historians, and particularly Tacitus, all too well. 'Cardinal Richelieu', wrote Guy Patin, 'read and practised Tacitus a great deal. That is why he was such a terrible man.'[52] Francisco de Melo wrote of Olivares:

The political and historical books which he had read left him with a number of maxims which were unsuited to the humour of the times. From this sprang a number of harsh actions, whose only object was to imitate the ancients; as if Tacitus and Procopius, of whom he took counsel, would not have altered their views if they had been alive now, considering the differences which every age introduces into the customs and interests of men.[53]

---

[47] He thought that Wallenstein's addiction to astrology was the worst of all his failings (cf. his *voto* of 18 May 1633 in AGS, Estado, legajo 2151). For his patronage of the alchemical experiments of Vincenzo Massimi at the Buen Retiro, see Brown and Elliott, *A Palace*, p. 217. For Richelieu's faith in astrology and the transmutation of metals, Fagniez, *Père Joseph*, II, p. 312.

[48] Brief accounts of the Olivares library and its history are to be found in Marañón, *Olivares*, pp. 160–6, and Gregorio de Andrés, 'Historia de la biblioteca del Conde–Duque de Olivares y descripción de sus códices', *Cuadernos Bibliográficos*, 28 (1972). There is an interesting attempt to discuss the contents of Richelieu's library in relation to his ideas in Wollenberg, *Richelieu*, ch. 3.

[49] Deloche, *Autour de la plume*, p. 14.

[50] Valdory, *Anecdotes . . . d'Olivarés*, p. 49.

[51] Batiffol, *Richelieu et Louis XIII*, p. 56.

[52] Quoted Thuau, *Raison d'état*, p. 44.

[53] Francisco Manuel de Melo, *Epanáforas de vária historia portuguesa*, ed. Edgar Prestage (Coimbra, 1931), p. 93.

It is difficult to know whether this judgement is fair, not least because both ministers seem to have made a point of observing a maxim once enunciated by Olivares: 'great men never cite authors, only reason'.[54] They shared a profound conviction in the overriding importance of reason, and of applying the principles of rational statecraft to the world of affairs, although both accepted that even reason had its limitations. 'Reason', observed Olivares, 'is worth very little in the world where considerations of interest predominate.'[55] Richelieu's view of the world was constructed, perhaps more systematically and coherently than that of Olivares, on a belief in the necessary primacy of reason. 'Reason', which he equated with 'natural illumination' (*lumière naturelle*),[56] is a word which figures repeatedly in his writings, especially if the *Testament Politique* can be regarded as representative of his thinking. But even Richelieu was forced to concede that the dictates of reason, however desirable, sometimes had to be ignored. When discussing that bane of the seventeenth-century French monarchy, the sale of offices, he observed that reason demanded that in a new state the best possible laws should be devised; but prudence did not allow this in old-established monarchies, where imperfections had become a habitual part of life.[57] This recalls a remark once made by Olivares that 'it would be better if many things were not as they are, but to change them would be worse'.[58]

This flexible and pragmatic response to long-established evils – a response which both ministers regarded as a sad necessity – was dignified in the seventeenth century with the name of 'prudence'. Richelieu drew a clear distinction between reason and prudence, which might well be at variance. 'It is sometimes a matter of prudence', we are told in the *Testament Politique*, 'to water down remedies to make them more effective; and orders that conform more closely to reason are not always the best, because sometimes they are not well suited to the capacities of those called upon to execute them.'[59]

The supreme evangelist of the gospel of prudence in the late sixteenth century was Justus Lipsius. As the editor of Tacitus, as the advocate of

---

[54] AGS, Estado, legajo 2050, *voto* of Olivares, 7 Dec. 1635.
[55] AGS, Estado, legajo 2521, *voto*, 1 July 1637.
[56] Richelieu, *Traité qui contient la méthode la plus facile . . . pour convertir ceux qui se sont séparéz de l'Eglise* (Paris, 1651), p. 65.
[57] *TP*, p. 234.
[58] AGS, Estado, legajo 2042, Olivares in junta of 27 June 1628.
[59] *TP*, p. 237. See F.E. Sutcliffe, *Guez de Balzac et son temps* (Paris, 1959), pp. 225–6.

Roman military and civic virtues, and as the purveyor of a philosophy of life designed to blend Christianity with the doctrines of the Stoics, Lipsius exercised an enormous intellectual influence during the years in which Richelieu and Olivares were coming to maturity.[60] Richelieu had the complete works of Lipsius in his library at the Palais Cardinal, and a copy of the *Civil Doctrine* in his more private library at Rueil.[61] His own views on reason and prudence are very close to those of Lipsius, and a systematic examination of his writings would certainly reveal Lipsian borrowings. Lipsius' teachings had in any event been popularized in France by Pierre Charron in his *La Sagesse*, of 1601. Charron, another author well represented in the Cardinal's library, links the world of sixteenth-century humanism with that of seventeenth-century rationalism as he deftly mingles the philosophies of Montaigne and Lipsius. It is in this period of transition between two mental worlds that Richelieu came to intellectual maturity; and if we can sometimes hear in the *Testament Politique* the voice of Lipsius, we can also hear that of Charron, as when Richelieu insists on the need to have a 'masculine virtue and do everything by reason'.[62]

Charron's claims for the moral autonomy of man inevitably led to accusations of atheism, and Olivares made the most of this when he accused Richelieu in the *Nicandro* of wanting to introduce Charron's irreligious wisdom into France.[63] But if Olivares ostentatiously disassociated himself from such pernicious tendencies, he too came from an environment permeated by Lipsian notions of the rationality of man. His uncle and political mentor, Don Baltasar de Zúñiga, had come to know and admire Lipsius while serving as ambassador to the Archdukes in Brussels.[64] His own library was well stocked with Lipsius' writings; and some of Lipsius' most enthusiastic followers were to be found in Seville, including Olivares' close friend, the future Count of La Roca, author of that quintessentially Lipsian handbook for diplomats, *The Ambassador*.[65]

What had Lipsius to offer a seventeenth-century statesman? In the

---

[60] For the European influence of Lipsius at this time, see Gerhard Oestreich, *Neostoicism and the Early Modern State* (Cambridge, 1982).

[61] Wollenberg, *Richelieu*, pp. 236 and 319, note 39.

[62] *TP*, p. 276; and see Sutcliffe, *Guez de Balzac*, pp. 65–7. For Charron and Lipsius, Church, *Richelieu and Reason of State*, pp. 75–8.

[63] *MC*, II, p. 268.

[64] Four letters from Lipsius to Zúñiga are included in Alejandro Ramírez, *Epistolario de Justo Lipsio y los Españoles, 1577–1606* (Madrid, 1966).

[65] *MC*, I, pp. xlvii–xlviii.

first place, a Tacitean view of the world, with its detached, ironical perception of the motivations of men, and its maxims of statecraft culled from the accumulated stock of historical experience – maxims that possessed all the practical advantages associated with the teachings of Machiavelli without the obloquy attached to his name. In the second place, a vindication of those Roman virtues that lent themselves so conveniently to the shaping of the seventeenth-century state – austerity, economy, authority, discipline and order. And finally a Stoic but Christian resignation in the face of adverse fortune.

The wisdom of Tacitus and Lipsius could be neatly encapsulated into maxims suited to the requirements of the seventeenth-century states-man. Both Richelieu and Olivares had a liking for maxims, which they either appropriated from the common stock of political wisdom or else minted freshly for themselves. There was certainly no lack of material to hand. Richelieu enjoyed citing the advice given to Henry IV by Antonio Pérez, that arch-devotee of Lipsius and through him of Tacitus, to the effect that the foundations of power should be Rome, council and the sea.[66] Olivares almost certainly drew on this same somewhat tainted fount of aphoristic political wisdom. His confidants included that great survivor from the age of Philip II, Pérez's disciple Baltasar Alamos de Barrientos, who spent his years in prison preparing his famous *Spanish Tacitus* (1614), with its long compendium of Tacitean aphorisms for the use of busy politicians.[67]

Yet both ministers were sceptical about the possibility of reducing politics to a firm set of rules, and both affected to despise political wisdom gleaned solely from books. There was always the unforeseen and the accidental, and the first rule of all, as Olivares insisted, was to be on the lookout for unexpected contingencies.[68] 'There is nothing more danger-ous for the state', observed Richelieu, 'than men who want to govern kingdoms on the basis of maxims which they cull from books. When they do this they often destroy them, because the past is not the same as the present, and times, places and persons change.'[69]

---

[66] *Maximes d'état et fragments politiques du Cardinal de Richelieu*, ed. Gabriel Hanotaux (Paris, 1880), p. 38; *TP*, pp. 348 and 401. *Les Aphorismes d'Antoine Pérez* was published in Paris in 1605. For Pérez and Lipsius see Gustav Ungerer, *A Spaniard in Elizabethan England: The Correspondence of Antonio Pérez's Exile* (London, 1974–6), II, pp. 348–50.

[67] For Alamos de Barrientos and Olivares, see the references in *MC*, I, pp. 40–1.

[68] AGS, Estado, legajo 2054, 'El Conde Duque sobre el reparo de las cosas de Alemania', 23 Oct. 1639.

[69] *TP*, p. 289.

27

Contingency and chance could make the best-laid plans miscarry. When this happened, the statesman had to fall back on his native wit and resolution, and on his own experience of men and the world. Here Richelieu had the advantage over Olivares. Not only had he held the office of secretary of state for a few months in 1616, but his years in the diocese of Luçon had given him valuable political and administrative experience. He had only been abroad once – to Rome in 1607 – but Olivares' experience of the world beyond Spain was confined to his childhood memories, and he never set foot outside the Iberian peninsula in his adult life. Both men, however, made a point of keeping themselves informed about foreign lands through their reading and through discussions with recently returned travellers.[70] Olivares had a special map-room in his quarters in the palace, where he would spend long hours poring over his maps and charts; and Flanders veterans were amazed by his detailed knowledge of the local topography.[71]

In spite of the impression created by some of his more spectacular policy failures, Olivares was temperamentally a cautious man who fussed over detail. The same is true of Richelieu, who saw to it that, as far as possible, nothing was left to chance. But in both men concern with detail was accompanied by the ability to think in terms of long-range objectives. Both would have subscribed to Seneca's dictum that a good statesman was defined by his ability to make for and attain his chosen objective, however many twists and turns were required along the route.[72]

Cunning and artifice were the natural stock in trade of two such wily politicians, and contemporaries watched in fascination as they wove their complicated plots. But Olivares is sometimes described, with something less than admiration, as 'capricious', 'chimerical', or even 'mysterious'.[73] This feeling that he indulged in mystery for the sake of mystery may derive, at least in part, from the character of his rhetoric. Both men were immensely proud of their rhetorical skills, and indeed it was Richelieu's speech in the Estates General of 1614 which helped to make

---

[70] Victor-L. Tapié, *La France de Louis XIII et de Richelieu* (Paris, 1967), p. 134.
[71] Conde de la Roca (Juan Antonio de Vera y Figueroa), *Fragmentos históricos de la vida de D. Gaspar de Guzmán*, in Antonio Valladares, *Semanario Erudito*, II (Madrid, 1787), pp. 266–7.
[72] Cited by Fernando Alvia de Castro in his *Verdadera razón de estado* (Lisbon, 1615), fo. 3. See José Antonio Maravall, *Estudios de historia del pensamiento español. Siglo XVII* (Madrid, 1975), p. 101.
[73] Valdory, *Anecdotes . . . d'Olivarés*, p. 49, and see Marañón, *Olivares*, p. 106.

his fortune. There is a persuasive luminosity about Richelieu's speeches, like the one he delivered to the Parlement of Paris in 1634.[74] The published text of this speech, however, seems to have been extensively doctored, if we are to believe Tallemant des Réaux, who describes Richelieu's team of literary experts as working over it line by line and word by word in a desperate attempt to make it fit for the printed page. But even Tallemant concedes that if on this occasion the Cardinal said very little of substance he said it very well. In Tallemant's opinion, Richelieu saw things very clearly, but was not good at developing his points at length. On the other hand, when he spoke succinctly, he was 'admirable et délicat'.[75]

Olivares, by contrast, favoured a more cloudy style of rhetoric, and could not conceivably be described as a man who talked succinctly. He preferred to batter his audience into submission with a bombardment of words. In his letters and state papers he is much the same. He indulges in long and complicated sentences, littered with sub-clauses and parentheses, and he frequently departs from his main point, sometimes for paragraphs on end. Then there suddenly comes a short, sharp phrase, some colloquial expression or popular proverb, which is all the more effective for surfacing through the heavy mass of verbiage. Richelieu's letters, on the other hand, are marked by an imperious brevity, although when he wrote for publication his literary vanity seems to have deprived his style of its usual hard precision.[76]

If indeed *le style, c'est l'homme*, we are faced with two very distinct personalities: one extravagant, inflated, and perhaps quintessentially baroque; the other cool, laconic, tightly controlled. The images of the two men transmitted to posterity tend to confirm the contrast – Olivares loud, bustling, over-emphatic in his speech and gesture; Richelieu taut, fastidious, almost feline in his movements. But can we safely take style as an expression of personality without knowing more than we know at present about the rhetorical traditions in which they were trained? There are affinities, for instance, between the style of Olivares and that of Lipsius, especially in their taste for the paradoxical and the epigrammatic, for abrupt transitions and contrived obscurity – features, too, of

---

[74] *Mercure français*, xx (Paris, 1637), pp. 5–24.
[75] Tallemant des Réaux, *Historiettes*, I (Paris, 1960), p. 269.
[76] Deloche, *Autour de la plume*, p. 10.

the prose style of the Bolognese writer Virgilio Malvezzi, much admired by Olivares who made him the historian of his regime.[77] But in Olivares one looks in vain for the brevity of Lipsius, which seems to have been jettisoned for the more ample oratorical effects of the Ciceronian style much favoured in early-seventeenth-century Rome. In this he was perhaps reacting, like other Spaniards of his generation, against the stylistic severity of the age of Philip II. Richelieu, on the other hand, rejected the theatrical excesses of the Ciceronian style as cultivated by the Jesuits, preferring a more austere and laconic version, purged of its excesses. Here he followed the example of his patron, Cardinal du Perron, whose style was anti-rhetorical, pungent and terse.[78]

But was it their training that led them in opposite directions, or did they select a style from among the various available options because it seemed to suit the image of themselves which they wished to present to the world? Are we faced, in other words, with conditioning or choice? It seems probable that there was a strong element of choice, if only because there were alternative rhetorical traditions to hand in both France and Spain.

Traditionally, eloquence was a powerful weapon in the statesman's armoury, to be sharpened and burnished with care. When Olivares' father sent him to Salamanca, his meticulous instructions for his son's education included a stipulation that every fortnight he should engage in set debates with members of his household.[79] The training presumably bore fruit – Siri tells us that the Count–Duke was 'naturally eloquent and spoke with ease'.[80] Richelieu, the founder of the Académie Française, was acutely sensitive to the possibilities of language as an instrument of power. It was for this that he exercised his rhetorical skills, and for this that – like Olivares – he courted the intellectuals. With language and reason he would convert and persuade. During the siege of La Rochelle, he tells us, he realized that it was for him 'to recover from heresy by reason those whom the king had recovered from rebellion by force'.[81]

---

[77] For the Lipsian rhetorical tradition, see Marc Fumaroli, *L'Age de l'éloquence* (Geneva, 1980), pp. 216–19.

[78] I am grateful to Dr Marc Fumaroli for advising me on the influence of Cardinal du Perron on Richelieu.

[79] BNM, Ms. 10,486, fos. 1–23, 'Instrucción que Don Enrique de Guzmán . . . dió a Don Laureano de Guzmán . . .', 7 Jan. 1601.

[80] Valdory, *Anecdotes . . . d'Olivarés*, p. 49.

[81] Richelieu, *Traité pour convertir*, p. 2.

Always an artist with words, he had a compelling belief in the power of words to win the minds and hearts of men.

It was in their fierce determination to control and reshape the world to their image through every instrument at their disposal, including that of language, that Richelieu and Olivares – in many respects so different – came together as one. But there is something paradoxical about this determination. Living, as Richelieu said, in a corrupt age when men were unwilling to be led by reason;[82] sharing an instinctive pessimism about men and events; aware that some sudden contingency could make the best-laid plans go awry; they fought for power with a tenacity born of the optimistic conviction that they could somehow use it to transform the world. Dangerous men, perhaps, but these were dangerous times.

[82] *TP*, p. 237.

31

2

‹‹

Masters and servants

In 1635 two great decorative programmes were in process of completion, one in Madrid and the other in Paris. One was devised, at least in part, by Olivares, and occupied the Hall of Realms, the great central hall of Philip IV's new pleasure palace in Madrid, the Buen Retiro. The other was devised by Richelieu for the so-called Galerie des Hommes Illustres in his own magnificent new palace, the Palais Cardinal.

As befitted a royal palace, the decorative scheme for the Hall of Realms was intended to celebrate the greatness of the dynasty – represented by Velázquez's equestrian portraits of Philip III and Philip IV and their consorts, and Prince Baltasar Carlos, the heir to the throne – and the recent triumphs of Spanish arms. Among the victories represented was the recovery of Brazil from the Dutch in 1625. On the right-hand side of this painting, by Juan Bautista Maino, the defeated Dutch are shown kneeling before a large tapestry. On this tapestry the young and somewhat uncertain figure of Philip IV in armour is being crowned with a wreath of laurels by two figures, also in armour. One is the goddess Minerva; the other, more startlingly, is the familiar and ponderous figure of the Count–Duke himself (fig. 3).[1]

The audacity of this juxtaposition of king and minister in a single painting may well be without parallel in seventeenth-century European art. But Richelieu's Gallery of Illustrious Men was also not without a certain daring. On the Cardinal's instructions, Philippe de Champaigne and Simon Vouet painted twenty-five illustrious men and women in the history of France, including Abbot Suger, Joan of Arc and Bertrand du Guesclin. As in the Hall of Realms, there were portraits of the royal family – Henry IV and Marie de Médicis, Louis XIII and Anne of Austria, and the king's brother, Gaston d'Orléans, heir presumptive to

[1] For the decorative programme for the Hall of Realms, see Brown and Elliott, *A Palace*, ch. 6.

3 Juan Bautista Maino, *The recapture of Bahía* (detail).

the throne. These were portraits twenty to twenty-four. The twenty-fifth illustrious figure was the Cardinal himself.[2] Between them, the Hall of Realms and the Gallery of Illustrious Men constitute important visual statements about how Olivares and Richelieu saw themselves in relation to their monarchs, and how they wished to be seen by the world.

The reign of Philip III of Spain (1598–1621) was preeminently the age of the royal favourite – the *privado* or *valido*, as he was known to Spaniards. Until 1618, when he was finally disgraced, the Duke of Lerma had in effect governed Spain for a monarch who was no more than a cypher; and Lerma's son, the Duke of Uceda, did his incompetent best to maintain the system during the last three years of Philip's life. In France, too, following the assassination of Henry IV in 1610, government had fallen into the hands of favourites: first the Italian adventurer, Concini – the favourite of the Queen Regent, Marie de Médicis – and then, on Concini's murder in 1617, the royal falconer Luynes, whose palace revolution transferred power nominally to the young Louis XIII, but in practice to himself.

Inevitably, in both France and Spain the ascendancy of the favourite provoked sharp critical comment, the theme of which was the duty of kings to be kings. In 1615 a Spanish Franciscan, Fray Juan de Santamaría, published a famous political treatise in which he asserted that it was no good having a king who, as in a painting by El Greco, looked splendid from afar but was nothing but streaks and smudges when seen close at hand. A true king, he wrote – and no one could doubt that he was writing for and about Philip III – 'should not be content with simply having the supreme power, and the highest and most prominent position, and then merely sleeping and relaxing; but should be the first in government, in council, and in all the offices of state . . .'[3] Two years later, when Concini was murdered in Paris, petitions flowed in from all over France urging Louis XIII to take control. 'It is time, Sir, for you to start speaking as a king, and to learn to distinguish between black and white.'[4]

The replacement of Concini by Luynes and of Lerma by Uceda suggests that neither Philip III nor Louis XIII took these strictures to

---

[2] See Bernard Dorival, 'Art et politique en France au XVIIe siècle: la galerie des hommes illustres du palais cardinal', *Bulletin de la Société de l'Histoire de l'Art Français* (1973), pp. 43–60.
[3] *República y policía cristiana* (Lisbon, 1621 edn), fos. 13–16.
[4] Quoted in Carré, *La Jeunesse*, p. 158.

heart. Favourites still governed, and it is no coincidence that both French and Spanish authors should have turned their attention in these years to the figure of the fifteenth-century Constable of Castile, Don Alvaro de Luna, whose spectacular rise and fall made him an object lesson for all modern favourites. In Spain two historical plays were written, probably by Mira de Amescua, chronicling his fortunes;[5] and in France, Richelieu – the effective head of the Queen Mother's party in its struggle against the government of the Constable, Luynes – is said to have sponsored the publication of a history of John II of Castile by Chaintreau, 'in order to compare the two Constables, de Luna and de Luynes'.[6]

A favourite was a man, often of low origins, who had risen to preeminence through his success – achieved, it was generally assumed, by sinister methods – in capturing the king's favour and dominating his will. The dilemma facing both Richelieu and Olivares in their bid for power was that they had to operate in a political climate which was increasingly hostile to the existence of a royal favourite, and yet had to win and keep the royal favour to attain their ends. Each, too, was faced with an initial and possibly insuperable obstacle in the attitude of the one person who mattered – the prince himself.

Richelieu, who owed his rise to the support of the Queen Mother and Concini, made the nearly fatal initial mistake of underestimating Louis. The murder of Concini and the subsequent palace revolution caught him by surprise. The years 1617–24 were exceptionally difficult for him – years of disgrace, of temporary exile to Avignon, and of uneasy association with a turbulent aristocratic opposition as the Queen Mother's faction resorted to rebellion, only to be defeated in 1620 at the battle of Ponts-de-Cé. His best hope of a return to court lay in the reconciliation of Marie de Médicis and her son, but his efforts to achieve this did not endear him to the king. When the Queen Mother tried yet again to secure his appointment to the King's Council in 1622, Louis refused point-blank, saying that he hated him like the devil.[7]

The twenty-one-year-old Louis, taciturn, suspicious, fiercely jealous of his authority but still very unsure of himself in spite of the success of his military expedition of 1620 against the rebellious province of Béarn, seems to have felt an intense personal antipathy towards a man whose

[5] *Comedia famosa de Ruy López de Avalos*, and *La segunda de Don Alvaro*, ed. Nellie E. Sánchez-Arce (Mexico, 1965, and Mexico, 1960).
[6] Thuau, *Raison d'état*, p. 223.
[7] Batiffol, *Richelieu et Louis XIII*, p. 3.

naturally authoritarian manner he feared and mistrusted. Olivares, in his capacity as a gentleman in the prince's household, was faced with just the same kind of antipathy in his initial dealings with the heir to the Spanish throne. Once again it seems to have been a question of a petulant adolescent, with deep personal insecurities, being instinctively afraid of the overwhelmingly powerful personality of an older, and obviously ambitious, man. More than once Olivares was tempted to give up and return to his native Seville.

In any event, his attempt to win the favour of the prince, even if successful, could only be regarded as a long-term political investment, since the king was hardly forty, and there was no reason to assume that he would not reign for many years to come. Yet some instinct seems to have persuaded him to hold on, even when Lerma, sensing danger, offered him distinguished alternative postings to get him away from the prince's household. By careful study of Prince Philip's moods and tastes, and obsequious self-abasement, which included on one memorable occasion kissing the prince's chamber-pot, he gradually won his confidence. Then suddenly his prospects were transformed. Philip III fell dangerously ill when returning from Portugal in 1619, and it became clear that his days were numbered. The rival court factions manoeuvred frantically for position, and when Philip III died after a few days' illness at the end of March 1621, the faction headed by Olivares and his uncle, Don Baltasar de Zúñiga, was poised to take power.

In the absence of any claims to high office based on governmental experience or unusual political wisdom, Olivares played the one card available to him by making the most of his physical proximity to the prince, just as the Duke of Lerma had done a generation earlier. In Spain, the classic story of the rise of a favourite seemed to be repeating itself once again. In France, the situation was rather different. Richelieu already had an established political base as principal adviser to the Queen Mother. He also had experience of government, and his high intelligence and diplomatic skills were widely recognized. As a prominent ecclesiastic he also enjoyed opportunities denied to Olivares. His chance came in December 1621 with the death of Luynes, who had blocked the Queen Mother's attempts to have him made a Cardinal. His elevation to the purple in September 1622 at the age of thirty-seven greatly strengthened his chances of securing a seat on the King's Council. Louis still resisted – the Tuscan ambassador reports as late as February 1624 that the king was reluctant to admit him to the Council because of his 'proud and domineering spirit'[8] – but on 29 April of that year Louis' resistance collapsed. Once again, Richelieu played the clerical card by immediately producing documentation to secure precedence in the Council by virtue of his rank as cardinal.[9] Four months later, in August, Louis dismissed and arrested his principal minister, La Vieuville, and entrusted Richelieu with the government.

How are we to explain Louis' capitulation to a man for whom he had felt such a deep antipathy? There were two vulnerable points in Louis' armour, and Richelieu made unerringly for both of them. One was his relationship with the Queen Mother. Where La Vieuville aimed to keep the king and Marie de Médicis apart, Richelieu came forward as the one man who offered some hope of healing their differences and ending the rift in the royal family.[10] Louis was even more vulnerable where his own high conception of his royal obligations was concerned. The death of Luynes at the end of 1621 had left him without a right-hand man capable of restoring the authority of the crown in a country that was being torn to pieces by the renewed outbreak of conflict with dissident nobles and the Huguenots. During 1622 and 1623, when policy was in the hands of the Brûlarts, the administration was plainly adrift. Their replacement by La Vieuville in the spring of 1623 did nothing to improve affairs. In particular, La Vieuville's conduct of foreign policy led to one humiliation after another, especially in the complex matter of the Valtelline, where it seemed that Paris was constantly being outmanoeuvred by Madrid.

In the midst of all this confusion and humiliating drift, Richelieu could plausibly put himself forward as the one man capable of restoring the royal authority.[11] He orchestrated a press campaign which played on the weaknesses and inadequacies of La Vieuville's policies, especially in the field of foreign affairs, and created a groundswell of sentiment on his own behalf.[12] But he also worked hard on the king, suggesting to him, in the words of the Venetian ambassador, 'ideas of glory and grandeur for his crown'.[13]

---

[8] Berthold Zeller, *Richelieu et les ministres de Louis XIII de 1621 à 1624* (Paris, 1880), p. 244.
[9] Avenel, II, p. 6.
[10] Fagniez, *Père Joseph*, I, p. 183.
[11] For the complicated circumstances attending Richelieu's rise to power, see especially Rémy Pithon, 'Les Débuts difficiles du ministère de Richelieu et la crise de Valteline, 1621–1627', *Revue d'Histoire Diplomatique*, 74 (1969), pp. 289–322, and A.D. Lublinskaya, *French Absolutism: the Crucial Phase, 1620–1629* (Cambridge, 1968), pp. 148–53, and 243–71.
[12] See Gustav Fagniez, 'L'Opinion publique et la presse politique sous Louis XIII, 1624–1626', *Revue d'Histoire Diplomatique*, 14 (1900), pp. 352–401.
[13] Zeller, *Richelieu et les ministres*, p. 267.

But to persuade Louis that he was the one to bring glory and grandeur to the crown, Richelieu had to manoeuvre with great care. In spite of his later attempts to represent himself as arriving at high office with a series of clear-cut plans for the future of France, there is no evidence that he had any proposals to lay before the king which represented a radical departure from the policies pursued by his immediate predecessors – policies aimed at destroying the political power of the Huguenots and seditious aristocrats, restoring order to the crown's finances, and holding Spain in check. All he could really offer was to pursue them more efficiently than the Brûlarts or La Vieuville. This would not have been difficult – no man was more helped to high office by his enemies than Richelieu in 1624. Yet ultimately the Cardinal could only attain his ends if he mastered the tortured personality of a monarch who needed the guiding hand of a strong minister but feared to acknowledge the need even to himself. By August 1624, through a shrewd mixture of deference, persuasiveness, and suppleness of manner combined with firmness of purpose, he had won, if not the king's confidence, at least his grudging consent.

Richelieu had in effect imposed himself on Louis through his ministerial qualifications rather than through the use of the traditional favourite's arts. But here, too, in consolidating his power, he showed himself a master. He took infinite pains to study Louis' unpredictable character, got to know his every passing mood, and took extreme care to avoid giving any impression that he was trespassing on the king's authority.[14] He was also shrewd enough to recognize Louis' continuing emotional need for a genuine favourite, and pushed forward young men who he thought would meet this requirement while presenting no threat to his own position. His one serious misjudgement came towards the end of his life, when Cinq-Mars proved to have political ambitions of his own.

Where Richelieu established his claims through his obvious ministerial abilities, Olivares of necessity took the favourite's classic route to power. He had secured his influence over the prince by constant personal attendance on him, and the attendance continued after Philip's accession to the throne in 1621. The new king appointed him groom of the stole in succession to the Duke of Uceda, and also, a year later, master of the horse. These two appointments, which the Duke of Lerma had also

---

[14] For the working relationship between the king and Richelieu, see especially Ranum, *Richelieu and the Councillors.*

combined in his own person, gave him privileged access to the king, both inside and outside the palace, where he lived in a suite of apartments with his wife and daughter. This was an advantage denied to Richelieu, who lived at some remove from his royal master. On coming to power he bought a mansion on the Rue St Honoré, which he then pulled down to construct the Palais Cardinal; but life in Paris was too much for his highly strung temperament, and he escaped whenever he could to one or other of his houses on the outskirts of the city.[15] Separated from the king for long periods, he kept himself informed on his every move through his confidants,[16] and maintained a regular correspondence with him. Olivares, living permanently within a few hundred yards of Philip, had no need to write.

From the first day of the reign, no one doubted Olivares' personal dominance over the new king. But there was an embarrassing ambiguity about this dominance. It looked suspiciously like a new government by favourite, and yet Olivares and his friends in the years of opposition to Lerma had waged an unrelenting campaign against this form of government. Prince Philip had had it drummed into his head that, when he came to the throne, he should take as his model, not his father, a *roi fainéant,* but his grandfather, Philip II, the epitome of a working king. On the first day of the reign he was heard to say that 'he had read in a book by a good author [almost certainly Fray Juan de Santamaría] that kings should not have favourites, but good councillors'.[17]

Olivares and his uncle, Don Baltasar de Zúñiga, tried to forestall the inevitable criticism by a careful division of functions. Zúñiga, as an experienced Councillor of State, was given formal responsibility for the state papers, while Olivares, nominally at least, occupied himself solely with his household duties. But there are some indications that behind the scenes he was taking an active interest in affairs of state – perhaps rather too active for the liking of his uncle. Zúñiga died in October 1622, and it was generally expected that Olivares would take over his duties. He was in fact now appointed to the Council of State, and so became for the first time a minister of the crown; but once again he held back from high office. For three years Zúñiga's duties were carried out on a collective basis by a

---

[15] Batiffol, *Richelieu et Louis XIII,* p. 26.
[16] Ranum, *Richelieu and the Councillors,* p. 79.
[17] Cited in Francisco Tomás y Valiente, *Los validos en la monarquía española del siglo XVII* (Madrid, 1963), p. 14.

triumvirate, to which Olivares did not even belong.[18] But it is doubtful if anyone was really deceived. As early as December 1622 the British ambassador reported that he was 'as absolute with this king as the Duke of Lerma was with his father';[19] and he emerged quite clearly as the king's principal minister, in fact if not in name, during the Prince of Wales' visit to Madrid in 1623. Indeed the assertive presence at Charles' side of the Duke of Buckingham may have hastened the process by making it essential to confront him with a Spanish counterpart.

Olivares' ascendancy over the sixteen-year-old king was, in the first instance, the result of patiently cultivating him during his years as prince. Philip, chafing at any attempt at control, but pathetically unsure of himself, had grown accustomed to the presence of this obsequious but reassuringly authoritarian figure, twice his own age, who offered him counsel and guidance. He needed these all the more when he found himself king. His first flush of enthusiasm for his royal duties quickly wore off, and he became vulnerable to the same criticisms as were being levelled at his brother-in-law, Louis XIII, who was firmly told in a pamphlet of 1624 that he should curb his 'extraordinary passion' for hunting at a time when his presence was required in the Council.[20]

When Philip turned reluctantly to his official duties it was helpful to have Olivares at hand to tell him how to respond to the *consultas* – those long and tedious reports of discussions in the councils which piled up day after day awaiting his decision. This arrangement might have seemed advantageous to Olivares, but there were good reasons, both personal and political, for him to want to put his relationship with the king on a different basis.

Philip, although he lacked application, had a good natural intelligence, and Olivares was astute enough to appreciate that a young king who was bright but capricious would sooner or later tire of finding himself in leading-strings. But, beyond this, the new ministers had come to power determined to make a clean break with the immediate past and reinstate effective kingship. This was politically necessary, not only in terms of public expectation, but also of their own diagnosis of the evils from which Spain was suffering. In their view, the restoration of Spain and Spanish power was dependent on a reassertion of the crown's authority, both at

---

[18] Roca, *Fragmentos históricos*, pp. 183–4.
[19] BL, Add. Ms. 36,449, fo. 34, Aston to Calvert, 19/29 Dec. 1622.
[20] 'La France en convalescence', *Mercure français*, x (Paris, 1625), p. 693.

home and abroad. This was impossible without the active cooperation of the king.

Like Richelieu, then, Olivares couched his appeal to his monarch in the form of a call to greatness. There were two words to which both ministers constantly resorted. These were 'authority' and 'reputation' – authority at home, reputation abroad. Naturally they presented themselves as ideally qualified to enable their monarchs to attain these high goals. But they also made it plain to their royal masters that there was no short-cut to success: that hard work and sacrifice were required if they were to play the exalted parts expected of them in the theatre of the world.

Both ministers developed, as a result, a tutorial relationship to royal masters who were also royal pupils. In some respects Philip, who was four years younger than Louis, proved more malleable. Louis was not a man for book-learning, and his attention span was limited. Richelieu therefore had to play on his anxiety to prove himself and on his high sense of his royal calling. He coached him as best he could in the skills of statecraft by inserting pieces of political wisdom into his memoranda,[21] and – once he had gained his confidence – by spending long hours closeted with him discussing affairs of state.[22] Philip, on the other hand, set out with Olivares' guidance on an intensive reading course. By the end of the decade he was a cultivated man with discriminating literary and artistic tastes.[23] He was also mentally well equipped to meet the bureaucratic requirements of Spanish kingship in the style of Philip II.

Early in the new reign Olivares drafted for Philip a long secret instruction on the government of Spain.[24] This was in contrast to Richelieu, who prepared his *Testament Politique* towards the end of his ministry to serve as a guide to Louis when he was no longer there to advise him in person.[25] Olivares' secret instruction, or Great Memorial, of 1624 was in part a programme of action for the reign; but it was also an educational document designed to instruct a new king in the character of his kingdoms and the art of governing them. But Philip at this time showed no great eagerness to let himself be instructed, and in 1626 Olivares was sufficiently perturbed by his pupil's lack of progress to write him a sharp note of rebuke for neglecting his duties, coupled with a threat

---

[21] E.g. Grillon, I, p. 185 ('Mémoire pour le Roi', 1625).
[22] Batiffol, *Richelieu et Louis XIII*, p. 152.
[23] See Brown and Elliott, *A Palace*, pp. 40–9, for the grooming of Philip.
[24] *MC*, I, doc. IV.
[25] *TP*, introduction, p. 36.

of resignation unless he changed his ways.[26] Philip expressed his contrition, but his behaviour does not seem to have changed until the autumn of 1627, when a nearly fatal illness helped to concentrate his mind wonderfully on the responsibilities of kingship.

Richelieu had comparable problems with Louis, and – like Olivares – had to combine fatherly persuasion with threats of resignation. But, unlike Olivares, he could also use the weapons of priestly admonition. Religiously, Louis, like Philip, was highly impressionable. 'No man', wrote Tallemant des Réaux unkindly, 'loved God less and feared the devil more, than the late king.'[27] Richelieu knew how to take advantage of this, and even if the king's spiritual guidance was formally entrusted to other hands, he could play to perfection the role of father-confessor. As a prelate he cut a formidable figure, and his rebukes were delivered with all the crushing weight of the authority that belonged as of age-old right to the church universal. In January 1629, in the presence both of the Queen Mother and of the royal confessor, he presented Louis with a startlingly frank analysis of his character defects – his congenital suspiciousness, his jealousy, his quickness of temper, and his tendency to lose himself in trivial detail to the neglect of great matters of state.[28] Louis, terrified of his own weaknesses, and confronted by the awesome presence of a man who offered at once formidable censure and a way of salvation, took the rebuke to heart.

Neither Richelieu nor Olivares would have issued such rebukes to their monarchs unless they had judged to a nicety exactly how far they could afford to go. They both recognized behind the outward stubbornness the sense of personal inadequacy, and knew that firm tutorial direction, even if initially unpopular, was the one way to keep their jobs. But there was more to their method than the calculation of personal advantage. In reality it was integral to their conception of kingship.

It is impossible to study the state papers and correspondence of Richelieu and Olivares without quickly becoming aware of the awe, amounting to veneration, with which they approached the office and person of the king. For each of them, God had specially chosen his royal master to forward His high purpose. The monarch must therefore prove worthy of his

[26] *MC*, I, doc. XI.
[27] Quoted by Jean Orcibal, *Les Origines du Jansénisme*, II (Paris, 1947), p. 561, note 2.
[28] Grillon, IV, doc. 11.

exalted calling. 'Kings more than all other men should act according to reason', Richelieu admonished Louis in the *Testament Politique*.[29] For Olivares the King of Spain was, by God's design, the greatest king on earth, and it was Philip's obligation to maintain and surpass the glorious tradition of Spanish kingship represented by the most distinguished of his predecessors – Ferdinand the Catholic (the 'king of kings'), Charles V, and Philip II ('first of kings in prudence').[30]

It was a heavy burden, then, which the two ministers were attempting to impose on the pathetically fragile figures of their respective monarchs – a burden charged with the double weight of divine command and human history. The extent of it was indicated by the sobriquets chosen for the monarchs, which in themselves constituted a programme for the reign. Philip was styled from 1625 Felipe el Grande, a king great at once in the arts of peace and war. Louis, for his part, was to be Louis le Juste, a worthy successor to his forebear, St Louis.[31] The final verdict on the two monarchs must unfortunately be that Philip was not great, nor was Louis just.

In setting a high ideal of kingship before their royal pupils, Richelieu and Olivares were in fact implying that the office of king transcended, and was capable of transforming, the man. Both kings were being called upon to serve something greater than themselves. This greater something was, for Richelieu, the state.

It seems to have been during the 1570s and 1580s, at a time when the religious wars and the consequent weakening of royal authority threatened the very fabric of the body politic, that a number of Frenchmen began to conceive of the state in its modern sense as an entity distinct from both the ruler and the ruled.[32] Although Jean Bodin still speaks of the 'republic' rather than the 'state', this conception of the state as a distinct apparatus of power emerges forcefully from the pages of his *Six livres de la République* (1576).[33] A few years later Henry III

---

[29] *TP*, p. 271.

[30] *MC*, II, p. 214, for Olivares' references to Ferdinand and Philip II.

[31] Dietrich Gerhard, 'Richelieu', in *The Responsibility of Power*, ed. Leonard Krieger and Fritz Stern (New York, 1969), p. 108. Louis' sobriquet, which seems to have been attached to him in his youth, is said to have been originally inspired by the fact that he was born under Libra. He could therefore be expected to keep the scales of justice in balance (see Pierre Chevallier, *Louis XIII* (Paris, 1979), p. 153).

[32] See the arguments advanced by Howell A. Lloyd, *The State, France and the Sixteenth Century* (London, 1983), especially ch. 6.

[33] Quentin Skinner, *The Foundations of Modern Political Thought*, II (Cambridge, 1978), p. 355.

himself referred to the state in a way which detached it from his own personal interests.[34] But while the new, Bodinesque, formulation helped to widen the terms of the political debate, old and new notions lived side by side and mingled together in a sometimes uneasy synthesis in early seventeenth-century France.

Pierre Charron, whose *La Sagesse* was published at the very beginning of the new century, provides a definition of the state likely to have enjoyed a wider circulation than the more sophisticated formulations of Bodin. 'The state', he writes, 'that is to say domination, or a fixed order in commanding and obeying.'[35] This idea of command and obedience was central to Richelieu's own vision of the state, which was for him an instrument of power. The word 'state' itself seems to have connoted for him Bodinesque ideas of sovereignty located in an apparatus of royal power that was rapidly being stripped of its Bodinesque limitations in the opening decades of the seventeenth century.[36] It was, however, power for a purpose. The king, in the majesty of his sovereignty, was responsible only to God, and the apparatus of his power must be used to sustain the common weal against selfish private interests. 'The public interest', wrote Richelieu in the *Testament Politique*, 'must be the sole end of the prince and his councillors.'[37] In fact, the king was expected to defer at all times to the needs of the state – an entity which subsumed the interests of king and kingdom and raised them to a higher level than could be obtained by either on its own. But the state was inseparable in his mind from the majesty of kingship, and the two were firmly conjoined when he wrote in his *Maxims* of his passion for the 'bien de l'Estat et de la Royauté'.[38]

Although Olivares speaks of 'matters of state' or 'reason of state'[39] he apparently does not employ the word 'state' (*estado*) as does Richelieu in order to designate a transcendent entity. The explanation for this may well be the very different character of the crowns of Spain and France.

[34] Lloyd, *The State*, p. 82.
[35] Book I, ch. 45 (Paris, 1671 edn, pp. 232–3).
[36] See Rudolf von Albertini, *Das politische Denken in Frankreich zur Zeit Richelieus* (Marburg, 1951), pp. 38 and 53, and W. F. Church, 'Cardinal Richelieu and the Social Estates of the Realm', *Album Helen Maud Cam*, II (Louvain–Paris, 1961), pp. 261–70.
[37] *TP*, p. 330.
[38] *Maximes d'état*, p. 55, and see Herbert H. Rowen, *The King's State* (New Brunswick, 1980), p. 63. For an admirably lucid and succinct survey of Richelieu's political ideas, see Gerhard, 'Richelieu'.
[39] E.g. *MC*, II, p. 167 ('I find no reason . . . that is not against all reason of state').

Where the King of France ruled over a single realm, the King of Spain was the ruler of a whole complex of kingdoms and provinces – the so-called *monarquía española*, whose individual components possessed varying forms of government. But although the word 'state' is largely absent from the Count–Duke's vocabulary, this does not necessarily imply a radical distinction between his view of kingship and that of the Cardinal. Instead, he speaks of the 'royal service' and the 'royal authority'.

In practice it is doubtful whether Richelieu's conception of the state is as abstract as it is sometimes represented, or Olivares' conception of kingship as personal as his vocabulary would suggest. Both ministers were in reality issuing a summons to king and subjects alike to sacrifice their private interests to a higher interest defined in terms of such abstract ideals as authority and obedience, responsibility and service. The realization of these ideals meant hard work and discipline for king, ministers and people, each according to his station in life.

Where the people were concerned, both Richelieu and Olivares, although concerned to improve their lot, insisted on the importance of keeping them under the strictest discipline. Richelieu notoriously compared them to mules, more easily spoilt by rest than by heavy labour. But equally, the labour should not be so heavy as to exceed their strength.[40] For Olivares, the people represented the greatest power in the realm, and he warned Philip in his Great Memorial that 'it is always important to pay attention to the voice of the people'.[41] But it remained unclear as to how the voice of the people was to make itself heard. The two ministers had little respect for representative assemblies, which Philip IV, in a moment of exasperation, once described as 'pernicious at all times and in all monarchies without exception'.[42] Cortes, Parlements and Estates were at best convenient forums in which the government could present its programmes and influence opinion. Richelieu, with his great belief in the persuasive powers of his own oratory, enjoyed taking the Parlement of Paris into his confidence and revealing to its members high matters of state, but his relations with Parlements in general, and the Parlement of Paris in particular, were almost uniformly bad. But, like Olivares, who in 1624 toyed with the idea of dispensing entirely with the

[40] *TP*, pp. 253–5 ('Du peuple').
[41] *MC*, I, pp. 61–3 ('Pueblo').
[42] Quoted in A. Waddington, *La République des Provinces-Unies* (Paris, 1895), I, p. 374.

Cortes of Castile,[43] he seems to have felt that on balance it was wiser to humour Parlements and Estates in small matters than to precipitate a major constitutional conflict by attempting to abolish them[44] – something which in any event would have been out of the question where Parlements were concerned, since members owned their offices.

For both ministers, however, there were strict limits beyond which corporate bodies and representative assemblies should not stray. Louis XIII, in a short speech to the Parlement of Paris in 1636, written for him by the Cardinal, said firmly: 'it is not for you to meddle in the affairs of my state'.[45] The *arcana imperii* were exclusively reserved for the king and his ministers, but the privilege of handling them was balanced by the heaviness of the responsibility, which required absolute dedication and unremitting hard work. Ministers, as the faithful executants of royal policies, must dedicate themselves night and day to the fulfilment of their arduous duties. Yet inevitably the highest responsibility of all fell on the monarch, upon whom God had laid the supreme burden of absolute power.

In seeking to equip their royal pupils for their high responsibility, Richelieu and Olivares reacted with delight or despair as they conformed, or failed to conform, to the exacting standards demanded of them. The Count–Duke, for instance, could hardly contain his excitement over Philip's achievement in 1629 in drafting unaided an important state paper, which he regarded as being of a quality not seen since the days of Ferdinand the Catholic. 'With this there is nothing more left to say, other than to give God many thanks, as we all do, for having given us such a king.'[46]

There are bound to be failures as well as successes in the arduous undertaking of grooming kings for greatness. The Count–Duke and the Cardinal could only work with the material to hand, and nothing could turn Louis XIII into another Henry IV, nor Philip IV into another Philip II. Louis, racked by ill-health, was a moody and unhappy man, ill-at-ease and irritable, and the victim of a stammer which left him taciturn and tongue-tied. But he had determination and courage – he was at his best in open country, on horseback with his army – and, if his intelligence was

[43] Andrés de Almansa y Mendoza, *Cartas, 1621–1626* (Madrid, 1886), pp. 295–6.
[44] Compare the comments of Olivares in *MC*, I, p. 62, and of Richelieu in *TP*, p. 274.
[45] Avenel, v, p. 541, and see Albertini, *Politische Denken*, pp. 69–70.
[46] ADM, legajo 79, Olivares to Aytona, 17 Aug. 1629.

limited, he acquired a shrewd judgement of men and events. Philip, once
he had settled down, became a conscientious working monarch, carefully
reading and responding to the endless stream of *consultas*, and well
capable of grasping and discussing complicated issues.

Both kings, too, had a high sense of their royal dignity – a quality that
was particularly necessary if, as their ministers intended, they were to be
systematically elevated to new heights of authority. Richelieu and
Olivares both saw that the court itself, with its formality and ceremonial,
its language of deference and respect, and its exact gradations of rank,
could be used as a major instrument of political discipline and social
control if the monarch could be taught to play his part correctly.

Louis' character, however, proved to be less well adapted than that of
Philip to this kind of enterprise. A sense of decorum and majesty had
been notably absent from the boisterous court of Henry IV, and in
Richelieu's eyes the reformation of the kingdom should properly have
started, as he observed in the *Testament Politique*, with a reformation of the
royal household.[47] Richelieu's life consisted of one long battle against
dérèglement – disorder – but where Louis' living habits were concerned,
he was doomed to defeat. A man of simple tastes, the king preferred to
live in the midst of what Richelieu described as a confusion running all
the way from the kitchen to the study.[48] The order, decorum and
grandeur which the Cardinal regarded as the only proper setting for a
King of France, would have to await the reign of Louis' son. Again it
remained for his son to show how a King of France could enhance his
authority through the judicious use of words: the cutting remark always
came more easily to Louis than the graceful compliment. On the other
hand, he was extremely sensitive to real or imagined slights, and both
king and minister were vigorous in their insistence on the proper marks of
deference to the crown.[49]

Philip IV, unlike Louis, developed under Olivares' guidance into the
very image of the ceremonial monarch. He possessed a natural bodily
grace and dignity of bearing; he cultivated to perfection the impassivity
and *gravitas* which suitably distanced a King of Spain from even the

[47] *TP*, p. 280.
[48] *Ibid.*, p. 281. For manners, or the lack of them, at the courts of Henry IV and Louis XIII, see in
particular M. Magendie, *La Politesse mondaine et les théories de l'honnêteté, en France, au XVIIe
siècle, de 1600 à 1660*, I (Paris, 1925), part I, chs. I and 2.
[49] See Orest Ranum, 'Courtesy, Absolutism and the Rise of the French State, 1630–1660', *Journal
of Modern History*, 52 (1980), pp. 426–51.

highest-born of grandees; and he was fascinated by the details of etiquette and ceremony, which allowed him to regulate with the maximum precision life inside the palace. Olivares shared Richelieu's determination to enforce the exact courtesies prescribed by rank, and with his help Philip succeeded in turning his court into what a contemporary called 'a school of silence, punctiliousness and reverence'.[50] At the same time, his aesthetic interests transformed the court into a brilliant centre of artistic and cultural life, which only heightened the contrast with the court of France. 'Foreigners who have come to France in my time', wrote Richelieu in the *Testament Politique*, 'are often astonished to see a state raised so high and a household sunk so low.'[51] Thwarted in his desire to make Louis XIII the focal point of a splendid and cultivated court, Richelieu created his own court at the Palais Cardinal. By contrast, Olivares, living an austere personal life, devoted his great gifts for stage-management to projecting the image of his monarch as the epitome of royal patronage and splendour, the *rey planeta*, Europe's first Sun King.[52]

In attempting, with more or less success, to mould Louis and Philip to a preconceived image of kingship, the two ministers were in reality consolidating their own personal dominance over their royal masters. Monarchs of whom so much was demanded were bound to feel with special intensity their own inadequacy. They therefore turned with relief mingled with resentment to men who were willing and able to guide them and to lighten their burdens. But in doing so they inevitably evoked the old image of the favourite.

This was something which clearly troubled Olivares. When he rebuked Philip for his idleness in 1626, he argued that, if he would only attend to his duties, 'the very reason for the name of *privado* would disappear'.[53] To avoid the opprobrium and justify their position to the world, he and Richelieu both insisted on their function as councillors. The good king, as Richelieu insisted in the *Testament*, was the king who took counsel.[54] It also followed that, as a good king, he would be blessed

---

[50] Alonso Carrillo, *Origen de la dignidad de grande de Castilla* (Madrid, 1657), fo. 12.

[51] *TP*, p. 280.

[52] See Brown and Elliott, *A Palace*.

[53] *MC*, I, p. 207.

[54] *TP*, p. 288, and see Madeleine Bertaud, 'Le Conseiller du prince, d'après les mémoires de Richelieu et son testament politique', in *Les Valeurs chez les mémorialistes français du XVIIe siècle avant la Fronde*, ed. N. Hepp and J. Hennequin (Paris, 1979), pp. 111–29.

in his choice of councillors. Richelieu for one had no compunctions on this score. 'The Cardinal', we are told in his memoirs, 'is the man whom God has chosen to transmit His counsels to His Majesty.'[55]

The convenient but often fictitious doctrine that Spain and France were ruled by monarchs who governed by advice but took their own decisions was institutionally embodied in their conciliar systems. The Spanish Monarchy was governed by an elaborate conciliar structure, consisting of twelve councils, headed by the Council of State, a body of anything up to eighteen members, whose meetings were only very rarely attended by the king. The French system, unlike the Spanish, had still to attain its definitive form. By the time of Richelieu's advent the Conseil du Roi effectively consisted of three different sections, with areas of competence that remained inadequately defined. Of these, the Conseil des Affaires, or Conseil d'en Haut, presided over by the king, was in process of asserting its preeminence.[56] When Richelieu was named to it in 1624 its membership rose to six, who were joined at their meetings by the four secretaries of state.[57]

Although they had their criticisms of certain features of the system, Richelieu and Olivares possessed neither the inclination nor the ability to change its fundamental character. The essential point for both of them was to establish their own preeminence within it. To do this they adopted the device of insisting on the necessity of having a single councillor who was superior to the rest; and they both used as their justification the intolerably heavy burden of business on the king. After making due obeisance to the divine character of monarchical government, Richelieu observed in the *Testament Politique* that 'if the sovereign cannot or will not personally keep a continuous eye on the chart and compass, reason demands that he should give one man responsibility over all the rest'.[58] Similarly, Olivares argued that there were many hours in the day when kings and princes, however industrious, could not attend to affairs of state. This suggested the need for a single minister with a universal knowledge of affairs, to see that 'all the material is brought before the prince in a suitably digested form, with all the considerations *pro* and *con*,

---

[55] Cited Bertaud, 'Le Conseiller', p. 114.
[56] See Roland Mousnier, 'Le Conseil du Roi de la mort de Henri IV au gouvernement personnel de Louis XIV', *Etudes d'Histoire Moderne et Contemporaine*, I, (1947), pp. 29–67, and the diagram on p. 7 of Bonney, *Political Change in France*.
[57] Batiffol, *Richelieu et Louis XIII*, pp. 10–12.
[58] *TP*, p. 307.

so that the prince can take the appropriate decision'.[59] The minister would in turn put it into effect. But the Count–Duke was very careful to make it plain that the minister was no more than the faithful executive of the king. 'When the prince makes up his mind', he wrote, 'the minister has to forget entirely the opinion which he held, and accept that his views were mistaken.'[60] Richelieu likewise went to infinite pains to make it clear that all decisions were those of the king in his council.[61]

The sheer inability of most princes to control single-handed the complexities of seventeenth-century government made the case for a superior minister highly persuasive; and during the 1620s the heavy demands of warfare and diplomacy argued forcefully for a concentration of power. 'The middling government of one person', observed Olivares, 'is considered superior to the good government of many because of the great risk of disturbance and confusion where many are involved.'[62] Circumstances, in fact, were pushing the monarchies of Western Europe towards a prime ministerial system, although neither Richelieu nor Olivares enjoyed the formal title. Olivares was no more than a minister – the king's 'faithful minister', as he liked to call himself.[63] In 1629, when the Council in France was being reorganized and reduced in size, letters patent confirmed Richelieu's preeminence and designated him, in recognition of his services, '*principal ministre* of our state'.[64] But *principal ministre* was a style which La Vieuville had also enjoyed.[65]

The title of 'prime minister' seems to have been officially used for the first time, not of Richelieu and Olivares, but of their successors, Mazarin and Don Luis de Haro, who appear in the documentation of the Treaty of the Pyrenees in 1659 as 'prime and principal ministers' of their two kings.[66] Yet this would not have happened if the idea of a first minister had not already gained wide currency. Indeed, as early as February 1623, within four months of Zúñiga's death, Olivares was complaining that the evil-intentioned were clamouring against him as the *primer ministro* of the king,[67] and sometimes he would receive a letter addressed to him as

[59] *MC*, II, p. 57 ('Instrucción al marqués de Leganés').
[60] ADM, legajo 79, Olivares to Aytona, 15 Oct. 1631.
[61] Georges Mongrédien, *10 novembre 1630. La Journée des Dupes* (Paris, 1961), p. 10.
[62] *MC*, II, p. 56.
[63] Tomás y Valiente, *Los validos*, p. 95.
[64] Grillon, IV, doc. 677 ('Lettres patentes', 21 Nov. 1629). I am indebted to Dr R.J. Bonney of Reading University for advice on this point.
[65] Batiffol, *Richelieu et Louis XIII*, p. 18.
[66] Tomás y Valiente, *Los validos*, p. 51, note 143, and p. 100.
[67] BAV, Barb. Lat. Ms. 8,599, fo. 7, Olivares to Pope, 17 Feb. 1623.

primer ministro of Spain.[68] Similarly, in France we find Jean Sirmond writing of Richelieu as 'this great man who today holds among us the rank of *premier ministre de l'Etat*'.[69] The new designation, first unofficial and then beginning to be formalized in mid-century documents of state, clearly reflected an important development in the structure and functioning of government. The preeminence of a single ministerial figure was coming to be recognized as necessary for the efficient conduct of affairs.

A first minister had to combine domination of the king with domination of his conciliar colleagues and the central government. The first might well be easier to achieve than the second. At certain moments both the Count–Duke and the Cardinal came up against strong resistance during their first years on the Council, and it was not until the 1630s that they acquired a relatively free hand. Richelieu had a much smaller group of councillors to manipulate and control, but among them was the awkward figure of Michel de Marillac, whose close ties with the Cardinal's opponents in court and country made him a formidable antagonist. Differences over policy were aggravated by differences of age: Marillac, born in 1563, was twenty-two years older than Richelieu. A similar generational divide confronted Olivares when he was appointed to the Council of State. Several of his fellow councillors had records of military and diplomatic service stretching well back into the reign of Philip II, and it was only in the later 1620s that the ranks of these survivors were drastically thinned by death.[70] The implications of this generational divide have not yet received the attention they deserve. How, for instance, did the experience of living through the French Wars of Religion or the revolt of the Netherlands and the defeat of the Armada affect the attitudes and judgement of these veteran councillors? Did they pursue a politics of nostalgia, as has been suggested for Marillac and his friends?[71] If so, was the nostalgia in Spain characterized by illusions of grandeur or intimations of disaster?

The presence at the council table of the venerable relics of an earlier

---

[68] AGS, Estado, legajo 2053, Don Cristóbal de Benavides to Olivares, 14 July 1638.

[69] Cited by Batiffol, *Richelieu et Louis XIII*, p. 18.

[70] The Count of Gondomar and Don Diego de Ibarra died in 1626; Don Pedro de Toledo in 1627; the Marquises of Hinojosa and Montesclaros in 1628; and Don Agustín Mexía, a veteran of the Flanders wars, in 1629.

[71] Mongrédien, *Journée des Dupes*, pp. 35–6. There is no adequate study of Marillac, but see Edouard Everat, *Michel de Marillac. Sa vie, ses oeuvres* (Riom, 1894).

age is in any event liable, in the nature of things, to create problems for ambitious younger colleagues. But Olivares' difficulties went appreciably further. He had to deal with a much more formalized and elaborate administrative system than Richelieu at the top levels of government. Spanish councillors, other than members of the Council of State, followed a rigid career pattern, which began with graduation from a handful of favoured colleges in the major universities, and proceeded by carefully regulated stages from one level of the judicial and administrative hierarchy to the next.[72] This left the Count–Duke with very little room for manoeuvre. He was surrounded by elderly professional bureaucrats who jealously guarded their privileges and looked narrowly out on the world with the suspicious eyes of men who had received a long training in the law.

Olivares' answer to this problem was to set up special *ad hoc* committees or *juntas*, which he filled as far as possible with his own hand-picked men. He would then use these juntas to circumvent the councils. But the device was only a moderate success. The councils sabotaged the work of the juntas, and it proved almost impossible to introduce genuine outsiders into the inner circles of the ministerial bureaucracy. Olivares' personal lawyer, José González, was almost alone in breaking into the system from outside and retaining his place in it after his patron's fall.[73]

At the lower administrative levels Richelieu was faced with a comparable problem in the well-entrenched French system of the sale of offices,[74] but he seems to have enjoyed more latitude than Olivares in the top reaches of government, especially after his victory over Marillac and his friends in 1630 had made his hold over the Conseil d'en Haut secure. Here, as in much else, Spain, which had been a leader in so many fields in the sixteenth century, was beginning in the seventeenth to pay a high price for pioneering. The Spanish bureaucratic structure was impervious to change. But in France as well as Spain, the only effective means of securing some control over the governmental machine was to build up a group of reliable dependants and place them whenever possible in strategic positions.

[72] See Richard L. Kagan, *Students and Society in Early Modern Spain* (Baltimore, 1974), and Janine Fayard, *Les Membres du Conseil de Castille à l'époque moderne, 1621–1746* (Geneva, 1979), ch. 2, for the career structures of councillors in Spain.
[73] For José González, see *MC*, II, p. 129, and Janine Fayard, 'José González (1583?–1668), "créature" du comte-duc d'Olivares et conseiller de Philippe IV', in *Hommage à Roland Mousnier* (Paris, 1980), pp. 351–67.
[74] See Roland Mousnier, *La Vénalité des offices sous Henri IV et Louis XIII* (Rouen, 1945).

Inevitably the Cardinal and the Count–Duke consolidated and exercised their power through an extensive system of patronage. Both turned in the first instance to their relatives. Olivares could never feel safe as long as the court was dominated by the great family connection of the Sandovals which the Duke of Lerma had built up during twenty years of power. Major court and governmental appointments during the first years of the reign therefore went to the interrelated families of Guzmán, Zúñiga and Haro, which would dominate Spanish political life for the next half century. Similarly in France it was the turn of the du Plessis and the La Portes.[75] Then there was the local connection, the Sevillians and the Poitevins, and family friends and clients. Finally, there were officials who attracted favourable attention, like Sublet de Noyers, Richelieu's secretary for war,[76] or Jerónimo de Villanueva, protonotary of the Crown of Aragon, who became Olivares' right-hand man.[77]

These various dependants holding diplomatic, military and governmental posts were known as the 'creatures' of the ministers – *créatures* in French, *hechuras* in Spanish. Absolute loyalty was the precondition of employment, and loyalty to the patron was equated with service to the king. 'I have no father, children or friend', wrote Olivares, 'except for him who serves the king well.'[78] Richelieu equally demanded total obedience, and carefully accumulated documentary evidence of misdemeanour for use in case of need. 'All those', wrote La Rochefoucauld, 'who were not devoted to his wishes were exposed to his hatred, and he would stop at nothing to elevate his creatures and destroy his enemies.'[79]

The two ministers were exacting taskmasters, requiring of their creatures and dependants that same absolute dedication to hard work in the royal service which they required of themselves. One of Richelieu's secretaries fell into temporary disgrace when he was discovered to have written a note to a friend complaining that he was unable to meet him 'because we live here in the harshest state of bondage in the world, and are dealing with the worst tyrant that ever was'.[80] 'My disposition is not good', Olivares warned his secretaries, in part because of lack of health, but also because 'those who are in a position of command over many must act with absolute integrity and close attention to detail, so that the

[75] Ranum, *Richelieu and the Councillors*, p. 30.
[76] *Ibid.*, ch. 5.
[77] See *MC*, I, p. 80, note 44, and Brown and Elliott, *A Palace*, pp. 25–6.
[78] ADM, legajo 79, Olivares to Aytona, 30 Dec. 1633.
[79] Orcibal, *Origines du Jansénisme*, II, p. 492, note 5.
[80] Cited in Deloche, *La Maison*, p. 61.

king (God preserve him) may be well served.'[81] Yet both men had a gentler side to their natures, and both were able to command affection as well as loyalty from those in their inner circle. Richelieu's principal secretary, Denys Charpentier, was a by-word for loyalty.[82] A similar devotion was displayed by Olivares' principal secretary, Antonio Carnero, half-Spanish, half-Flemish, whose family had served the Counts of Olivares for three generations.[83]

The Cardinal and the Count–Duke took full advantage of their power over their dependants. They used them – as Richelieu used his family dependants, the Bouthilliers[84] – as their eyes and ears in the court, and as the executants of policies which they could trust no one else to force through regardless of the obstacles. They bullied and badgered them mercilessly, to make them achieve the impossible and surpass themselves in their loyalty to the king, whatever the personal cost. It was to his creatures that Olivares turned when he wanted the palace of the Buen Retiro built for Philip IV at breakneck speed, and to his creatures that he looked for gifts with which to furnish it, reducing the Marquis of Leganés to tears when he rebuked him for giving only his second-best pictures to the king.[85]

Caught on one side by the relentless demands of their exacting masters, and on the other by the general hostility which their zeal in their masters' service provoked, the creatures of Richelieu and Olivares inevitably developed their own *esprit de corps*. They saw themselves as privileged beings, suffering in a higher cause – that of the royal service. Olivares once wrote graphically to his brother-in-law, the Count of Monterrey, that the king regarded him as one of those 'embarked in our ship'.[86] They were all in the same boat, and would reach port or sink together. The knowledge of this gave them a certain exhilaration, and served as some compensation for the incidental discomforts of the voyage. Storm-tossed and almost permanently embattled they tended to develop over the years, almost in self-protection, a special brand of arrogance which only added to their unpopularity in court and country, and in the long run set them perilously apart. Government through

---

[81] *MC*, I, p. 33 ('Instrucción a los secretarios', Oct. 1624).
[82] Deloche, *La Maison*, pp. 116–17.
[83] See *MC*, I, p. 28.
[84] Ranum, *Richelieu and the Councillors*, p. 32–7.
[85] Brown and Elliott, *A Palace*, p. 116.
[86] AGS, Estado, legajo 2713, Olivares to Monterrey, 30 Oct. 1639.

creatures was the best, and perhaps the only way, to get things done in those difficult decades of the seventeenth century. But it was, by definition, government exercised in dangerous isolation.

Beyond the exhilaration, there were also the rewards. The Marquis of Leganés, who was a nonentity before his cousin, the Count–Duke, raised him to high office, once observed that the greatest of his many services to the king was to have 'followed the Count–Duke's direction in performing them, seeking to imitate him in his zeal and love for Your Majesty and the royal service, in conformity with my obligation to be exclusively his creature (*hechura*) and hence Your Majesty's'.[87] Leganés may have had to surrender some of his choicest pictures to the royal collection, but his services as a councillor and a general were to bring him ample recompense.

Naturally it was impossible to demand of relatives and dependants unstinting dedication to the royal service without offering them some expectation of reward. This in turn required that the ministers themselves should visibly be the recipients of the highest royal favour. Continuing manifestations of the king's esteem were a necessary precondition of their own ability to command the continuing loyalty of their creatures, and both ministers were in fact rewarded with a continuous stream of favours. At the very beginning of the reign of Philip IV, Olivares was granted the coveted grandeeship which had so consistently eluded his father. Simultaneously he began to use his position and influence to carve out for himself a large fiefdom in the region of Seville, designed to rival that of his kinsman, the Duke of Medina Sidonia. In 1625 he married his daughter to an impoverished representative of his own house of Guzmán, which claimed greater antiquity than the Medina Sidonias; and the culmination of his efforts to establish the fortunes of the cadet branch of the Guzmáns came a few days after his daughter's marriage, when the king raised him to a dukedom under the title of Duke of San Lúcar la Mayor.[88] It was from this moment that, as Count of Olivares and Duke of San Lúcar, he became known to contemporaries as the Conde-Duque, the Count–Duke of Olivares.

The shattering of his hopes of direct succession by the death of his daughter in childbirth in the following year seems to have taken the heart

[87] AHN, Consejos, libro 7157, petition from Marquis of Leganés, 19 Nov. 1641.
[88] The document elevating Olivares to a dukedom, dated 5 January 1625, is reproduced in Roca, *Fragmentos históricas*, pp. 233–5.

out of Olivares' plans for family aggrandizement. Any conflict of loyalties that he may previously have felt now gave way to an all-consuming dedication to the interests of the crown, and to an almost obsessive insistence on probity in his own public life and that of his dependants. His own hands, especially by seventeenth-century standards, seem to have been clean, and although he continued to receive gifts and honours from the king, he could also claim to have spent heavily – as did Richelieu[89] – in the service of the crown. But he signally failed to extend his own standards to his dependants and relatives, some of whom, like his brother-in-law Monterrey, became notoriously rich on the perquisites of office.

Richelieu also claimed to be disinterested, but seems to have built up his own fortune and that of his family with fewer inhibitions. The death in a duel in 1619 of his elder brother, the Marquis of Richelieu, ended the hope of succession in the male line,[90] but this did not deter him from doing everything in his power to enhance the greatness of his house. As a cleric he was able, unlike Olivares, to accumulate benefices, which added a quarter of a million *livres* a year to his income.[91] Then in 1631 Louis XIII made him a duke. He collected titles and offices with great assiduity, built up an enormous fortune, and spent prodigally.[92] He also engaged in an ambitious if not entirely successful marriage policy for his sisters and nieces, in an attempt to establish his family among the greatest in France.[93] Part of this may be seen as deliberate political strategy to impose himself on the great nobility, whose ambitions represented a more immediate threat to the crown than those of the grandee houses of Spain, but it also reflects the intensity of his aspirations for himself and his family.

The aggrandizement of the two ministers, and with them a circle of clients and dependants, inevitably exposed them to bitter attack. Mathieu de Morgues was scathing about Richelieu's systematic accumulation of new offices for which he was unqualified, and his invention of new titles to go with them: 'Généralissime and Eminentissime, and it

---

[89] Batiffol, *Autour de Richelieu*, pp. 15–16.

[90] Carré, *La Jeunesse*, p. 208.

[91] Louis J. Lekai, *The Rise of Cistercian Strict Observance in Seventeenth Century France* (Washington, 1968), p. 63.

[92] Batiffol, *Autour de Richelieu*, ch. 1, and Jean-Pierre Labatut, *Les Ducs et pairs de France au XVIIe siècle* (Paris, 1972), p. 262, for Richelieu's fortune. In addition to the dukedom of Richelieu he also acquired the dukedom of Fronsac in 1634. Aiguillon was established as a *duché-pairie* in favour of his niece in 1638 (see Labatut, pp. 78 and 173).

[93] See Ranum, 'Richelieu and the Great Nobility', *French Historical Studies*, 3 (1963), p. 201.

would not take much for him to have himself called Ministrissime and Admiralissime.'[94] The ministers responded to these attacks by insisting with a vehemence bordering on shrillness that their sole motivation was the disinterested service of the king. Olivares was represented in a play by Quevedo as a second Spanish Seneca, the wise and disinterested counsellor, whose foresight and prudence brought his monarch victory;[95] and the theme found its visual counterpart in Maino's picture of his crowning Philip with laurels in the Hall of Realms. Richelieu, in creating a Gallery of Illustrious Men, gave his contemporaries a lesson in their duties to the prince and the state, while simultaneously confirming his own credentials by having himself portrayed as the latest in the line. ' It is my glory', he wrote to Bouthillier in 1630, at a time when the air was thick with conspiracy, 'to be exposed to everyone for the service of the king, thanks be to God. What consoles me is that I have no personal enemies, and that I have never offended anyone save in the service of the state.'[96]

By identifying themselves so closely with the service of the crown, as wise and disinterested ministers uniquely equipped with the necessary qualities of industry and prudence, the Cardinal and the Count–Duke hoped to exorcise the image of the favourite. But yet, as they could never forget, they depended entirely for their survival on the royal favour, and all the time they were bound to ask themselves how long this would last. In June 1626, following the Chalais conspiracy, Louis XIII made a solemn promise to Richelieu: 'Be assured that I will always protect you against all comers, and that I will never abandon you . . . Rest assured that I will never change and that anyone who attacks you will find me as your second.'[97] This was a remarkable promise, but could Richelieu take the king at his word? He had seen with his own eyes the mob tearing to pieces the body of his own patron Concini, assassinated on the specific orders of the king. He knew better than anyone the streak of cruelty and vindictiveness in his master, and he remained a prey to gnawing anxiety throughout his ministerial career.

Olivares also suffered from continuous anxiety, although the toppling of favourites tended to be managed in a more civilized fashion in Madrid. By a paradox full of ironies, therefore, ministers who had succeeded in

---

[94] Morgues, 'La très humble . . . remonstrance', *Recueil*, p. 24.
[95] Francisco de Quevedo y Villegas, *Cómo ha de ser el privado*, in *Obras completas*, ed. Felicidad Buendía, II (6th edn, Madrid, 1967).
[96] Grillon, V, p. 195.
[97] Grillon, I, pp. 353–4 (9 June 1626); and see Georges Pagès, *La Monarchie d'ancien régime en France* (Paris, 1952), p. 82.

making their monarchs so dependent on themselves, found themselves no less dependent on their monarchs. In Quevedo's play, *The Perfect Favourite*, the Marquis of Valisero (an anagram of Olivares) says that he is a 'tiny atom' beside the king.[98] Richelieu wrote of himself in similar vein in 1628: ' I was zero, which means something only when there are numbers in front of it; and now that it has pleased the king to put me at the front, I am the same zero, which, as I see it, signifies nothing.'[99] The cringing self-abasement which they sometimes displayed in their relations with their masters reflects a realistic awareness that monarchs who had raised them from nothing could with equal ease return them to the place from which they had come.

In retrospect it may seem as if their fears were exaggerated, but there were critical moments in the careers of both ministers when their fall was confidently predicted. Court intrigue was a constant menace to both, and there was always a danger that unfriendly voices would succeed in gaining the ear of the king. While the two ministers did what they could to shield their masters from malign influences, it was impossible to seal off from the world a monarch who moved around as much as Louis XIII; and not even Philip IV, who was much more of a prisoner in his own palace, could be surrounded by a totally impermeable *cordon sanitaire*. With two monarchs whose religious consciences were as scrupulous as those of Louis and Philip, ecclesiastics – whether royal confessors, court preachers or papal nuncios – were bound to enjoy a special degree of influence, and it was not easy to prevent them from speaking their minds, or serving as conduits for special interests. Philip IV's confessor, Fray Antonio de Sotomayor, for instance, seems to have used his influence to block measures which would have eased the entry of Jews into the peninsula;[100] and the papal nuncio, Cardinal Monti, lobbied persistently and successfully in the royal closet to thwart Olivares' plans for clipping the powers of the church in Spain.[101] Similarly, not all of Louis' Jesuit confessors proved amenable to Richelieu's direction, as the dismissal of Father Caussin in December 1637 for his outspoken comments on the horrors of war and of Protestant alliances makes plain.[102]

[98] *Cómo ha de ser el privado*, p. 596 (Act 1).
[99] Grillon, III, p. 61 (Richelieu to Cardinal de La Valette, 11 Feb. 1628).
[100] José Espinosa Rodríguez, *Fray Antonio de Sotomayor y su correspondencia con Felipe IV* (Vigo, 1944), pp. 35–6.
[101] Quintín Aldea Vaquero, *Iglesia y Estado en la España del siglo XVII* (Comillas, 1961), pp. 43–5.
[102] Orcibal, *Origines du Jansénisme*, II, pp. 560–1; Avenel, V, pp. 811–14.

Neither minister, therefore, could ever feel absolutely secure, and each felt keenly the isolation of his exposed position. On the one hand the two men were faced with the hatred of their enemies, whether covert or open, and the hostility of a public opinion which seemed incapable of appreciating the ideals for which they struggled. On the other, they were confronted by sudden changes of mood in their masters which might presage some violent storm. Both kings could, when they wished, be exceptionally stubborn. 'I have never', wrote Olivares, 'met a man as difficult to move as the king.'[103] The six feet of Louis' study notoriously gave Richelieu more trouble than all the rest of Europe together,[104] and he counted himself lucky if the king accepted two out of every four proposals that he made.[105] 'If you knew', wrote Olivares to the Marquis of Aytona, 'on how many matters of importance His Majesty has decided against my opinion . . . you would cross yourself.'[106]

Both ministers may have been exaggerating for effect, but there were many occasions when they felt themselves mistrusted, misunderstood and agonizingly alone in the world. 'One man alone', writes Richelieu to Louis, 'cannot do everything.'[107] 'Sir, I can do no more, I am all alone', writes Olivares to Philip.[108] Each struggled to establish and preserve with his master a genuine working partnership in which one would give the other assistance and support. To a surprisingly large extent this working partnership was achieved, and with it a relationship which went beyond mere formal esteem. But the collaboration by its very nature was characterized by constant tensions and daily uncertainties. To live the life of the statesman, according to Richelieu, was to be condemned to eternal torture.[109] 'Todo es trabajos', 'it is all hard work', complained Olivares as he toiled through the long hours of his endless working day.[110] The Cardinal and the Count–Duke demanded much of themselves and much of their monarchs; and it would be hard to say, as we contemplate those eighteen or twenty years of partnership between the two kings and their ministers, which were the masters, and which the servants.

[103] *MC*, II, p. 48 (Olivares to Count of Castro, 13 Aug. 1629).
[104] Aubery, *Histoire*, p. 589.
[105] Grillon, IV, p. 549 (Richelieu to Cardinal de Bérulle, Aug. 1629).
[106] ADM, legajo 79, Olivares to Aytona, 24 May 1631.
[107] Grillon, II, p. 664 (Memoir for king, 23 Nov. 1627).
[108] AGS, Estado, legajo 2656, *voto* of Olivares, 2 Oct. 1635.
[109] *TP*, p. 296.
[110] ADM, legajo 79, Olivares to Aytona, 19 Sept. 1627.

3

Restoration and reform

The Europe in which Olivares and Richelieu came to power in the early 1620s was a continent in turmoil. Between 1618 and 1621 the peace so precariously established in the early years of the century collapsed with impressive suddenness. When reports of the Defenestration of Prague reached Paris in the early summer of 1618 Luynes inquired whether Bohemia had a sea-coast.[1] At least he was in good company. But the ignorance would soon be dispelled. The Bohemian rebellion, followed in 1620 by the revolt of the Valtelline against its Protestant Grisons overlords, and the expiry in 1621 of the Twelve Years' Truce between Spain and the United Provinces, marked the beginnings of a great European upheaval into which one state after another would be sucked.

Puysieulx, who effectively assumed responsibility for the conduct of foreign affairs in France after the dismissal of Richelieu in 1617, prophesied that, unless the revolt in Bohemia was quickly brought under control, it would lead to a general European war that would be at once a war 'of religion and state'.[2] He was a better prophet than politician. It was the combination of religious and political issues repeating itself across the continent, and occurring both between and within states, that made the crisis of 1618–21 so intractable. For this was a confrontation not only between Catholics and Protestants, at the national and international level, but also between monarchical power and aristocratic and constitutionalist opposition. In a pamphlet published in 1617 Richelieu argued that it was Protestants, not Catholics, who threatened the

---

[1] 'How unfit this man was for the credit he had with the King may be argued by this; that when there was question made about some business in Bohemia, he demanded whether it was an inland country, or lay upon the sea?' *The Autobiography of Edward, Lord Herbert of Cherbury*, ed. Sidney W. Lee (London, 1886), pp. 104–5. Herbert must have heard the story a few months later when he arrived in Paris as the ambassador of James I.

[2] Victor-L. Tapié, *La Politique étrangère de la France et le début de la guerre de Trente Ans, 1616–1621* (Paris, 1934), p. 239.

authority of kings.[3] The Bohemian rebellion seemed to bear him out. So, too, did the unrest in Béarn, a Bohemia in miniature, where Louis XIII ordered the restitution of all church property in 1617. The provincial Estates reacted strongly to an edict which they regarded as a threat to their liberties as well as their religion.[4] Everywhere the combination of radical Protestantism with representative assemblies seemed a guarantee of political upheaval.

France and Spain, as the two leading Catholic monarchies in Europe, were therefore bound to feel tremors of apprehension at the spread of Protestant-inspired revolt through the lands of the Holy Roman Empire. But developments in the Empire touched France even more intimately than they touched Spain, not only because of geographical proximity, but because they resembled so closely what was happening at home. The same combination of forces was at work in France as in the Empire, although constitutionally the King of France's position was incomparably stronger than that of the Emperor. Among the French provinces only Béarn and Navarre possessed something approaching semi-autonomous status on the Bohemian model; and in 1620, when the Emperor Ferdinand II was reducing Bohemia by force, Louis XIII led his army into Béarn, and followed up his expedition by announcing the formal incorporation of Béarn and Navarre into the kingdom of France.

But Louis' real as distinct from his nominal authority over his kingdom was severely restricted in the first years of his reign. Life was certainly complicated by the division of France into *pays d'élections* and *pays d'états*, where the survival of provincial Estates imposed a serious check on the crown's tax-raising powers.[5] But Bourbon France was a corporate society, in which there was always scope for a skilful ruler to play off one corporate body or administrative institution against another: Estates against Parlements, and Parlements against the provincial governors.[6] Although it was always difficult for a regency government to maintain authority, no administration in France since 1610 had been conspicuous for its political skills, and the effects of this were everywhere apparent.

[3] *Ibid.*, p. 417.
[4] For Béarn, see Lublinskaya, *French Absolutism*, pp. 170–3, and Tapié, *Politique étrangère*, pp. 235–8.
[5] For an exhaustive treatment of provincial assemblies and Estates, see J. Russell Major, *Representative Government in Early Modern France* (New Haven–London, 1980).
[6] For the governors, see Robert R. Harding, *Anatomy of a Power Elite. The Provincial Governors in Early Modern France* (New Haven–London, 1978).

The activities of an ambitious and undisciplined aristocracy; the degree of independence enjoyed by the provincial governors and by an office-holding class which owed its offices to purchase rather than to royal concession; and the presence of an entrenched Protestant minority, especially in the west and south, had all conspired in the years between 1610 and 1620 to subvert the royal authority. Disaster was temporarily averted in 1620 when the royal army defeated the Queen Mother's faction at the battle of Ponts-de-Cé; but at any moment a new alliance of the dissident elements could plunge the country into chaos.

The internal dangers also had an external dimension, for there were close links between the Dutch, the German Calvinist princes, and the Huguenots, who looked to their foreign friends for military and financial help. The defeat of Calvinist rebellion in the Empire would therefore redound to Louis' domestic advantage. But it was a tradition of French foreign policy to protect the liberties of the German princes, Protestant and Catholic alike, against the power of the Habsburgs; and although the recent royal marriages had encouraged the rapprochement of France and Spain, France's wish to see revolt suppressed in the Empire was counterbalanced by its fear that the successful suppression of revolt would make the House of Austria excessively powerful. Between 1618 and 1621 the principal object of France's foreign policy was therefore to achieve a general pacification in the Empire before matters got out of hand. But uncertainty of purpose, shortage of money, and recurrent domestic crises meant that it failed to pursue effectively a policy either of intervention or non-intervention, and made the worst of every world.[7]

Intervention in the affairs of the Empire also posed problems for Spain, but of a different kind. In comparison with France, the Spanish Monarchy – as the dominions of the King of Spain were collectively known – possessed a high degree of stability. The extent of effective royal control varied greatly from one kingdom or province to another, but even in those parts of the Monarchy where constitutionalism survived most strongly – Catalonia, for instance, or the Basque provinces – there was no Protestant minority to give aid and comfort to political dissidents. For a century now there had been no revolt in Castile, the heart of the Monarchy, and the great Castilian aristocrats, held in check by a highly

---

[7] Tapié, *Politique étrangère*, examines in detail the dilemmas and failures of French foreign policy during these years.

developed royal bureaucracy, had to seek power through palace intrigue or by obtaining seats on the Council of State.

The Duke of Lerma's twenty years of preeminence as the favourite of Philip III represented a weakening of the strong personal monarchy established by Philip II, and the capture of the crown and, to a lesser degree, of the governmental system by a powerful aristocratic faction. Lerma remained committed to the traditional lines of policy of the Spanish Habsburgs – the defence of the faith, and the conservation of a world-wide Monarchy that was beginning to look over-extended – but a combination of inclination and circumstance had led him to seek peace with England and to sign a truce with the rebellious Dutch. But by the time of his fall in 1618 his prudence was being condemned as pusillanimity, and the Council of State found itself under intense pressure from Spain's viceroys in Italy and its ambassadors in the leading capitals of Europe to stand up forcefully for the defence of what were perceived as the vital interests of the Monarchy.

The activists argued that these interests were best defended by vigorous Spanish support for the Austrian branch of the Habsburgs as it battled against heresy and rebellion, and by the renewal of war with the Dutch, who had taken advantage of the truce to encroach on the king's overseas territories, undermine the Castilian economy, and give general encouragement to the enemies of the House of Austria. Under the guidance of Don Baltasar de Zúñiga, with his long experience of affairs in central and northern Europe, the Council of State took a series of decisions between 1618 and 1621 which ensured Spain's active involvement in Germany, asserted its control over the military corridors that linked Milan to Vienna and Brussels, and led it in the spring of 1621 to resume hostilities with the Dutch.[8]

The heavy new military and naval expenditures made necessary by Spain's return to war in 1620-1 came at an awkward moment. As in France during the regency period, the royal finances in Spain had been badly mismanaged by a corrupt and incompetent administration, and the

---

[8] For Spanish foreign policy in the last years of Philip III, see H. R. Trevor-Roper, 'Spain and Europe, 1598–1621', *The New Cambridge Modern History*, IV (Cambridge, 1970), ch. 9; Jonathan I. Israel, *The Dutch Republic and the Hispanic World, 1606–1661* (Oxford, 1982); and the following articles by P. J. Brightwell: 'The Spanish System and the Twelve Years' Truce', *English Historical Review*, 89 (1974), pp. 270–92; 'The Spanish Origins of the Thirty Years' War', *European Studies Review*, 9 (1979), pp. 409–31; 'Spain and Bohemia: the Decision to Intervene, 1619', and 'Spain, Bohemia and Europe, 1619–1621', *European Studies Review*, 12 (1982), pp. 117–41 and 371–99.

crown had enormous debts. Now more money was urgently needed, and it was needed just when remittances of American silver for the crown had slumped dramatically. The shortfall would have to be made good by taxation, and this meant in the first instance taxation in Castile, the crown's traditional mainstay. But the Cortes of Castile, which were beginning to show a new vitality in the later years of Philip III, could justifiably protest that the country was in no shape to pay still more in taxes. Competition from cheap foreign goods during the years of peace had undermined still further an already weak economy; and the great plague at the turn of the century had reduced Castile's population by around half a million to a total of some six million, as compared with the sixteen million of France. Pressure was therefore growing in Castile for greater financial assistance from other parts of the Monarchy: the Italian viceroyalties of Naples and Sicily, and the various non-Castilian kingdoms and provinces of the Iberian peninsula: Portugal, the Basque provinces, Navarre, Aragon, Valencia and Catalonia. But all these retained their own customary laws and representative assemblies, so that any attempt to extract larger financial and military contributions could well lead to disruptive constitutional conflict.[9]

In both France and Spain in the 1620s, war was to be the precipitant of change. In both countries, war aggravated old problems – especially the problems of finance – and created pressing new needs. The ministries of Richelieu and Olivares cannot be abstracted from this context of war: European war, in which Spain was already an active participant when Olivares came to power, and – in France – civil war in addition, as Louis XIII sought to reconquer substantial areas of his own realm from the Huguenots and the dissident nobles.

The shadow of war made all the darker a scene which the two ministers depicted in the most sombre colours. 'The present state of these kingdoms is probably, for our sins, the worst that has ever been seen', wrote Olivares in his Great Memorial for Philip IV in 1624.[10] 'I can truthfully say', wrote Richelieu in the *Testament Politique* of the situation which he found in France in that same year, 'that the Huguenots shared the state with [Your Majesty], that the *grands* behaved as if they were not

[9] For the pressures building up in Spain at the end of Philip III's reign, see J. H. Elliott, *The Revolt of the Catalans* (Cambridge, 1963, reprinted 1984), pp. 182–93.
[10] *MC*, I, p. 52.

your subjects, and the governors of the provinces as if they were sovereign powers.'[11]

Reforming statesmen have a natural tendency to depict the scene that confronts them on their attainment of high office as one of utter darkness and confusion. Richelieu and Olivares had indeed inherited formidable problems both at home and abroad, but if they were the prisoners of the immediate past, they were also – and to a far greater extent than they would ever have been prepared to admit – its beneficiaries. They came to power at a moment when decisive action was expected, and indeed demanded, by a large body of informed and uninformed opinion in societies where the idea of 'reformation' was gaining new momentum. In the final years of Philip III the ministers in Spain were attempting, however inadequately, to respond to a general demand for *reformación* of social customs, the tax structure, the royal administration, and almost anything else capable of being reformed.[12] In France, not even the *église prétendue réformée* had succeeded in giving *réformation* a bad name.[13] Early-seventeenth-century French society was being swept by the same powerful currents for internal reformation of the Catholic church as had swept Spain a generation earlier.[14] This in itself was enough to create a climate of opinion which eagerly embraced the idea of reformation and extended it instinctively to civil life.

Reformation did not, in practice, preclude innovating change. But in societies which still tended to look askance at the very idea of novelty, programmes of action were naturally conceived and presented as programmes of restoration and reform. Richelieu and Olivares, for both of whom the royal authority was paramount, measured that authority in their own days against the record of the past, and found it sadly wanting. It was their mission to restore it – restore it in Spain to what it had been in the days of Philip II or Ferdinand the Catholic, and in France to what it had been before the Wars of Religion caused it to collapse. Any innovation which might be involved in achieving this was seen as an

---

[11] *TP*, p. 93.

[12] See J. H. Elliott, 'El programa de Olivares y los movimientos de 1640', *Historia de España Ramón Menéndez Pidal*, xxv (Madrid, 1982), especially pp. 335–42, and 'Self-Perception and Decline in Early Seventeenth-Century Spain', *Past and Present*, 74 (1977), pp. 41–61.

[13] In spite of the assertion of Thuau, *Raison d'état*, p. 383, to the contrary. See, for example, the tract entitled 'La Réformation de la France' in the *Mercure français*, ix (Paris, 1624), pp. 417–23, which puts forward proposals for 'reforming the disorders of the state and its principal parts'.

[14] For the reform movement in French Catholicism in the early years of the century, see especially Orcibal, *Origines du Jansénisme*, ii.

incidental necessity. When Olivares was challenged on this very question of innovation, he had his answer ready: 'if we are not to apply remedies to deeply rooted evils, then what will become of the world?'[15] The language in Spain and France remains that of remedy, reformation and restoration, as when Guez de Balzac describes Louis XIII in 1631 as 'this most necessary *Réformateur* . . . who has raised the royal authority as far as it can go without becoming tyranny'.[16]

The idea of restoration naturally presupposed the existence of a traditional order that had been disturbed by the passions of men and the ravages of time. In the *Testament Politique* Richelieu compares two kinds of architect. One tears down an ancient building and starts afresh; the other employs his skills to correct its defects and reduce it to a tolerable symmetry. The second, in his view, was much more deserving of praise than the first.[17] As a reformer in both church and state he hoped to give symmetry and order to an antiquated and ramshackle edifice, and Olivares was engaged in a similar process in Spain. Inevitably their priorities were different, as Richelieu's reference to the Huguenots and the *grands* makes clear. Spain's problems, and especially its economic problems, were deep and intractable, but it was not afflicted by deep religious divisions, nor was the crown challenged by armed faction and revolt. Such differences in the respective conditions of France and Spain naturally led to differences in response. Yet, for all the differences, the reconstruction programmes of the two ministers would still have much in common.

Some of the resemblances may be explained by conscious imitation, but many more derive from the similarity of problems in a context determined on the one hand by the pressures of war and financial strain, and on the other by a shared perception of the need to reassert a diminished royal authority. For both ministers, domestic reform possessed a high priority. But so, too, did the restoration of their respective monarchs to what they regarded as their rightful preeminence among the princes of Europe. Olivares was heir to the great reforming movements of the last years of Philip III, but he was also the heir to the foreign policy activists of those years, beginning with his uncle, Don Baltasar de Zúñiga. Richelieu's position was initially more equivocal. As

---

[15] BL, Add. Ms. 28,452, fo. 6, exchange between Olivares and Montesclaros, 9 May 1624.
[16] *Le Prince*, in *Oeuvres de J-L. De Guez, sieur de Balzac* (Paris, 1854 edn), I, p. 89.
[17] *TP*, p. 236.

the client of Marie de Médicis, his affiliations were with the 'Spanish' party of the *dévots*, who looked to him to restore religious unity to France and bring about much-needed reformation in church and state while preserving peace with Spain. But at the same time he carried with him the hopes of the *bons français*, anxious to see a reassertion of the King of France's claims to be the defender of the liberties of European states, whether Catholic or Protestant, against Spanish aspirations to world-wide monarchy. As a result, both their ministries would see a continuing tension between war and reform, which at some moments were mutually reinforcing, and at others mutually incompatible.[18] The degree to which this tension could be controlled, contained and directed would determine the fate of their programmes.

As Olivares looked around him at the start of Philip IV's reign in 1621, he saw on one side the massed ranks of Spain's enemies moving into action, and on the other a penniless king and a ramshackle Spanish Monarchy under the faltering leadership of a bankrupt Castile. In company with many of his contemporaries, he believed that Castile, and, with it, Spanish power, was in a state of decline – *declinación* – but that the progress of the wasting disease could still be checked by applying the right remedies. One of the first acts of the new administration was to establish a ten-man Junta de Reformación entrusted with the task of reforming manners and morals.[19] In societies in which national misfortunes were directly attributed to divine displeasure, moral regeneration was seen as a prime necessity. In Richelieu's France it was bound up with the still incomplete process of reform within the Catholic Church, and sustained by a powerful and spontaneous movement for spiritual renewal. In the Spain of Olivares, on the other hand, the heroic days of the Catholic Reform movement were over, and there seems to have been no instinctive spiritual groundswell in support of a new morality.

The deliberations of the reform junta culminated in the publication in February 1623 of the famous *Articles of Reformation*.[20] These included measures to ban sartorial extravagance, cut the number of municipal

---

[18] See Fagniez, 'L'Opinion publique'.
[19] Angel González Palencia, *La Junta de Reformación* (Valladolid, 1932) prints the documentation of this junta.
[20] *Ibid.*, doc. LXVI.

officials in Castile by two-thirds, close the brothels, and reduce the number of grammar schools in order to prevent the young from acquiring useless education. The regime also took steps to prevent the publication of novels and plays, in the belief that they were corrupting Castilian youth.[21] When censorship failed to produce the desired results, Olivares turned his energies towards educational reform in the hope of moulding a new and less hedonistic generation with a stronger sense of public service.[22]

Exemplary punishment was meted out to a handful of ministers of the preceding regime, and royal officials were ordered to produce inventories listing their possessions. By exhortation, example and decree Olivares and his colleagues clearly hoped to introduce a new and austere moral climate favourable to the process of national recovery. The key to this process was, in Olivares' opinion, to be found in the full restoration of the crown's authority.

The condition of Castile, as he described it in his Great Memorial of 1624, was that of a society which had lost its internal equilibrium.[23] The church was too rich; the grandees encroached on the royal authority; the standards of government and justice had deteriorated. In comparison with the France of the early 1620s Castile was in reality a tranquil and much governed country, but Olivares was measuring it not against the France of Louis XIII but the Castile of Philip II, where – at least in the popular memory – justice was upheld and the king's commands obeyed. Indeed, in his more alarmist moments he seems to have felt that twenty years of misgovernment by the Duke of Lerma had undone the work of the great rulers of the sixteenth century, and that Castile was in danger of reverting to the anarchical days of the later Middle Ages, when the crown was little more than a pawn in the hands of overbearing grandees.

The crown therefore had to restore the former standards of government, and revert to its proper role as the guarantor of social harmony. This was traditionally done by excluding the grandees from effective power, and favouring the lesser nobility and *hidalgos* against the high nobility. In advocating such measures Olivares was simply seeking to revive the social and political order established by Ferdinand and Isabella

---

[21] Angel González Palencia, 'Quevedo, Tirso y las comedias ante la Junta de Reformación', *Boletín de la Real Academia Española*, 25 (1946), pp. 43–84.
[22] See *MC*, II, preliminary study to docs. XI and XII.
[23] *MC*, I, doc. IV.

and upheld by Philip II – an order in which the public interest prevailed over the private under the overarching authority of the crown.

But how could royal authority be effectively restored when the king was so deeply in debt? Zúñiga and Olivares drew up plans to recover alienated royal revenues and reduce expenditure by limiting the flow of treasury grants and introducing economies in the royal households. From the beginning, Olivares took a direct interest in the crown's finances, and was soon personally involved in the laborious business of negotiating the annual contracts or *asientos* with the royal bankers. The majority of these were Genoese financiers who, in the common opinion, held the crown up to ransom with their exorbitant rates of interest. Olivares concluded that financial salvation depended on his ability to break the Genoese stranglehold, and laid his plans accordingly.[24] Early in 1626 he made a clean sweep of the Council of Finance, whose members were tarnished by their close association with the Genoese, and placed at the head of the new council a minister in whom he had complete confidence, Gilimón de la Mota.[25] In the Portuguese business community, many of whose members were crypto-Jews anxious for protection from the attentions of the Inquisition, he found a potential alternative group of financiers who had the additional advantage of being vassals of the crown.[26] By bringing these into play against the Genoese in return for tacit royal protection, he was able to suspend payments to the bankers in January 1627, converting short-term into long-term debts and forcing down the rates of interest.

But the attempted reorganization of the financial structure was only one element in a much wider programme for increasing the royal revenues and economic productivity. The tax system in Spain, as in France, was both inequitable and grossly inefficient. Portugal, the Basque provinces and the Crown of Aragon, all of them sheltering behind their contractual relationship with the king, contributed proportionately far less in taxes than Castile.

The Castilian tax system itself seemed to Olivares to be socially unjust

[24] For a history of royal finances and financial policies in the reign of Philip IV, see Antonio Dominguez Ortiz, *Política y hacienda de Felipe IV* (Madrid, 1960); and, for the crown's Genoese bankers, Felipe Ruiz Martin, 'La banca en España hasta 1782', in *El banco de España: una historia económica* (Madrid, 1970), ch. 4.
[25] *MC*, I, doc. VI.
[26] See Julio Caro Baroja, 'La sociedad criptojudía en la corte de Felipe IV', in his *Inquisición, brujería y criptojudaísmo* (Madrid, 1970), and James C. Boyajian, *Portuguese Bankers at the Court of Spain, 1626–1650* (New Brunswick, 1983).

in its application, economically harmful in its impact on potentially productive members of society, and highly inefficient as a means of generating revenue. He therefore proposed radical plans for fiscal reform. From 1624 the *millones*, a tax on essential articles of consumption, was to be abolished, and he hoped to move towards a single consolidated tax, possibly on flour, to replace the existing multiplicity of taxes. In place of the *millones*, which played a part in the Castilian fiscal system comparable to that of the *taille* in France,[27] the towns and villages of Castile were to share out on a proportional basis the responsibility for maintaining 30,000 paid soldiers to man the garrisons and frontier fortresses. This, he believed, would operate more efficiently and equitably than the *millones*, and would ensure regular annual appropriations for national defence.[28]

The fiscal reform programme was coupled with an ambitious scheme for the creation of *montes de piedad* and national banks, to be financed initially by a 5% levy on property and income. The banks were intended to help reduce public and private debt and encourage the revival of Castilian industry and agriculture by providing the necessary capital for economic enterprise at reasonable rates of interest. In addition, juntas were set up to devise plans for repopulating deserted regions, for making rivers navigable and promoting overseas trade. Like his contemporaries in other parts of Europe, Olivares was deeply impressed by the successes of the Dutch. It was necessary, he told the king, to turn Spaniards into merchants.[29] This difficult feat was to be accomplished by conferring privileges and titles of nobility on those who engaged in commerce,[30] and by organizing overseas trading companies on the model of the Dutch East India Company. The first of these companies, the Almirantazgo de los Países Septentrionales, was established in Seville by royal decree in 1624 for trade with northern Europe, and the intention was to follow it with a Levant Company based in Barcelona, and an India Company in Lisbon.[31]

---

[27] The *millones* were by now producing 30% of the revenue available annually to finance current expenditures. See Charles Jago, 'Habsburg Absolutism and the Cortes of Castile', *American Historical Review*, 86 (1981), p. 317.

[28] See González Palencia, *Junta de Reformación*, doc. LXII, and *MC*, I, p. 44.

[29] *MC*, I, p. 98 ('Gran Memorial').

[30] *MC*, II, pp. 145–9.

[31] *MC*, I, pp. 46–7, and II, pp. 141–5. The fate of the India Company, launched in 1628, is studied in A. R. Disney, *Twilight of the Pepper Empire* (Cambridge, Mass., 1978). For the Almirantazgo, see A. Domínguez Ortiz, 'El Almirantazgo de los países septentrionales y la política económica de Felipe IV', *Hispania*, 7 (1947), and Israel, *The Dutch Republic*, especially pp. 204–9.

These various fiscal and economic reforms reflected the belief of Olivares and his colleagues that national wealth could be increased by the proper application of carefully devised policies. Some of the projects, like the banking scheme, had been under discussion at least since the later sixteenth century. Others, like the trading companies, were directly borrowed from the Dutch, and were worked out in consultation with a handful of advisers, like Manuel López Pereira, a Portuguese merchant who established himself as a confidant of Olivares in fiscal and commercial questions.[32] But although the regime was responsive to the pressure of interest groups, like the textile manufacturers of the towns of central Castile with their pleas for protection, it showed a notable lack of enthusiasm for more formal modes of consultation. In particular, it was extremely reluctant to associate the Cortes of Castile with its reforming projects.

Since so much of the initial impetus for reform had come from the Cortes in the later years of Philip III, it might have paid Zúñiga and Olivares to capitalize on its reforming enthusiasm in order to give their programme a solid basis of support. But they judged otherwise, presumably out of a fear that the vociferous constitutionalist element in the Cortes would impose unacceptable conditions on the crown. They therefore decided to bypass the Cortes, and put their case directly to the city councils of Castile in a long royal letter of October 1622 outlining the government's reform proposals. But several of the cities adamantly refused to approve financial measures which had not been the subject of parliamentary discussion, and Olivares was compelled to summon the Cortes again in the spring of 1623, having first ensured his own selection as deputy for Madrid. It soon became clear that there was strong opposition to the central features of the reform programme, the banking scheme and the abolition of the *millones*, and Olivares' attempts to cajole his fellow-deputies into agreement were strikingly unsuccessful. The urban oligarchies of Castile had their own reform priorities, and their own special interests to protect. As a result, the programme began to be eroded, and the reforming impetus was lost.[33]

---

[32] Olivares' dependence on López Pereira is made clear in a note to the king on 25 May 1641 (AGS, Estado, legajo 2056) when Pereira was ill.

[33] For the reaction of the urban patriciate, see especially Ruiz Martín, 'La banca', pp. 74–96. Further information on the constitutional conflict is to be found in Jago, 'Habsburg Absolutism', and Jean Vilar, 'Formes et tendances de l'opposition sous Olivares: Lisón y Viedma, *defensor de la patria'*, *Mélanges de la Casa de Velázquez*, 7 (1971), pp. 263–94.

Richelieu and Olivares

The effect of this conflict between crown and parliament in the early 1620s was to reinforce the authoritarian elements already inherent in Olivares' programme. If Castile refused to cooperate in its own salvation, he would save it in spite of itself. The whole thrust of his regime therefore became increasingly interventionist and *dirigiste*. Looking at the successes of the Dutch, who had raised themselves from nothing to challenge the massed might of the Spanish Monarchy, he hoped through government initiative and action to achieve a comparable miracle in Spain. From the very beginning of his ministry he was obsessed by the need to make Spain more effectively competitive in a world where the balance of power seemed to be shifting against it; and he saw economic policy – the promotion of national growth – as an integral part of his plans for the restoration of Spain's international power.

Any programme for the revival of Spanish power was bound to take as its starting-point the unique character, at once global and fragmented, of the Spanish Monarchy. 'A scattered empire', wrote Giovanni Botero in his *Reason of State* (1589), 'is weaker than a compact one because the distance between the parts is always a source of weakness.'[34] This awkward fact of life dominated the thinking of Olivares, who drew from it the conclusion already drawn by Botero: that the only way to counter the effects of geographical dispersion was to arrange for mutual help in times of individual need, and to maintain effective communications by means of naval power. The point was not lost on Richelieu, who comments in the *Testament Politique* that the separation of the constituent parts of the Spanish Monarchy made communication between them so difficult that Spain's only hope was to maintain substantial Atlantic and Mediterranean fleets. He added with a certain complacency that 'the providence of God, who desires to keep everything in balance, has ensured that France, by virtue of its geographical position, should separate the states of Spain and weaken them by dividing them'.[35]

A naval reconstruction programme was already under way before the accession of Philip IV,[36] and a special committee for naval affairs, the Junta de Armadas, was revived under Olivares' presidency in January 1622.[37] The new regime's commitment to the strengthening of the fleet

[34] Trans. and ed. Waley (London, 1956), p. 11 (Book I, ch. 7).
[35] *TP*, pp. 407–8.
[36] See I. A. A. Thompson, *War and Government in Habsburg Spain, 1560–1620* (London, 1976), pp. 198–200, and Israel, *The Dutch Republic*, p. 43.
[37] C. Fernández Duro, *Armada española, desde la unión de los reinos de Castilla y Aragón* (9 vols., Madrid, 1895–1903), IV, p. 10.

was symbolized by the official visit of the king and his minister to the port towns of Andalusia in 1624, and Olivares made the appropriation of regular funds for the maintenance of naval squadrons one of his first priorities.[38] The plans for Spain's naval revival, like those for the reorganization of the military system in Castile, formed part of an extremely ambitious programme designed to mobilize the Monarchy's resources more efficiently and achieve a higher degree of unity and cooperation between its different component parts. This programme came to be known as the Union of Arms.

It was Olivares' acute awareness of the military and financial weaknesses of the Spanish Monarchy as then constituted which prompted this, the most radical of all his reforming schemes, and the one which finally was to be his undoing. The Union of Arms was an attempt to give institutional form to the mutual assistance which Botero regarded as essential for the survival of a ' scattered empire '. The scheme prepared by Olivares in 1625 was based on a quota system by which all the provinces of the Monarchy, from Flanders to Peru, would serve with a fixed number of paid men, out of a grand total of 140,000, in the event of any one of them coming under attack.[39] Apart from its military advantages, the scheme would also help to promote Olivares' most cherished aim – the genuine unification of the Monarchy, beginning with the Iberian peninsula itself. His object, in the words of his Great Memorial of 1624, was that Philip should no longer be merely ' King of Portugal, Aragon and Valencia, and Count of Barcelona ', but should become the ' King of Spain '.[40]

Unity conceived as uniformity was to be the Count–Duke's answer to the deep-seated problem of the diversity of the Spanish Monarchy. The enhancement of royal authority through the curbing of obstreperous representative assemblies, and the abolition of obnoxious provincial rights and privileges, seemed to him essential for the Monarchy's survival in a hostile world where constitutionalism, as an impediment to efficiency and discipline, was a luxury that could no longer be afforded. But kingdoms like Aragon and Valencia could not be expected to agree to the sacrifice of treasured liberties without some compensation in the form of new opportunities. He therefore envisaged a genuinely integrated

---

[38] See the king's letter to the cities of October 1622, González Palencia, *Junta de Reformación*, p. 408.
[39] *MC*, I, doc. IX, for his document on the subject, with a preliminary study. Also, Elliott, *Catalans*, pp. 204–8.
[40] *MC*, I, p. 96.

Monarchy, in which customs barriers would be eliminated, laws be made uniform, and offices be bestowed by merit without regard to province of origin. He scorned the kind of sentiment which set province against province. 'I am not *nacional*', he liked to say, 'that is something for children.'[41] In his Monarchy the king would be the focal point of loyalty, and the provincial aristocracies, welded together through intermarriage, would constitute a service nobility motivated solely by its sense of duty to the crown.

In attempting to impose cohesion on the Spanish Monarchy, the Count–Duke was grappling with a problem of a very different order of magnitude from that which faced Richelieu. For all the continuing vitality of its provinces and the survival of provincial sovereign courts and Estates, France, in comparison with the Spanish Monarchy, was by the seventeenth century a relatively compact and unified territorial state. Philip IV may not have been King of Spain but no one questioned that, where provincial rights were concerned, Louis XIII was indeed King of France. The problems of the Spanish Habsburgs were much more akin to those of their Austrian cousins, who were also the rulers of disparate kingdoms and provinces, and who would likewise attempt to weld them together into some form of supranational community with the person of the Emperor as the focus of loyalty.[42] The eventual triumph in modern Europe of the compact, unified nation-state should not blind us to the existence of these larger political units, which were not necessarily doomed to extinction, but which depended for their survival on the ability of their rulers to formulate a different set of answers, like those towards which Olivares was groping in the 1620s.

The early 1620s in Spain, then, appear as a period of major policy initiatives, and Olivares as a great reforming minister, in terms at least of intention if not of achievement. As we observe him in all his reforming zeal, it is hard to remember that this was also the man who once said that 'it would be better if many things were not as they are, but to change them would be worse'.[43] But Spain's situation, as he saw it, was so grave that he simply had no choice. Survival in his eyes depended on reform.

---

[41] BNM, Ms. 1630, fo. 186v, Olivares to Marquis of Torrecuso, 4 Jan. 1640. Similar remarks occur elsewhere in his correspondence.

[42] For this process, see in particular R. J. W. Evans, *The Making of the Habsburg Monarchy, 1550–1700* (Oxford, 1979).

[43] See above, p. 25.

Against Olivares as a visionary with impossibly grandiose reforming designs, Richelieu tends to be represented as a man of moderation, a coolly calculating pragmatist. But this is to ignore the Richelieu of the mid-1620s, to all appearances as committed a reformer as his Spanish colleague. His reforming net, indeed, was to be cast wider than that of Olivares, since his status as a churchman involved him personally in the movement for religious reformation which ran parallel to that for the reformation of the state. Louis XIII's commitment to the ideal of a general monastic reform, and the inability of Cardinal La Rochefoucaud as apostolic visitor to make more headway in his reforming mission, created opportunities for personal intervention which Richelieu, in his zeal for discipline and order, found irresistible. Appointed coadjutor to the abbot of Cluny in 1627, and then abbot in 1629, he embarked on an ambitious scheme for the union into a single body of all the Benedictine congregations in France, beginning with the great houses of Cluny and Saint-Maur. In 1635 the Cistercians and Premonstratensians also came under his rule; but, for all this accumulation of power, he was to find the reformation of monasteries as frustrating a task as the reformation of the state. Confronted on the one hand by the resistance of the monks, and on the other by the suspicions of Rome, he achieved no more than limited and temporary success. In the church, as in the state, his death was to be the signal for a powerful reaction in the form of a virtual monastic insurrection – a Fronde of the monks that parallelled the Frondes of the parliamentarians and the princes.[44]

The violence of the reaction that swept France in the 1640s reflects the strength of feeling aroused by nearly two decades of interventionist government in the name of discipline, order and reform. In the early 1620s, however, there was no doubt about the strength of the reforming impetus in France, as in Spain. Just as the Cortes of Castile had championed the reform movement in the years immediately preceding Olivares' rise to power, so too the French Estates General of 1614, in which Richelieu had participated, had put forward comprehensive proposals for reform: moral, economic, administrative and financial.[45]

---

[44] For the monastic reform movement, see Lekai, *Cistercian Strict Observance*, and Dom Paul Denis, *Le Cardinal de Richelieu et la réforme des monastères bénédictins* (Paris, 1913).
[45] See J. Michael Hayden, *France and the Estates General of 1614* (Cambridge, 1974), pp. 209–15, and R. J. Bonney, *The King's Debts. Finance and Politics in France, 1589–1661* (Oxford, 1981), pp. 79–84.

Much of their programme had in fact been included in an edict of 1618, but this had never been registered by the Parlement and remained a dead letter.[46] The civil and religious conflict during the regimes of Concini and Luynes in any event made the time unpropitious for reform. But Richelieu shared Olivares' awareness of the political advantages to be gained by capitalizing on the widespread desire for a general reformation of the state. In reality, his immediate predecessor, La Vieuville, as *surintendant des finances* in 1623–4, had already embarked on an ambitious programme of financial retrenchment of the kind demanded by the reformers, and succeeded, with the help of a new peace with the Huguenots in October 1622, in securing an impressive reduction of royal expenditure during his nineteen months in office.[47] But Richelieu and his supporters found it expedient to ignore La Vieuville's successes and preferred instead to point to his failings.

Like the reformers in Spain they resorted to medical imagery to further their cause. François de Fancan, who had entered Richelieu's service as a publicist in 1617, attacked the Brûlarts and La Vieuville in a pamphlet dramatically entitled *Dialogue de la France mourante*.[48] La Vieuville's fall in 1624 was followed by the appearance of an anonymous pamphlet called *La France en convalescence*,[49] which purported to show that Louis XIII, in dismissing La Vieuville and entrusting his administration to more capable hands, had set France on the road to recovery. After demanding the prosecution of La Vieuville, in a manner reminiscent of the campaign against the fallen ministers of Philip III in Spain, the pamphlet urged Louis XIII to adopt the financial reforms requested by the Estates General of 1614: the creation of a *chambre de justice* to investigate the activities of the financiers; the appointment of judges with clean hands; the abolition of the sale of offices; and the recovery of alienated royal demesne.

Richelieu was not deaf to these pleas, which indeed he may personally have inspired.[50] La Vieuville was prosecuted and imprisoned, and a *chambre de justice* established. Like Olivares, Richelieu devoted much time and energy in the opening years of his ministry to overhauling the administration of the royal finances.[51] A collegiate system of financial

---

[46] Hayden, *Estates General*, p. 215.
[47] Bonney, *King's Debts*, pp. 110–11.
[48] Fagniez, 'L'Opinion publique', p. 367.
[49] *Mercure français*, x (Paris, 1625), pp. 678–94.
[50] Deloche, *Autour de la plume*, p. 240.
[51] Bonney, *King's Debts*, pp. 115–21.

control was introduced, with himself at its head; but in practice Michel de Marillac had effective charge of the finances until his appointment as Keeper of the Seals in 1626, when he was replaced by a more able *surintendant des finances*, and one more to Richelieu's liking, the Marquis d'Effiat.

But in his attempts at fiscal reform, Richelieu ran into the same kind of difficulties as Olivares. It was easier to launch a campaign against the crown's bankers than to dispense with their services. He did not have Olivares' problem of attempting to extract the royal revenues from the clutches of foreigners, since most of the bankers of the French crown, unlike those of the Spanish, were by now of native origin.[52] But he remained throughout his career deeply preoccupied by their dominance. They were, as he said in the *Testament Politique*, 'a group apart, prejudicial to the state', and yet, as he had to admit, 'necessary'.[53] But although he argued that it was essential to remedy what he called the *dérèglement* of the financiers, he was as incapable as Olivares of achieving this, and left his finance ministers, d'Effiat and Bullion, to handle the recurrent financial crises as best they could.

A comment made in 1625 by the president of Spain's Council of Finance, the Marquis of Montesclaros, provides a good indication of why financial reform was one of the first casualties of the reform programmes of the new regimes in France and Spain. 'The lack of money', he told his colleagues, 'is serious, but it is more important to preserve reputation.'[54] Coming from a treasury minister the sentiment is unusual. In Spain the first attempts at retrenchment and financial reform were wrecked by the heavy military and naval commitments which brought Spanish arms a string of victories in that *annus mirabilis* of the reign of Philip IV, 1625. In France they were wrecked by military involvement in the Valtelline, which was followed almost at once by the revolt of Soubise in January 1625, and a renewal of the insurrection of the Huguenots of La Rochelle.[55]

Any hopes of immediate reform in France, therefore, went by the board. Richelieu's first task was to restore the king's authority at home, and salvage what he could from his attempt to assert a French presence in the Valtelline and North Italy. But the events of 1625 made it clear that it

---

[52] *Ibid.*, p. 81.
[53] *TP*, p. 250.
[54] AHN, Estado, libro 738, fos. 313–17, draft consulta of Council of State, 22 Oct. 1625.
[55] Bonney, *King's Debts*, p. 123, and Lublinskaya, *French Absolutism*, p. 216.

was impossible to pursue both these aims simultaneously. Marillac and his colleagues were pressing the Cardinal to reach a settlement with Spain and concentrate his resources on war against the Huguenots.[56] He himself favoured a compromise peace with the Huguenots in order to give first priority to what he saw as the danger from Spain; but in the end he had to compromise on both fronts, partly as the result of the crown's financial difficulties, and partly because of the continuing insecurity of his own position and the bitter opposition to his policies. The Peace of Paris with the Huguenots in February 1626, and the Peace of Monzón with Spain a month later, were disappointing short-term settlements to long-standing problems, and they revealed the persistent underlying weaknesses of the crown.[57]

One of the most valuable lessons learnt by Richelieu in those first difficult years of his ministry, 1624–6, was the critical importance of creating a permanent war-fleet for France.[58] Just as Olivares, then, threw his energies into reviving Spain's power at sea, so Richelieu took personal control of the attempt to endow France with a navy. In 1626 he eased the Duke of Montmorency out of his hereditary post of Admiral of France, and assumed the duties of the office himself, under the grandiloquent title of Grand Maître de la Navigation et du Commerce de France.[59] He continued systematically to concentrate control over maritime affairs in his own hands, acquiring the governorships of Le Havre, Brest and Brouage, and establishing a Conseil de la Marine of hand-picked men, comparable to Olivares' Junta de Armadas. The creation of a French war-fleet was one of the most successful and permanent of the Cardinal's accomplishments, but it was paralleled by Olivares' success in making Spain at least as powerful on the sea as it had been in the great days of Philip II.[60]

---

[56] Bonney, *ibid.*, p. 124.

[57] For the Peace of Monzón, see Pithon, 'Les Débuts difficiles', p. 21, and Lublinskaya, *French Absolutism* pp. 278–81.

[58] When he came to power, the crown had only ten galleys in the Mediterranean, and no ships in the Atlantic and Channel ports. See Lublinskaya, *French Absolutism*, p. 283.

[59] For a detailed but not entirely sympathetic treatment of the Cardinal's naval programme and policies, see L.-A. Boiteux, *Richelieu 'grand maître de la navigation et du commerce de France'* (Paris, 1955).

[60] José Alcalá-Zamora y Queipo de Llano, *España, Flandes y el Mar del Norte, 1618–1639* (Barcelona, 1975), p. 358. The Spanish fleet in 1637 consisted of seventy-one galleons and seventy galleys, excluding the overseas squadrons and numerous smaller vessels. France by this date had a war-fleet of about forty-six ships, roughly the number planned by Richelieu (Boiteux, *Richelieu 'grand maître'*, p. 153).

Although much of Richelieu's energy during the first two years of his ministry was devoted to the immediate tasks in hand, his state papers make it clear that he was also thinking in terms of a wide-ranging reform programme to be set in train when circumstances allowed. Already by 1624 Olivares was well embarked on his reforms. The Spanish *Articles of Reformation* of 1623, with their sumptuary measures and administrative and social reforms, were reproduced in full in the *Mercure français* for that year,[61] and Richelieu kept himself well informed on developments in Madrid. It would not be surprising, therefore, if he took a leaf out of Olivares' book as he set out to prepare a programme of his own.

A short memorandum among his papers of 1624 'to remedy the most pressing disorders'[62] bears some striking resemblances to the kind of documents being produced by Olivares and his circle. Like Olivares' proposals, the memorandum began with the assumption of decline. It argued that the two clearest indications of the 'decadence of this state' were the total disregard for royal authority, which encouraged people to participate in conspiracies and cabals, and excessive luxury, which had obliterated social distinctions and provoked every kind of disorder. What were the remedies for this unfortunate state of affairs? These, too, might have been devised by Olivares. The first was to secure regular funding for the maintenance of a permanent army, 'sufficient to defend the realm externally and keep it dutiful internally'. The second remedy was to publish a solemn edict against extravagant social habits, and clear the court of parasites.

During 1625 the Cardinal worked out a more systematic and detailed programme, a *Règlement* for all the affairs of the realm, which – like Olivares' great secret memorandum of 1624 – proposed a wide range of reforms including reform of the church, reform of the royal household, sumptuary measures, prohibition of the sale of office, and the suppression of surplus offices.[63] But it was only with the return of domestic and foreign peace in 1626 that Richelieu found himself in a position to think seriously about putting these reforms into effect. Like Olivares, he had to carry public opinion with him; but, again like Olivares, he was reluctant to submit his programme to a representative assembly in the form of France's nearest equivalent to the Cortes, the

---

[61] *Mercure français*, IX (Paris, 1624), pp. 1–80 ('Ordonnances pour la Réformation . . .').
[62] Grillon, I, p. 141–2.
[63] Grillon, I, pp. 248–69.

Estates General. Instead, he decided to repeat an experiment he had already tried with success in 1625, during the debate over France's involvement in the Valtelline, and summon an Assembly of Notables. The advantage of this was that its members were chosen by the crown. The Assembly, fifty-five strong, opened at the Tuileries on 2 December 1626 to the accompaniment of speeches by Marillac, Schomberg and Richelieu.[64]

When the three principal ministers divided among themselves the presentation of the reform programme to the assembly, Richelieu significantly reserved for himself the theme of financial reform.[65] As he observed in the *Testament Politique*, finance was like the fulcrum of Archimedes which, when once established, could move the world.[66] The reduction of expenses and the increase of revenues were central to his programme; and to make the inevitable sacrifices more palatable, Louis XIII spontaneously offered to reform his household – an offer comparable to that made by Philip IV to the Cortes of Castile in 1623.[67] The centrepiece of his reform programme was to be the same as that of Olivares: the redemption of alienated royal revenues, which he hoped to achieve with the help of the Notables in the course of six years.[68] The Cardinal also hoped to lighten the tax burden by reducing the *taille*, and he may already have been nurturing hopes that he would eventually be able to abolish the *taille* entirely, replacing it by a uniform salt tax throughout France, coupled with a sales tax, just as Olivares hoped to abolish the *millones*.[69]

The similarity of the crown's financial problems in France and Spain pointed to similar remedies; but there may have been a piece of direct borrowing in the proposals presented to the assembly by Richelieu on 11 January 1627 for reforms in the military establishment.[70] Olivares had wanted Castile to provide and pay for a standing army of 30,000 men. Richelieu proposed to the Notables a standing army of 18,000–20,000,

---

[64] For a detailed study of the Assembly of Notables and its work, see Jeanne Petit, *L'Assemblée des Notables de 1626–1627* (Paris, 1936).
[65] See Lublinskaya, *French Absolutism*, p. 300.
[66] *TP*, pp. 427–8.
[67] Grillon, 1, p. 559, for the reference in Richelieu's speech to household economies. Compare Olivares' reference to the same subject in his speech to the Cortes of Castile on 16 September 1623 (*MC*, 1, p. 20).
[68] Grillon, 1, p. 561; Lublinskaya, *French Absolutism*, p. 296.
[69] Bonney, *King's Debts*, p. 131; Hauser, *Pensée et action*, p. 177.
[70] Petit, *L'Assemblée*, part 11, ch. 2.

which was to be raised and paid for on a quota basis by all the provinces of France. Although frontier provinces had sometimes been called upon to assume this burden, the idea of extending responsibility for the provision and maintenance of a military establishment among all the provinces seems to have been a new one in France, and it would not be surprising if the inspiration came directly from Madrid. In this same year, 1627, Secretary Coke proposed that Charles I should follow the Spanish example and 'unite his three kingdoms in a strict union and obligation each to other for their mutual defence'.[71] In Spain, France and England it would seem that the Union of Arms was an idea whose time had come.

The borrowing from Spain was even more explicit in Richelieu's plans for commercial and economic revival.[72] He saw the Assembly of Notables as a convenient forum in which to gain support for his plans for the development of France as a maritime power with trading companies and a war fleet of forty-five ships. The organization of trading companies had in fact already begun in 1625, with a scheme for two companies headed by the Cardinal.[73] It is clear that, like Olivares, he had been impressed by the example of the Dutch, and hoped, again like Olivares, to reproduce it in the very different environment of an authoritarian monarchical society. These first schemes coincided with Olivares' creation of the Almirantazgo in Seville for Spanish trade with Flanders, details of which were sent to Richelieu in the summer of 1626 by du Fargis, the French ambassador in Madrid. Du Fargis proposed a similar system of reserved monopoly trades and armed convoys for France, but in the end the proposal proved too ambitious and expensive, although Richelieu took from it what he could.[74]

When Olivares told Philip IV that it was necessary to turn Spaniards into merchants, he was in effect acknowledging that his plans for naval and commercial revival demanded a fundamental change in social habits and attitudes of mind. Richelieu seems to have been equally aware that it was going to be a hard task to turn Frenchmen into merchants, and he had recourse to similar devices. In an attempt to persuade nobles to go into trade he reissued on several occasions the edicts which guaranteed

[71] See Conrad S. R. Russell, 'Monarchies, Wars and Estates in England, France, and Spain, c. 1580–c. 1640', *Legislative Studies Quarterly*, (1982), p. 216.
[72] Examined by Hauser in *Pensée et action*.
[73] *Ibid.*, ch. 6; Boiteux, *Richelieu 'grand maître'*, pp. 202–3, and chs. 7 and 8; Lublinskaya, *French Absolutism*, pp. 283–4.
[74] Boiteux, *Richelieu 'grand maître'*, pp. 50–2; Hauser, *Pensée et action*, pp. 54–6.

that trade implied no derogation of nobility; and the Code Michaud of 1629, in which Marillac attempted to codify the reform programme of these years, contained provisions for grants of personal nobility to those who fitted out and maintained a ship for five years or more – the same kind of inducement as was being offered in Madrid.[75]

Olivares and Richelieu were in reality struggling against deeply entrenched social values which in both countries impeded the kind of changes they considered essential for survival in a highly competitive world. They both saw the need to raise trade and industry to a new level of importance, and they were well aware of the strength of rival attractions to hard work and entrepreneurial enterprise. This awareness explains the preoccupation of reformers in Spain with the proliferation of religious foundations, and the inclusion in the Spanish *Articles of Reformation* of a provision to reduce the number of grammar schools, where children were 'wasting their time with Latinity, instead of employing themselves in occupations more useful to themselves and the republic'.[76] It is not surprising, then, to find Richelieu following suit, and attempting to close down monasteries and grammar schools in France.[77] Several years later, in the section on 'Letters' in the *Testament Politique*, he was still expatiating on the consequences of too much education, and arguing that, in a well-regulated state, there should be more masters of mechanical than liberal arts.[78]

This *cri du coeur* was a sign of failure. It was one thing to persuade the Assembly of Notables to endorse the crown's plans for economic and social reform. It was quite another to carry them into effect, as Olivares was simultaneously finding in Spain. Both ministers were faced on the one hand by an entirely justified scepticism about participating in trading projects sponsored and controlled by the crown, and on the other by established attitudes and patterns of behaviour which placed economic activity relatively low on the scale of social values. Social advancement in both France and Spain was more easily secured through office than trade; and the massive bureaucratic apparatus with which both countries were burdened provided ample opportunities for gratifying the consuming thirst for office.

[75] Boiteux, *Richelieu 'grand maître'*, pp. 197–9; *MC*, II, p. 147.
[76] González Palencia, *Junta de Reformación*, p. 452.
[77] Grillon, I, p. 256 (*Règlement* of 1625); Boiteux, *Richelieu 'grand maître'*, p. 197; Hauser, *Pensée et action*, p. 65.
[78] *TP*, pp. 204–6.

Richelieu's *Règlement* of 1625 makes it clear that it was one of his ambitions to reduce the number of offices, and abolish their sale, with all its disastrous consequences for French government and society.[79] Here his difficulties were of a different order from those of Olivares. In Spain, the proliferation of offices constituted a more immediate problem than venality. Although lesser offices had for long been up for sale, the crown had retained its control over the disposal of the more important posts, and there was no formal system, as in France, for hereditary transmission. In practice, this had not prevented the rise of office-holding dynasties with a monopoly on power – a development which Olivares deplored and which he attempted to restrain.[80] In France, on the other hand, the venal and hereditary character of office-holding had for long crippled effective royal government, and constituted a major obstacle to Richelieu's designs for the restoration of the crown's authority.

Yet in spite of the Cardinal's recognition of this fact, abolition of the sale of office and the *droit annuel* did not appear in the reform programme presented to the Assembly of Notables.[81] He seems to have realized that too many vested interests were at stake, and that compensation for existing office-holders, which alone would have made such reforms palatable, was far beyond the financial means of the crown. Olivares ran into exactly the same difficulties on a lesser scale with his scheme to reduce by two-thirds the number of municipal offices in Castile. There was simply no money for buying out the holders of offices on an equitable basis; and under combined pressure from the urban patriciates and the Cortes, he was forced to abandon his scheme.[82]

Olivares grasped the nettle and was stung. Richelieu preferred not to grasp it at all. This may perhaps enhance his claims to be considered the more pragmatic reformer of the two, but the fact remains that, like Olivares, he had suffered a major defeat. He suffered another in his proposals for fiscal reform. The establishment of a fund to redeem alienated crown lands over a six-year period was central to the programme of reform. The Cardinal and d'Effiat failed in their attempts to get it endorsed by the Notables, who opted instead for a repurchase scheme spread out over sixteen years. This was effectively to consign the

[79] Grillon, I, pp. 260–1.
[80] *MC*, I, p. 72 ('Gran Memorial'), and see Kagan, *Students and Society*, ch. 7.
[81] Tapié, *Louis XIII et Richelieu*, pp. 163–4; Mousnier, *Vénalité*, book IV, ch. 5.
[82] See Elliott, 'El programa de Olivares', pp. 357–9.

plan to oblivion.[83] It was a failure comparable to Olivares' failure to carry the Cortes with him in his project to accumulate capital and buy back alienated royal revenues through the creation of a national banking system. Both ministers were condemned by the rejection of their financial proposals to the continuation of a hand-to-mouth existence.

Although the Notables approved the plan for establishing a navy of forty-five ships at a cost of 1.2 million *livres*, they were unable to suggest where the money was to be found. The Cardinal's plan for the regular funding of the army, however, fared marginally better. The Notables agreed to the provincial quota system, although only if two-thirds of the cost were borne by the treasury[84] – a proviso which drastically reduced the importance of the change. There are some indications that the new system was put into effect: in Provence at least it seems to have been in operation in the 1630s.[85] But any successes achieved by the new quota system did not have the significance that comparable successes would have possessed in Spain. There is no evidence that, like Olivares, Richelieu saw his plan for sharing out among the provinces the costs of defence as the first stage of a project for national unification.

The absence among Richelieu's papers of any mention of the problem of provincial rights and institutions is perhaps the most striking difference between what are otherwise the markedly similar programmes for reform in France and Spain. The omission is curious. Even if the provinces of France enjoyed less autonomy than those of Spain, the disparity between *pays d'états* and *pays d'élections* was a continuing preoccupation of ministers concerned with the royal revenues. It is possible that Marillac had plans for abolishing the distinction and establishing uniformity, but the evidence is not clear.[86] Richelieu, for his part, may well have felt that the autonomous powers of the provincial governors represented a more pressing danger to the crown than the autonomous powers of the provinces themselves, and decided to make it his first concern to reduce the governors to subservience. He may also have believed that the powers of the Estates were more likely to succumb to a series of oblique measures than to frontal attack.

---

[83] Bonney, *King's Debts*, p. 134.
[84] *Ibid.*
[85] Petit, *L'Assemblée*, p. 145, note 123.
[86] Major, *Representative Government*, pp. 568–70.

Apart from providing Richelieu with a general endorsement for his programme, and redefining the crime of *lèse-majesté* to give him even greater powers against those whom he classified as enemies of the state,[87] the positive achievements of the Assembly of Notables of 1626–7 were few. Richelieu's ambitious programme for domestic reform seems in retrospect as visionary as that of Olivares. Here were two statesmen with a set of reforming proposals which, if implemented, would have gone beyond a reformation to a transformation of the state. One after another their proposals had to be watered down or abandoned. Are we to assume from this that their grand designs were simply unrealistic, in terms of the capacity of the early-seventeenth-century state to initiate and direct change? Did they expect too much of the state and too little of society, which they were so unwilling to associate with them in their reforming programmes? Or was reformation from above perhaps the only way forward in these custom-bound societies of the Ancien Régime?

Society was no doubt deeply resistant to reform, but perhaps the reformers themselves were also at fault. If 'reformation' was one of the watchwords of Richelieu and Olivares, another was 'reputation'. 'I have always desired with the greatest anxiety', said Olivares in 1625, 'to see Your Majesty enjoying a reputation in the world equal to your greatness and qualities.'[88] 'Reputation', wrote Richelieu, 'is so very necessary to a prince that the one who enjoys it does more with his mere name than can be achieved with their armies by those who do not.'[89] The rhetoric of reputation, which constituted the guiding principle of these two statesmen in foreign and domestic policy alike, imposed a logic of its own on their programmes for reform. Prestige brought power; power brought prestige; and prestige, if skilfully exploited, could sometimes make it unnecessary to resort to arms. But reputation, with all its overtones of honour derived from the military and aristocratic ethos of Early Modern Europe, had at all times to be defended, whatever the price; and the price to France and Spain in the later 1620s was to be the definitive sacrifice of reform to war.

[87] Petit, *L'Assemblée*, pp. 195–8.
[88] AGS, Estado, legajo 2039, consulta, 29 June 1625.
[89] *TP*, p. 373, and see Church, *Richelieu and Reason of State*, p. 500.

4

Mantua and its consequences

In a famous article published in 1937 Georges Pagès gave us a new appreciation of the *grand orage* – that great storm which reached its climax on the Day of the Dupes, now dated 11 rather than 10 November 1630,[1] when it looked as if Richelieu had finally been swept from power by his enemies.[2] Traditionally the story had revolved around the clash of ambition between the Cardinal and the Keeper of the Seals, Michel de Marillac, whose affiliation to the party of Marie de Médicis forced an unhappy Louis XIII to choose between his mother and his minister. Without discounting the high personal drama of the occasion, Pagès argued persuasively that it needed to be set into the wider context of a struggle between two irreconcilable policies. In 1630 Louis was compelled to choose not only between Richelieu on the one hand and Marie de Médicis and Marillac on the other, but also between war and reform. His choice, in favour of Richelieu, and consequently of war, was to prove a turning-point in the history of France.

There is no need to tell again the story told so well by Pagès; but it has so far escaped notice that a comparable drama involving the will of the king and the fate of his minister was simultaneously being played out south of the Pyrenees. Spain, too, was to have its *grand orage*. The same winds were blowing in Madrid as Paris, and, as they rose to gale force during those critical years 1627–30, they left the political landscape of Europe permanently transformed.

The year 1627 began for both Spain and France with the promise of better times to come. Olivares saw this as the critical year 'which will

---

[1] The Day of the Dupes has been convincingly redated to 11 November by Pierre Chevallier on the basis of foreign diplomatic despatches. His findings, which first appeared in article form, are reproduced in his *Louis XIII*, pp. 379–401. See also Grillon, v, pp. 641–2.
[2] 'Autour du "grand orage". Richelieu et Marillac: deux politiques', *Revue Historique*, 179 (1937), pp. 63–97.

decide the fate of this Monarchy, and will determine whether we can achieve universal peace with honour, or see the collapse of all or part of this hope'.[3] He badly wanted peace, and it was beginning to look as if peace might be within his grasp. In 1625–6 the balance of European power was tilting in favour of the House of Austria. Spain had scored major victories over the English and the Dutch, and the armies of the Emperor had defeated the Danes. As London's relations with Paris deteriorated, there were grounds for hope that the English would soon tire of their war with Spain. There also seemed a strong possibility that the Emperor, triumphant over his enemies in Germany, would lend Spain his military support against the United Provinces. If Imperial forces came to the assistance of the Spanish army in the Netherlands, and if the economic blockade already in operation against the Dutch could be strengthened and extended, perhaps by establishing a Spanish naval base in the Baltic to intercept the Dutch carrying trade, then there was at least a possibility that the United Provinces would start thinking seriously about reaching peace with Spain.[4]

But, in the Count–Duke's words, it had to be ' peace with honour', by which he meant a settlement shorn of the humiliating clauses that had discredited the truce of 1609. In northern and central Europe alike he disclaimed any expansionist ambitions for his royal master, and there seems no reason to doubt his disclaimer. His argument was that Spain, as the greatest power in the world, was the one that most needed peace. But, for this very reason, it could least afford to give the impression of seeking it. Like a lion in the forest, it would always be friendless, but it would not be attacked so long as it was feared. It was therefore ' hoping for peace but not proposing it' that he made his dispositions for 1627.

France's domestic difficulties, and its worsening relations with the England of Charles I, made this a particularly propitious moment for a major diplomatic initiative. Why not extend the hand of friendship to Richelieu, and unite the forces of Catholic France and Spain against a Protestant enemy? This idea was not entirely far-fetched. In the spring of 1626, after the Treaty of Monzón, Richelieu (although he subsequently denied it) had made tentative approaches to Olivares about the possibility

[3] AGS, Estado, legajo 2040, 'Parecer de S.E. el Conde Duque', 12 Dec. 1626.
[4] For the international situation and Madrid's foreign policy in these years, see Rafael Ródenas Vilar, *La política europea de España durante la guerra de treinta años, 1624–1630* (Madrid, 1967), part II, and Eberhard Straub, *Pax et Imperium. Spaniens Kampf um seine Friedensordnung in Europa zwischen 1617 und 1635* (Paderborn, 1980), ch. 7.

of a joint Franco-Spanish enterprise against Charles I. In doing this he was motivated partly by domestic considerations – the desire to win the support of the *dévots* – and partly by the hope of preventing a peace settlement between Spain and England. Although the Spanish ambassador in Paris, the Marquis of Mirabel, warned the Count–Duke not to trust Richelieu, Olivares decided to play along with the Cardinal, in the hope that this would split Spain's northern enemies, deprive the Dutch of French support and embroil France in war with England.[5]

Duplicity in Paris was therefore matched by duplicity in Madrid, as Richelieu and Olivares each sought to turn the follies of the Duke of Buckingham's foreign policy to account. On 20 March 1627 Olivares agreed with the French ambassador in Madrid, du Fargis, on an offensive alliance against England, and a month later the treaty was ratified. Its ratification did not prevent the opening in the summer of informal talks between representatives of Spain and England about the possibilities of a peace settlement, nor did it prevent the French from breaking a verbal promise not to renew their three-year-old subsidy treaty with the Dutch.[6]

The superficial reconciliation with France, the attempt to shift the war in the Netherlands from expensive land campaigns to economic and naval blockades, and the first approaches to a peace with England all gave Olivares something of a breathing-space in those first months of 1627, and an opportunity to concentrate on domestic reform. His first priority was the restoration of the crown's finances and the Castilian economy. On 31 January the crown won a little more room for manoeuvre by suspending its payments to the Genoese bankers.[7] To relieve the pressure of the defence budget on the royal treasury the Count–Duke now took the first steps towards extending the Union of Arms to other parts of the Monarchy outside the Iberian peninsula.[8] He also turned his attention to what had become the most pressing of all his problems – the high rate of inflation in Castile.

---

[5] For the story of the attempted Franco-Spanish collaboration against England, see Georg Lutz, *Kardinal Giovanni Francesco Guidi di Bagno* (Tübingen, 1971), part II, chs. 2 and 3; Straub, *Pax et Imperium*, pp. 253–88; Luis Suárez Fernández, *Notas a la política anti-española del Cardenal Richelieu* (Valladolid, 1950), pp. 26–35; and Michel Devèze, *L'Espagne de Philippe IV*, 2 vols. (Paris, 1970–1), I, pp. 137–8.

[6] Lutz, *Bagno*, pp. 237–8; Alcalá-Zamora, *España, Flandes*, pp. 226–7.

[7] Domínguez Ortiz, *Política y hacienda*, p. 31.

[8] Orders had already been sent in October 1626 for its introduction into Flanders (see Elliott, *Catalans*, p. 246). In April 1627 instructions to the same effect were sent to the viceroys of New Spain and Peru. See Fred Bronner, 'La unión de las armas en el Perú', *Anuario de Estudios Americanos*, 24 (1967), pp. 1133–77.

In France, too, reform was the order of the day. The final ceremony of the Assembly of Notables was held on 24 February 1627, and there seemed a real possibility that Richelieu, fortified by the Assembly's support, would be able to embark systematically on his programme for the restoration of royal authority and the introduction of significant reforms. Inevitably, the restoration of authority took precedence. The Cardinal was resolute in his determination to concentrate power exclusively in the hands of the crown. Arms were to be deposited in the royal arsenals, and private fortresses to be razed.[9] Although the crown's campaign against duelling – a form of private violence more common in France than in Spain – was partly intended to prevent the unnecessary shedding of blood, the execution of Montmorency-Bouteville on 22 January was a signal to a fractious nobility that the king was in future to have the monopoly of force.[10]

The Chalais conspiracy of 1626 had given Richelieu good reason to distrust the high nobility, who combined armed faction in the country with conspiracy at court. The immediate effect of the revelation of the conspiracy was to strengthen the king's commitment to his minister, but the queen and Gaston d'Orléans both opposed him, and from 1626 to the end of 1630 there was a perennial danger of his being overthrown by a *coup d'état* engineered by the high nobility in association with members of the immediate royal family. He was also faced by the threat of a renewed alliance between the *grands* and the Huguenots. Between them, Gaston, Condé, and the Count of Soissons, as the three leading princes of the blood, were capable of plunging France into chaos, and one of Richelieu's most important successes in 1626–7 was to win Condé to his side.[11]

The loyalty of Condé was to provide an element of stability during that highly unstable period of aristocratic challenge and Huguenot revolt which was only brought to a close with the defeat of the Duke of Montmorency's rebellion in 1632. In July 1627 an English expedition under the command of the Duke of Buckingham was despatched to the Ile de Ré to offer assistance to La Rochelle. Two months later La Rochelle reluctantly came out in revolt.[12] From the summer of 1627,

[9] Grillon, ii, doc. 119; Gerhard, 'Richelieu', p. 107.
[10] Ranum, 'Richelieu and the Great Nobility', p. 200. See also Richard Herr, 'Honor versus Absolutism: Richelieu's Fight against Duelling', *Journal of Modern History*, 27 (1955), pp. 281–5.
[11] Ranum, 'Richelieu and the Great Nobility', pp. 194–5; Bonney, *King's Debts*, pp. 129–30.
[12] David Parker, *La Rochelle and the French Monarchy* (London, 1980), pp. 15–16.

therefore, the crown was at war both with domestic and foreign enemies, and all thoughts of reform were once again set aside.

Louis responded to the news of Buckingham's plans by deciding to go in person to the coast of Saintonge. On 28 June, just as he was starting out on his journey, he was struck down by a fever, which brought him to the brink of death.[13] Louis' later and more famous illness in 1630, the immediate prelude to the Day of the Dupes, has eclipsed this earlier illness of July 1627 in the histories of the reign. But it was a critical moment for Richelieu. 'On the king's health depends that of the state', he wrote, as he prayed for his master's recovery.[14] Louis was still childless, and his feckless brother Gaston was the heir apparent. Although Richelieu had done his best to maintain good relations with Gaston, there was every possibility that his succession would lead to a change of government. Cardinal Bagno, the papal nuncio, reported that the populace was bitterly hostile to Richelieu, and that its hostility extended to the king, whose death was eagerly awaited by Gaston's friends.[15]

Cardinal Barberini in Rome was sufficiently alarmed by Bagno's report to send a set of instructions for use in the event of Louis' death.[16] But from 20 July – the day on which the English fleet arrived off the Ile de Ré – the king began to recover, although his convalescence was slow. It was only on 20 September that he was able to leave Paris for the camp at La Rochelle, where Richelieu took personal charge of the operations to dislodge the English and reduce the city by siege.

By a quirk of fate, just as Louis XIII was on the road to recovery, his brother-in-law, Philip IV, came down with a fever. On 23 August his condition suddenly worsened. For a few agonizing days, during which – in Olivares' graphic words – the sea and sky changed places, it seemed that the end was at hand. But then, on 4 September, Philip began to recover, and on the 10th, although still very weak, he was able to get out of bed.[17]

Philip's illness in 1627, which has passed unnoticed in Spanish historiography, was of major political significance for contemporaries.

---

[13] Batiffol, *Richelieu et Louis XIII*, p. 175.
[14] Grillon, II, p. 296 (Richelieu to Brézé, 17 July 1627).
[15] Lutz, *Bagno*, pp. 79–80.
[16] *Ibid.*, appendix A.
[17] See *MC*, I, docs. XII and XIII, for Philip IV's illness and its implications; and, for the domestic conjuncture at this moment, Elliott, 'El programa de Olivares', pp. 400–7.

Like Louis' illness in France, it suggests the unpredictability of events, and the acute vulnerability of royal ministers who depended for their own survival on that of their king. The situation in Spain at this moment bore some striking resemblances to the situation in France. In both instances, the king was without an heir of his body, although the Queen of Spain was pregnant. If, as seemed not improbable, she had another miscarriage, or the child died soon after birth, the succession would devolve upon the elder of Philip's two brothers, the Infante Don Carlos. Although it was already clear that Don Carlos was no Gaston d'Orléans, he and his brother, the Cardinal-Infante, both of them living in the palace under close surveillance, represented a natural focus of loyalty for the aristocratic opposition to Olivares. The existence of young Infantes was a novelty in Habsburg Spain, and the Count–Duke's mind no doubt went back to the succession struggles in later medieval Castile. He may also have reflected on the disturbing example of Gaston in France. The palace intrigues around the persons of the Infantes during the two weeks of Philip's illness suggest that his fears were not quite as exaggerated as they seem in retrospect.

Besides bringing aristocratic intrigue into the open, Philip's illness, like that of Louis, revealed the extreme unpopularity of his government. The ambassador of the Republic of Lucca was sufficiently alarmed to resort to cypher when reporting that the churches of Madrid were nearly empty when prayers were offered for the king's recovery.[18] Matías de Novoa, a dissident courtier, noted in his memoirs that many people were hoping for Philip's death in the belief that this was the only way to rid themselves of the Count–Duke and his tyranny.[19] It was the same reaction as the papal nuncio had noted in France. How are we to explain the intense hostility, both aristocratic and popular, to an administration that had been welcomed with such enthusiasm six years before?

Lucca's ambassador attributed the general desire for a change of regime to heavy taxation, high prices, and what he called the 'rigorous character' of the Count–Duke, who was parsimonious with patronage and kept the affairs of state in his own hands and those of his dependants. But he also thought that Olivares was paying the price for circumstances beyond his own control: the weakness of Spain after the long period of

[18] Archivio di Stato, Lucca, ATL 647, no. 37 (despatch of 25 Sept. 1627).
[19] *Historia de Felipe IV, Rey de España*, Colección de documentos inéditos para la historia de España LXIX (Madrid, 1878), p. 62.

government by Lerma; the high costs of war; and the effects on Castile of the circulation of a debased copper currency.

As the ambassador noted, many of these were inherited problems, but they had been aggravated by the failure of the Olivares regime to handle them effectively. It was above all high taxation and soaring prices which had made the government so unpopular in Castile at large. Olivares was paying the penalty for his failure to carry through his programme of fiscal reform, and for his resort to the minting of debased copper currency, known as *vellón*, to cover the crown's deficits during the first five years of the reign. When minting was eventually suspended in 1626 the Castilian currency was already out of control. Having decided that the only answer to rising prices was a drastic deflation which would have instantaneously reduced the nominal value of the *vellón* coinage by 75%, the Count–Duke was met by the solid resistance of the Council of Castile, which was afraid that Castile in its present precarious state could not stand the shock.[20] The Council resorted instead to an abortive attempt at price-fixing. When this failed it turned in the spring of 1627 to an ingenious scheme, which proved equally abortive, for the creation of special banks to 'consume' the *vellón*.[21] As fears of popular disturbances increased, the government responded in June by tightening the censorship, as Richelieu's government had tightened it a few months earlier.[22] The king's last action before he fell ill in August was to order the Council of Castile to 'do something, even if you do it badly' to halt the rise in prices.[23]

The king's illness therefore came at a moment of growing discontent over rising prices in Castile. This discontent obviously created a favourable climate in which to engineer the downfall of Olivares in the event of Philip's death. It is not easy to identify the dissident nobles who were manoeuvring for favour with the Infante Don Carlos in anticipation of this happy event, but it seems likely that the moving spirit, and the cleverest, was the Marquis of Castel Rodrigo, the son of the influential Portuguese-born minister of Philip II, Don Cristóbal de Moura. The faction drew its strength from the relatives and supporters of the late Duke of Lerma, who looked forward to a change of monarch to recover

---

[20] Roca, *Fragmentos históricos*, p. 279. The conflict between Olivares and the Council of Castile over financial policy will be discussed in greater detail in my forthcoming *The Count–Duke of Olivares*.
[21] Ruiz Martín, 'La banca', pp. 104–7; Domínguez Ortiz, *Política y hacienda*, pp. 256–7.
[22] *MC*, II, p. 184 (law of 13 June 1627). For France, Petit, *L'Assemblée*, p. 198.
[23] AHN, Consejos, legajo 51,359, expte. 6, king's reply to letter from Cardinal Trejo of 22 Aug. 1627.

power from the hands of the newly promoted families of the Olivares connection; and it was reinforced by those nobles who had been alienated by the Count–Duke's brusque ways. What is not clear, however, is whether the dissident aristocrats had a programme, other than the removal of Olivares from power. Although Olivares' handling of foreign policy had its critics both inside and outside the Council of State, there is no evidence of the kind of sharp and continuing division over the general direction of policy which in France pitted the *dévots* against the *bons français*. But Councillors of State who were accustomed to look upon France as the most dangerous enemy of Spain were shaken by the revelation of Olivares' unexpected plans for an alliance with the French and the despatch of a Spanish fleet to help Louis XIII defeat the Huguenots of La Rochelle.[24]

With the king's recovery, all the high hopes and expectations of those heady days were dashed. The opposition was temporarily silenced, and a pretext was found for getting Castel Rodrigo out of the country. The revelation of the number and strength of his enemies seems to have taken Olivares by surprise; and yet the opposition in Spain looks pallid and ineffectual beside the opposition to Richelieu. In spite of obscure hints of a murder plot in 1623,[25] the Count–Duke does not seem to have lived under the constant threat of assassination which induced Louis to give Richelieu a permanent armed guard of fifty men after the discovery of the Chalais conspiracy in 1626.[26] Although the Infantes provided a natural rallying-point for dissidents at court, they were closely guarded, and lacked the room for manoeuvre which Gaston enjoyed in France. Above all, the Spanish nobility was a domesticated nobility which displayed none of the French nobility's addiction to armed faction and rebellion.

This meant that the Count–Duke did not have to meet the kind of open challenge to the crown's authority which created such continuous problems for Richelieu in his early years in office, and made the suppression of revolt the first priority in France. In Spain, the problems were of another, and perhaps more intractable, character. Olivares was faced with the need to find the means to sustain an expensive foreign policy and defend an extended empire at a time when silver supplies from

[24] Straub, *Pax et Imperium*, pp. 277–8.
[25] BL, Add. Ms. 36,449, fo. 54, Aston to Calvert, 28 July/7 Aug. 1623.
[26] Batiffol, *Richelieu et Louis XIII*, p. 149, and *Autour de Richelieu*, ch. 2 ('Les Gardes et mousquetaires du Cardinal').

the Indies were dwindling, the crown's debts were becoming un-manageable, and the Castilian economy was in no shape to generate new sources of wealth. His attempts to tackle these problems had provoked intense resistance, and his opponents were skilled at working within the system to block changes of which they disapproved. After six years in the management of affairs he found himself frustrated at every turn, and his government subjected to a barrage of criticism for policies which earned it growing unpopularity without the compensations which would have come with success.

It is not surprising, then, that the Count–Duke should have reacted to the crisis of the king's illness by seeking to vindicate his policies and inject new life into his programme for reform. His first step was to strengthen his own position by offering to resign[27] – an offer which, as he had anticipated, the king turned down. Philip, apparently chastened by his illness, now became a much more active partner in government, and at this point placed his personal authority squarely behind his minister. The councils were ordered to produce specific reform proposals,[28] and in a long state paper the king took the Council of Castile to task for failing to deal with the disorders of the Castilian coinage, and accused it of being responsible for the current discontent.[29]

Prodded and goaded by Olivares, the Council of Castile moved gingerly over the course of the next nine months towards the goal he had in mind – a sharp deflation which would restore some order to the currency. It came in August 1628 when the scheme for 'consuming' the *vellón* currency by the establishment of special banks was abandoned in the face of strong opposition from the cities, and the nominal value of the *vellón* coinage was reduced at a stroke by 50%.[30] This spectacular deflation brought heavy loss to private individuals with currency holdings in *vellón*, but instant relief to the royal treasury, which had been paying enormous premiums to the bankers for the conversion of copper into silver for foreign transactions. Taken in conjunction with the suspension of payments to the bankers in the previous year and the resulting reduction in rates of interest, it offered a new and possibly

---

[27] *MC*, I, p. 227 (10 Oct. 1627).
[28] Roca, *Fragmentos históricos*, p. 259.
[29] *MC*, I, doc. XIII. This state paper was in fact drafted by the Count–Duke (see *MC*, I, p. 231).
[30] Ruiz Martín, 'La banca', p. 107; Earl J. Hamilton, *American Treasure and the Price Revolution in Spain, 1501–1650* (Cambridge, Mass., 1934), p. 83, and 'Spanish Banking Schemes before 1700', *Journal of Political Economy*, 57 (1949), pp. 134–56.

unrepeatable opportunity to place the crown's finances and the Castilian currency on a more stable footing.

But the opportunity was not followed up, primarily because of the heavy new foreign policy commitments into which Olivares had entered a few months earlier. Duke Vincent II of Mantua had died at the end of 1627, and the succession to Mantua and Montferrat, which were fiefs of the Empire, was claimed by his nearest male relative, the French Duke of Nevers. The governor of Milan, Don Gonzalo de Córdoba, had repeatedly warned Madrid of the dangers to Spain's position in Northern Italy if a Frenchman succeeded to the duchy; and on 29 March 1628, on the receipt of orders from Madrid, which mistakenly assumed that he was already on the move, he sent his troops into Montferrat and prepared to lay siege to the strategic stronghold of Casale.[31] It was this act of war by the Spanish army of Milan, claiming to be upholding the right of the Emperor to determine the Mantuan succession, that was to lead Spain into a direct confrontation with France – a confrontation that would transform the political configuration of Europe.

In retrospect, Spain's military intervention in Mantua looks like the most serious mistake of Olivares' political career, although if Gonzalo de Córdoba had shown himself a more decisive commander, the verdict might have been very different. How was it that a minister who until now had been noted, and indeed criticized by his more bellicose colleagues, for the cautiousness of his foreign policy should suddenly have embarked on what many of his contemporaries regarded as a piece of unjustified opportunism?

While the answers to this question will never be fully known, it is possible to guess at some of the considerations which are likely to have been uppermost in the Count–Duke's mind. In the first place, he was understandably alarmed about the consequences for Spain's political and strategic position in Northern Italy if a client of the French were installed in Mantua. Then, too, there was the generally favourable conjuncture of events for the House of Austria in Europe, as the Imperial army under Wallenstein swept to victory in Germany. Olivares had good reason for confidence at the end of 1627. France, neutralized by the war against the English and the Huguenots of La Rochelle, was now Spain's ally. A

---

[31] Manuel Fernández Alvarez, *Don Gonzalo Fernández de Córdoba y la guerra de sucesión de Mantua y del Monferrato, 1627–1629* (Madrid, 1955), p. 65. For the Mantuan War see also Straub, *Pax et Imperium*, ch. 8.

possible joint invasion of England was under discussion, and a Spanish fleet had been sent to help the French against the Duke of Buckingham's expeditionary force, although it contrived to arrive too late to take any part in the fighting. Finally, it is a fair assumption, although impossible to prove, that Olivares, as a result of the events surrounding the king's illness, felt under pressure to produce some spectacular success which would confound his domestic critics. The capture of Casale would be a brilliant coup, making Spain's position in Northern Italy impregnable.

The assumption was fair, but it was based on what proved to be two fatal miscalculations – that Casale would be quickly taken, and that Louis XIII, preoccupied with the siege of La Rochelle and the problem of the Huguenots, would have no option but to accept a *fait accompli*. In fact, Gonzalo de Córdoba's army became hopelessly bogged down outside the walls of Casale, and by the autumn of 1628 it was a race for time as to which of the besieged cities, Casale or La Rochelle, would be the first to fall. In the event, it was La Rochelle, which surrendered on 28 October.

Even now, Olivares believed that time was on his side. He expected Casale to fall at any moment, and thought that, even if the French should decide to intervene in Italy, their army would not be ready before the early summer of 1629. In November Richelieu sent an envoy, Bautru, to Madrid to assure Olivares of France's peaceful intentions. Behind the Count–Duke's bravado in his discussions with Bautru it is not difficult to detect a certain uneasiness.[32] One source of anxiety was that the treasure-fleet was overdue. It had in fact been captured in September by a Dutch flotilla commanded by Piet Heyn, but the news only reached Madrid in late December after tense weeks of waiting. Olivares also suspected that Richelieu was negotiating an agreement with the Huguenots in order to free his hands for intervention in Italy; and on 5 January 1629 he warned the papal nuncio that if French troops crossed the Alps, it would be the beginning of a thirty-year war between the Crowns of France and Spain.[33] His prediction was almost uncannily accurate. The Treaty of the Pyrenees was signed in November 1659.

Olivares was right to be worried, although the speed of the French operation took him, and everybody else, by surprise. At the end of February 1629, Louis XIII and Richelieu led an army across the Alps, and defeated Charles Emmanuel of Savoy at Susa in the first week of

---

[32] AAE., Correspondance politique, Espagne, tome 15, fos. 284–306.
[33] AV, Spagna, 69, fo. 61, nuncio's despatch.

March.[34] Olivares was badly shaken when the news reached Madrid, and saw little chance of averting what he called 'total ruin' unless the Emperor immediately sent his forces into Italy.[35] Gonzalo de Córdoba was forced to raise the siege of Casale under the pressure of the French advance, and by the end of March 1629 the first and most significant stage of the Mantuan War was over.

Richelieu was vindicated by the success of the Italian campaign, but – like Olivares – he took an enormous risk in deciding to intervene in Mantua. Both ministers, beset by acute domestic problems and bitter opposition, had placed foreign adventure before domestic reform. In doing so, they put their own future at stake.

In Madrid, there is no evidence of opposition to the intervention in Mantua, although there was plenty of recrimination when the intervention failed. The pressure for intervention came first from Gonzalo de Córdoba, as governor of Milan, and Olivares and his fellow-Councillors of State allowed themselves to be carried along by what seemed the logic of events, although covering themselves with a moral justification by assembling a junta of theologians, which decided that the use of force was justified to uphold the Emperor's rights.[36] In France, on the other hand, the king's council was divided, and the Queen Mother, Marillac and Cardinal Bérulle, the leader of the *dévots*, were all opposed to a foreign policy adventure which was bound to lead to confrontation with Spain.[37] The arguments on their side, as Pagès has shown, were strong. Although La Rochelle had fallen, the Protestants of Languedoc remained to be subdued. Marillac was deeply troubled by the continuous outbreaks of unrest provoked by the crown's attempts to levy new taxes, and by the mounting resistance of the parlements to the registration of fiscal edicts.[38] He and his allies had no doubt that a conflict with Spain – which, as a Catholic power, was properly France's natural ally in the struggle against heresy – was an act of folly, or worse, and that the immediate priority was for the government to devote itself to what Marillac called the 'soulagement des sujets' and the 'bons règlements de l'Etat', for which peace was indispensable.

---

[34] For France and Savoy, see Jacques Humbert, *Une Grande Entreprise oubliée. Les Français en Savoie sous Louis XIII* (Paris, 1960).
[35] ADM, legajo 79, Olivares to Aytona, 26 March 1629.
[36] AGS, Estado, legajo 2331, fo. 48, undated letter from Olivares.
[37] Bonney, *King's Debts*, p. 149.
[38] Pagès, 'Grand orage', p. 66.

Richelieu's priorities were different. Since the Peace of Monzón in 1626 he had seemed to favour the policy of the *dévots*, putting domestic considerations first. In 1627 the Cardinal imprisoned his confidential adviser and publicist Fancan, whose enthusiastic endorsement of an anti-Spanish foreign policy based on an alliance with Protestant powers had made him a political liability.[39] This apparent renunciation of a bellicose foreign policy may have been a temporary response to the strength of the opposition and the pressure of events, although it may also have reflected the genuine desire of at least part of his nature to give France the tranquillity or *repos* which it so badly needed. But the Spanish intervention in Mantua reawakened all his old suspicions of Madrid's intentions, which Spain's failure to get its fleet to La Rochelle on time to fight the English had done nothing to allay. He could now turn round to the *dévots* with evidence that Olivares was not to be trusted and that rapprochement with Spain did not work.

There were moments during the siege of La Rochelle when the Cardinal was ready to abandon it in despair,[40] but, as Father Joseph pointed out to him, success would open up a whole new vista of opportunities both at home and abroad. 'After La Rochelle', he wrote to Richelieu, the king would be in a position to 'give a new face to affairs in the realm', and to assume, 'with greater justice than ever, the role of arbiter of Christendom.'[41] The consequence of the surrender of La Rochelle was, as Father Joseph had predicted, to enhance enormously the domestic and international prestige both of Louis and his minister. Richelieu was acclaimed in the wake of the victory as 'the greatest statesman that ever lived' and as 'greater than Cardinal Ximenes' – that other great cardinal-warrior who had also saved his nation.[42] The aura of success immeasurably enhanced the Cardinal's authority, and greatly strengthened his relationship with Louis, who saw him as the architect of his glory.

The Cardinal was able to capitalize on his enhanced authority to press his case for military intervention in Italy. According to his memoirs he

[39] See G. Fagniez, 'Fancan et Richelieu', *Revue Historique*, 107 (1911), pp. 59–78.

[40] Fagniez, *Père Joseph*, I, p. 398.

[41] *Ibid.*, p. 392.

[42] Batiffol, *Richelieu et Louis XIII*, p. 191. For the popularity among contemporaries of parallels between Richelieu and Ximenes, see Thuau, *Raison d'état*, pp. 184 and 393. Maxim CLI of Richelieu's *Maximes d'état* is inspired by Cardinal Ximenes, and is probably drawn from Gómez de Castro's *De rebus gestis a Francisco Ximenio Cisnerio*.

put it to Louis that glory was no small reason for coming to the help of the
new Duke of Mantua, and that it would be an action which would surpass
'all the great expeditions of the Romans'. Great affairs, he went on, were
sometimes the matter of a fleeting moment which, if once allowed to pass,
would never again return; and – no doubt thinking of Piet Heyn's capture
of the treasure-fleet – he argued that Spain had never been in greater
financial distress.[43] The famous *Avis au roi* of 13 January 1629, in which
he dissected the king's character so mercilessly,[44] began with the enticing
prospect that Louis could, if he wished, make himself 'the most powerful
monarch and the most esteemed prince in the world'; and it skilfully tied
the security of France to the need for 'a perpetual design to arrest the
course of Spain's progress', while doing everything possible to avoid full-
scale war with Spain. By ending with an offer of resignation the Cardinal
effectively forced Louis to accept his own ordering of priorities. But, like
Olivares, who was also dealing with a pious monarch, he too had recourse
to the theologians to calm the royal conscience.[45] Louis was, after all,
about to make war on two of his brothers-in-law, the King of Spain and
the Duke of Savoy. He was already at war with the third, the King of
England.

Richelieu was well aware of the need to justify French military action
to his compatriots and the world, and he found his justification in the
theme of Spanish aspirations to universal monarchy. It was a simple but
effective theme which he exploited unremittingly for the rest of his
ministerial career. In order to disarm his *dévot* critics he insisted that
Spain was simply using Catholicism as a cloak to cover its secular
ambitions; and to forge the anti-Habsburg coalition which he realized
was essential for success, he represented the King of France as the
liberator and the arbiter of Christendom. France was the natural counter-
weight – the '*contre-poids*' – to Habsburg expansionism.[46]

Did the Cardinal really believe his own propaganda? His reading of
Madrid's intentions does not square with what is known about the
designs of Olivares, whose aim was not universal monarchy but a general
peace. In reality, two views of Christendom confronted each other in
1629. The Count–Duke's was of a Christendom, relatively diverse and
pluralistic, enjoying all the benefits of order and tranquillity that flowed
from a *pax austriaca* which was guaranteed by the close cooperation of

---

[43] *Mémoires*, IV, pp. 4–9.   [45] O'Connell, *Richelieu*, p. 191.
[44] Grillon, IV, pp. 24–47.   [46] Wollenberg, *Richelieu*, p. 142.

Vienna and Madrid, acting in close harmony with the papacy. The Cardinal's was of a Christendom in which the King of France resumed his rightful place as the first among monarchs; in which the French church spoke for the cause of international Catholicism; and in which peace was preserved by a system of collective security among European states under the beneficent direction of a powerful France.

Olivares, by intervening in Mantua, played straight into Richelieu's hands. His action alienated the papacy, alarmed the Italian princes, and lent credence to Richelieu's claim that the Habsburgs would stop at nothing to achieve universal dominion. For the Count–Duke, France was the true disturber of the European peace, but most of the world – including many of the most influential figures at the court of the Emperor – did not see the Mantuan affair in this light. The lure of 'reputation' had led him on, just as it led Richelieu on during the opening months of 1629.

For Richelieu, as for Olivares, the winning of reputation in the Mantuan affair carried with it a major political prize. Both ministers were thinking in terms of military and diplomatic successes which could then be turned to account at home. Capitalizing on his triumph at La Rochelle, Richelieu hoped to unite a divided country behind him in a glorious foreign campaign; and then, capitalizing this time on victory abroad, turn round to deal more effectively with his domestic difficulties. This is precisely what he achieved in the first half of 1629. The king, returning victorious from Italy at the end of April, was able to impose the Peace of Alais on his Huguenot subjects in June. This guaranteed them their religious rights, while destroying their political and military organiz-ation. But a definitive settlement in Italy, securing the Duke of Nevers' rights in Mantua, had eluded the Cardinal.

Where Richelieu was temporarily enjoying the sweet taste of victory in the early months of 1629, Olivares was savouring the bitter taste of defeat. The spring and summer months of 1629 were among the most dangerous and critical of the Count–Duke's political career. The raising of the siege of Casale was a devastating blow, damaging to his own prestige and that of his royal master, and likely to wreck the elaborate plans on which he had been working over the last two years for the restoration of Spain's international position. 'I have quite lost my navigating aids', he wrote to Gonzalo de Córdoba in May, 'my quadrant and compass.'[47]

---

[47] AGS, Estado, legajo 2713, letter of 4 May 1629.

In effect he now had two wars on his hands, one in the Netherlands and the other in Italy, and he was well aware that Spain lacked the resources to pursue them both at once. He had been counting on Imperial troops under Wallenstein to join in the war against the Dutch, but instead they were now required for Mantua. In the spring of 1629 Spain's position in the Netherlands was beginning to crumble as a result of the financial strains imposed by the Mantuan campaign and the loss of the treasure-fleet, and Olivares came under intense pressure from Ambrosio Spínola and the Council of State to settle with the Dutch on terms which he considered totally unacceptable, in order to allow Spain to restore its position in Northern Italy.[48]

Flanders or Italy was an old Spanish dilemma. Now in 1629 the dilemma led to a domestic crisis in which Olivares' hold on power suddenly looked precarious. The failure at Casale gave new courage to Olivares' enemies. The opposition somehow had to shake Philip's confidence in his minister, and here it played on the king's jealousy of his brother-in-law, and his thirst for glory on the battlefield. According to Richelieu's memoirs – not perhaps the most impartial of sources – the praises of Louis XIII were loudly sung at the Spanish court after his triumph in Italy, and his portrait was to be seen in every artist's studio in Madrid.[49] Not surprisingly, Philip – now twenty-four, and beginning to tire of being in leading-strings – aspired to follow Louis' example. The opposition encouraged him in this, and in June, as the fate of Italy and Flanders hung in the balance, it addressed him directly in a widely circulated manifesto.[50]

The manifesto accused a tyrannical Olivares of ruining Spain through his 'presumption and mistaken policies'. He was trying to set the world right with 'imaginary and fantastical machinations'; he was destroying Spain with his futile reforming pragmatics, his ill-timed devaluation of the coinage, and his wars in Italy, capriciously begun and capriciously planned, and fought 'without troops, without money, without reason'. The king was urged to imitate Philip II and Charles V. 'Your Majesty is not a king, but a person whom the Count–Duke seeks to conserve in order to make use of the office of king – a mere ceremonial ruler.' It was

---

[48] For the sequence of events in the spring and summer of 1629, see *MC*, II, pp. 5–18.
[49] *Mémoires*, X, pp. 278–9.
[50] BL, Add. Ms. 14,004, fos. 428–30v, for one among several manuscript copies to have survived. The manifesto was also incorporated into Novoa's *Historia de Felipe IV*, Documentos inéditos LXIX, pp. 74–6. See *MC*, II, p. 8.

time for Philip to rule by himself, and turn for advice, when he needed it, to his grandees and loyal subjects.

The manifesto reads like an attempt by the high nobility to recover what they saw as their natural influence with the king. As a direct appeal to Philip to shake off the Count–Duke's tyrannical government it was psychologically well-timed, and it hit its mark. Unwilling to be seen any longer as a 'mere ceremonial ruler', Philip was suddenly galvanized into unwonted activity, and informed Olivares, to his horror, that he planned to take personal command of his forces in Italy.

In a remarkable document, dated 17 June 1629, the Count–Duke put to the king a series of questions about his intentions, and Philip replied in the margin.[51] What was His Majesty's intention as regards Mantua and Montferrat? 'It is my aim and intention that not a single Frenchman should remain in Italy . . .' Did the king intend to maintain peaceful relations with France, once the Mantuan question was settled? 'My intention is to get my revenge on France for its recent behaviour, but I do not know when or how . . .' Did he want peace with the Dutch, even on unfavourable terms, in order to fight in Italy, since two simultaneous wars were out of the question? Philip indicated that he did, and reiterated his determination to command an army in Italy. 'One cannot win fame without undertaking some great enterprise in person . . . Once I have led this expedition I shall, with God's help, do with the world what I want . . . To get a good general peace, we must first have a good and honourable war . . .'

In the weeks that followed, Olivares found himself frequently overruled. In spite of his objections, the Council of State agreed to wind up the war in the Netherlands, even if this involved a peace settlement on unsatisfactory terms. Philip seemed determined to press ahead with his plans for an Italian campaign to take his revenge on Louis XIII, although the Count–Duke, who found himself dealing with a very petulant master, tried to impress upon him that this was not a matter for 'anger and precipitation, but for mature wisdom and constancy, and for extreme caution in not spending a single *real* unnecessarily'.[52]

Little by little the will of the Count–Duke prevailed in this battle of wills, although he lived through some very difficult months, in which he found himself partially excluded from the decision-making process,

---

[51] *MC*, II, doc. I.
[52] *MC*, II, p. 39 (22 June 1629).

while the king handled a great deal more business by himself. Philip was extremely reluctant to listen to his minister when he elaborated on the dangers of leaving Castile in its present unsettled state and entrusting its government to a regency council.[53] In gradually winning the upper hand, Olivares benefited from the lack of any obvious candidate to take his place. There seems to have been no Marillac in Madrid. All the diplomatic threads were in his hands, and, for all the criticisms that were levelled against him, he had shown extraordinary skill and perseverance in keeping Spain's armies in the field. He was helped, too, by the beginnings of a Habsburg recovery in Northern Italy, as Imperial troops moved down into Mantua in the summer of 1629, and Spínola began a new siege of Casale. But he was not yet out of danger. In the autumn, Spain was threatened with a debacle in the war against the Dutch, and Philip, to whom a son and heir had just been born, announced that he was going in person to take command of his army of Flanders.[54] 'God give us peace this winter', Olivares wrote in desperation to Spínola, 'and so help to calm these unfortunate royal humours.'[55]

In the end, the king's bid for independence petered out in farce. Instead of leaving Madrid to take command of an army, he left it without Olivares in January 1630 to accompany his sister on the first part of her journey to join her husband, the King of Hungary, in Vienna. For a moment everyone believed that Philip had at last thrown off the shackles that bound him to his favourite and was about to dismiss him.[56] But then he abruptly turned round, and in a few days was back at court as if nothing had happened. It was the nearest Spain ever came to having a Day of the Dupes.

The comic, or pathetic, ending to the drama of the tense relationship between the king and the Count–Duke in 1629–30 should not be allowed to disguise its significance. Philip, like Louis XIII, resented being told that he was not his own master, and not unnaturally wished to prove the world wrong. But his attempt to assert his authority came at a moment when the Mantuan fiasco made Olivares particularly vulnerable. The Count–Duke's enemies now had a series of powerful arguments against his stewardship, and had there been a personality of real stature among

---

[53] *MC*, II, pp. 12–13.
[54] AHN, Estado, legajo 727, royal order, 27 Oct. 1629.
[55] Brown and Elliott, *A Palace*, p. 52.
[56] *MC*, II, p. 16.

them, the story might have ended differently. But the older generation of councillors was dying out, and there was no convincing figure to head the opposition.

Among the arguments deployed by the opposition there was one to which the king had proved particularly susceptible – that a real king should lead his armies into battle like Louis XIII in Italy. Olivares' enemies would return to it again in the 1630s, as they huddled together in their little groups to vent their spleen against him. Behind it there lurked a substantive issue about the character of kingship in seventeenth-century Europe. Did a king's duties lie primarily with his ministers at court or his soldiers on the battlefield? Olivares had various reasons for attempting to dissuade Philip from going to war, not all of them bad. There was genuine cause for concern, as there was with Louis XIII, about the king's health on campaign, especially before he had an heir. There was also good reason to be worried about the shattering blow to prestige in the event of defeat. Olivares was therefore justified in arguing that careful planning and a great deal of money were needed before the king went campaigning. But inevitably he was especially concerned about the opportunities that his own absence abroad, and that of his royal master, would give to his enemies.

This consideration was also uppermost in Richelieu's mind when he was planning the Mantuan campaign. If the king left for Italy at the head of his army, the Queen Mother would act as regent – a disturbing prospect, and all the more so since Marie de Médicis was fiercely opposed to French intervention in Mantua on behalf of the Duke of Nevers, whom she detested.[57] The Cardinal had originally intended that Louis should remain in Paris, while Gaston commanded the army of Italy, but this idea foundered on Louis' refusal to see his brother win glory on the battlefield. In the circumstances the Cardinal had no choice but to let Louis have his way, and run the risk of leaving his flank uncovered in Paris while the king was on campaign.[58]

Richelieu's anxiety was well founded. The Queen Mother's advisers inevitably gained in influence during her temporary regency. So too did the opposition elements at court, which played on her maternal fears about the health and safety of her son. Marillac and Bérulle warned, too, that Richelieu would not be satisfied with raising the siege of Casale, but

---

[57] Batiffol, *Richelieu et Louis XIII*, p. 227.
[58] Grillon, IV, pp. 14–15; Bonney, *King's Debts*, p. 150.

would plunge the country into war with Spain – a war which threatened to be 'immortal'.[59]

Louis' triumphant return to France after raising the siege of Casale temporarily silenced the opposition, especially as he took the opportunity to subjugate the Huguenots in the Midi on the way back to Paris. This was exactly what the *dévot* opposition had been demanding of Richelieu. But the failure to reach a definitive settlement in Italy meant that the question of priorities – of war or reform – was only postponed, not resolved; and as soon as the situation became critical again in Italy in the winter of 1629 with the second siege of Casale, the question came to the forefront once more. As the opposition had suspected, once French prestige had been committed, there could be no drawing back for Richelieu. He rejected the arguments of his opponents that there was no money for war,[60] and pressed the case for a new military intervention in Italy. In the considerations which he submitted to the king on 21 November 1629, he made it clear that the choice was between *réputation* and *repos*.[61] 'It is difficult', he wrote, 'for a prince to have great *réputation* and great *repos*, since frequently the esteem of the world is gained only by great actions, and ordinarily those which engender esteem excite the envy and hatred of neighbours . . .'

This time the behaviour of Gaston, who had fled to Lorraine, made it impossible for Louis to leave the country. Richelieu was appointed lieutenant-general of the army of Italy on 24 December 1629, and set off for a second time to rescue a Casale under siege. He was well aware that in leaving for Italy alone he was taking a serious risk. His relations with the Queen Mother were deteriorating, and in his memorandum of 21 November to the king he almost challenged Louis to protect him while he was out of the country.[62] But Cardinal Bérulle, whose personal sanctity had given the *dévots* much of their influence at court, had died in October,[63] and Marillac appeared to be loyal.[64] Richelieu seems to have been reckoning, then, on repeating the pattern of the spring of 1629, and

---

[59] Pagès, 'Grand orage', pp. 77–8.
[60] Bonney, *King's Debts*, p. 151.
[61] Grillon, IV, doc. 678.
[62] *Ibid.*, p. 679.
[63] See Pierre de La Vaissière, *Un Grand Procès sous Richelieu. L'affaire du Maréchal de Marillac, 1630–1632* (Paris, 1924), p. 26, and M. Houssaye, *Le Cardinal de Bérulle et le Cardinal de Richelieu, 1625–1629* (Paris, 1875).
[64] Pagès, 'Grand orage', p. 80.

turning the tables on his domestic opponents by means of victory in Italy. The difficulty about this strategy was that victory, as much as defeat, brought its problems. On 29 March 1630 the French army in Italy captured the fortress of Pinerolo; and, as Pagès pointed out, it was the capture of Pinerolo that precipitated *le grand orage* and brought the struggle at the French court to a head. If Louis decided to hold on to Pinerolo, wrote Richelieu in his famous memorandum of 13 April 1630, he had 'made the greatest conquest imaginable' and would be in a position to become 'the arbiter and master of Italy'. But Richelieu put the choice squarely before his master. The retention of Pinerolo meant war – indefinite war with Spain and also with Savoy, which threatened open alliance with Spain if Pinerolo were not restored to it; and 'if the king decides on war, it will be necessary to abandon all thought of tranquillity (*repos*), of economies and reorganization within the realm'. Once again, it was *repos* or *réputation*. Louis chose *réputation*, and in May 1630 led his army against Savoy.[65]

Louis' victorious campaign in the following weeks brought Richelieu no more than a temporary respite. Marillac, although prepared at the time to agree to France's retention of Pinerolo,[66] had quickly been assailed by doubts. On 13 May, before the start of the campaign, at an important meeting in Lyon with Louis, the Queen Mother and the Cardinal, along with the governor of Languedoc, the Duke of Montmorency, he had argued strongly in favour of peace. The people were crushed by taxes and ready to revolt; the issues of war were uncertain; the king would be exposed to grave personal danger. A survivor of the troubled France of the sixteenth century, he could not forget the misfortunes that earlier French interventions in Italy had brought in their train.[67] During the course of the summer, Marillac's agitation increased. He begged Richelieu to consider the glory that could be acquired by 'bringing order to the kingdom and relieving the people' – a direct challenge to the assumption that reputation was primarily won on the battlefield.[68] Marillac's correspondence in these months shows him to be a man deeply, and justifiably, concerned by the miserable condition of France; but it also reveals him as a man gnawed by anxiety and fear. 'There is

---

[65] See *ibid.*, pp. 82–5. The text of Richelieu's memorandum of 13 April 1630 is printed in full in Grillon, v, doc. 196.
[66] Grillon, v, p. 221, note 7.
[67] Grillon, v, p. 259.
[68] Grillon, v, p. 275.

sedition everywhere in France', he wrote in July. 'The parlements punish nobody.' This complicity of the parlements made him deeply concerned for the authority and dignity of the king.[69] He was worried, too, and with good reason, by the state of the royal finances. 'The shortage of money makes me very afraid . . .'[70] 'I am afraid' was a constant refrain.[71]

Did the voice of this timorous and elderly man really speak to the concerns of the country, or was Richelieu, with his robust anti-Spanish sentiments, more in tune with the times? It may well be that the Cardinal's policies, with their promise of the recovery of national unity through a victorious war against a traditional enemy, were better suited than those of Marillac to the mood of the new generation in France.[72] Yet Marillac's pleas for peace and reform also answered to an obvious and deeply felt need, however much Richelieu might protest that 'the aversion of the people to war is not a strong reason in favour of peace'.[73]

This aversion was manifested in continuous outbreaks of public discontent, which lent credence to the arguments of Marillac and his friends. Their arguments, together with their fears, seemed increasingly persuasive to the Queen Mother, who worried about the effect of campaigning on her son's precarious health, and became openly defeatist about the war after the Emperor's forces captured and sacked Mantua in July.[74] Persuaded, like others, that Richelieu was deliberately prolonging the war in order to make himself more absolute, she apparently came to the conclusion during the summer of 1630 that the Cardinal must be dismissed.[75]

Marillac's camp was strengthened, too, by the adhesion of the younger nobility who looked to Gaston as their leader and yearned for release from the oppression of the Cardinal's authoritarian government.[76] This group was largely motivated, like the aristocratic opposition to Olivares, by thwarted ambition, petty hatreds and vendettas. It overlapped with the

[69] Grillon, v, p. 398 (Marillac to Richelieu, 15 July 1630). The publication by Grillon of several of Marillac's letters makes it possible to appreciate better than hitherto the character both of Marillac's arguments and of the man himself.
[70] Grillon, v, p. 522 (Marillac to Richelieu, 15 Aug. 1630).
[71] Cf. his letter to Richelieu of 17 Aug. 1630 (Grillon, v, p. 540).
[72] I am much indebted to Orest Ranum for discussions on this point.
[73] Grillon, v, p. 260 (*Avis* of Richelieu, mid-May 1630).
[74] La Vaissière, *Un Grand Procès*, p. 39.
[75] Bonney, *King's Debts*, pp. 152–3.
[76] La Vaissière, *Un Grand Procès*, p. 43.

entourage of Anne of Austria which had ties to the Spanish ambassador, the Marquis of Mirabel. Unlike the Marillac party it seems to have had no programme beyond the overthrow of Richelieu. But opposition to the war gave it a rallying-cry from 1630, and in September it made common cause with Marillac.

On 21 September Louis came down with fever while at Lyon. On the 29th he received extreme unction. During his illness, the Duke of Guise, Bassompierre and Marillac's half-brother, the Maréchal de Marillac, met secretly at Lyon to decide on Richelieu's fate – exile, prison or death – when Gaston acceded to the throne.[77] But then on the 30th the king began unexpectedly to recover, and by 19 October, although still weak, was able to begin the return journey to Paris.

The Queen Mother may have extracted a promise from her son during his illness to dismiss the Cardinal once he was back in the capital.[78] But the final break was precipitated by Richelieu's unexpected rejection of the treaty which the French envoys, Brûlart and Father Joseph, had negotiated at Ratisbon on 13 October after a ceasefire had been reached in Italy. In making peace with the Emperor and the Empire, the envoys had in effect committed France to abandoning its allies. If the treaty stood, it would wreck the Cardinal's plans for the creation of a European coalition against the Habsburgs. He was understandably plunged into gloom, and during these weeks of mental anguish over Louis' illness and the Ratisbon affair he visibly aged. But in the end, with characteristic skill and luck, he turned a potential disaster into a triumph, and boldly decided to repudiate the treaty on the grounds that France's representatives had exceeded their powers.[79]

The rejection of the treaty, over the protests of Marillac, saved the situation in Italy, where French troops continued their march on Casale and forced the Spaniards once again to abandon their siege. But domestically it brought the struggle between the Cardinal and his enemies to a climax. The repudiation of the Ratisbon agreement effectively opened up the prospect of endless conflict between France and

[77] Mongrédien, *La Journée des Dupes*, pp. 61–2.
[78] Pagès, 'Grand orage', p. 95.
[79] For the Treaty of Ratisbon and Richelieu's reactions to it, see Fagniez, *Père Joseph*, I, pp. 492–535; D.P. O'Connell, 'A *Cause Célèbre* in the History of Treaty-Making: the Refusal to Ratify the Peace Treaty of Regensberg in 1630', *The British Year Book of International Law*, 42 (1967), pp. 71–90; Wollenberg, *Richelieu*, pp. 55–9.

the House of Austria.[80] To prevent this, the Queen Mother and her friends had to act at once. On the Day of the Dupes – 11 November 1630 – she thought that she had secured the Cardinal's dismissal, only to find at the moment of apparent victory that the king was not prepared to sacrifice his minister. It was an ironic coincidence that in Madrid at the very moment when events in Paris were reaching their climax, Olivares was denouncing the Treaty of Ratisbon in words that might have been written for him by Richelieu, as 'the most unauthorized peace that we have ever experienced'.[81]

Richelieu followed up his triumph by arresting Marillac and stripping him of his post as Keeper of the Seals. During the days of crisis the Cardinal's 'creatures' had stood beside him, and he now systematically consolidated his hold on the government. The Duke of Guise went into exile; Bassompierre was sent to the Bastille; and the Maréchal de Marillac, placed under arrest in Italy where he was in command of the army, was convicted by thirteen votes to ten on a series of largely trumped-up charges, and went to his death in May 1631.[82]

In 1629–30, then, both Olivares and Richelieu emerged triumphant over their enemies, although in France, unlike Spain, there was a prolonged aftermath of confusion and revolt. Gaston fled the court at the end of January 1631, and took refuge at Orléans. Here he began to raise money and men. Then in March, with royal forces approaching, he took refuge in the Spanish Franche-Comté and then Lorraine. The Queen Mother, in retreat at Compiègne, crossed the frontier into the Spanish Netherlands in July, and never again set foot in France.[83] The fact that his closest relatives should turn to Spain for refuge and help was a source of obvious embarrassment to the king. It also opened up ominous new possibilities for Spanish exploitation of domestic unrest. At the end of March the king declared Gaston's advisers and followers guilty of *lèse-majesté*. A month later, Gaston responded from Nancy with a manifesto denouncing Richelieu and his policies,[84] which may be seen as the equivalent of the manifesto produced in Madrid in 1629 by the Duke of

[80] Bonney, *King's Debts*, p. 154; Mongrédien, *La Journée des Dupes*, p. 59.
[81] AGS, Estado, legajo 2331, fo. 126, consulta of Council of State, 10 Nov. 1630.
[82] La Vaissière, *Un Grand Procès*, p. 214; Mongrédien, *La Journée des Dupes*, p. 88.
[83] For the Queen Mother in exile, see P. Henrard, *Marie de Médicis dans les Pays-Bas, 1631–1638*, Annales de l'Académie d'Archéologie de Belgique XXXI (Antwerp, 1875).
[84] Georges Dethan, *Gaston d'Orléans. Conspirateur et prince charmant* (Paris, 1959), pp. 102–4; Church, *Richelieu and Reason of State*, pp. 207–8.

Sessa and his friends. Richelieu – 'this inhuman and perverse priest' – was accused of wanting to make himself 'sovereign of this monarchy under the title of minister'. He forbade access to the king; he had crushed public liberties; and with his taxes and fiscal extortions had 'reduced France to the last extremity'.

It was fortunate for the Cardinal that Gaston's deeds failed, as usual, to measure up to his words. Although several leading nobles joined him in Lorraine, and he could count on widespread anti-Richelieu sentiment inside France, his rebellion was badly managed and badly led. It ended in fiasco in September 1632 when his characteristically quixotic supporter, the Duke of Montmorency, having attempted to raise his province of Languedoc in revolt, was defeated by royalist forces at Castelnaudary.[85] In the defeat and execution of Montmorency, the verdict of the Day of the Dupes was resoundingly confirmed.

Although Richelieu had emerged victorious, the events of 1630 and their aftermath left him deeply scarred. In Paris, as in Madrid, there was a palpable atmosphere of hatred in these years.[86] Yet in retrospect it seems unlikely that Louis and Philip ever had any serious intention of dropping their ministers.[87] At the height of the crisis, both kings were under heavy pressure, which was all the more difficult to resist because to some extent it coincided with their own deepest inclination, to throw off the shackles of dependence and rise to the full majesty of kingship. It was not easy for Philip to ignore the complaints that he was nothing but a 'ceremonial ruler', or for Louis to turn a deaf ear when he was exhorted to resume his sceptre and rule by himself, like his great ancestors.[88] Yet in the end both kings held firm. In success, and even in defeat, Richelieu and Olivares were formidable figures, and their stature seemed all the greater when set against the puny figures of most of their opponents. By successfully identifying themselves with what they represented as the true interests of the king and the state, they could depict their enemies as frustrated power-seekers, who put private interest before the public weal.

---

[85] See Dethan, *Gaston*, part I, ch. 9 for Montmorency's revolt.
[86] For first-hand reactions of the two ministers to the atmosphere of hostility which surrounded them, see – for Olivares – *MC*, I, doc. XII, and for Richelieu the disturbing 'Journal de monsieur le cardinal de Richelieu, qu'il a faict durant le grand orage de la court . . .', in *Archives Curieuses de l'Histoire de France*, ed. F. Danjou, 2nd series, V (Paris, 1838), pp. 5–107.
[87] For Richelieu, see Pagès, 'Grand orage', p. 96.
[88] 'Louis, reprends ton sceptre et règne par toi-même/Comme tes grands aïeux . . .', quoted in Batiffol, *Richelieu et Louis XIII*, p. 313.

Both ministers, however, were badly shaken by the experience, and both responded by seeking to mobilize opinion in their favour. The circulation in Paris and Madrid of pasquinades and subversive manifestoes made it clear that even the more repressive measures of censorship that had recently been adopted at the instigation of the two ministers were inadequate to stifle the opposition. In France and Spain there was an insatiable interest for news of events at court, and a public opinion which had to be wooed and won.

Over the winter of 1629 Olivares mobilized a team of propagandists – among them Quevedo, a man of unrivalled polemical skills – to vindicate his ministerial record.[89] In France, with its long history of domestic division, pamphlet warfare was a more firmly established tradition than in Spain. From the earliest years of his ministry Richelieu had drawn on the skills of the publicists, but the dissensions within the royal family and the bitterness of the struggle made the pamphlet war unusually intense in 1630–1, and he spared no effort to ensure favourable publicity for his cause. When Théophraste Renaudot started his *Gazette* in the spring of 1631, the Cardinal moved quickly to take it under his wing, and obtained for Renaudot an exclusive right to the printing of gazettes, relations and newsletters.[90]

The Count–Duke and the Cardinal both sought to cultivate an image of themselves as wise, far-sighted and disinterested ministers, and they both looked for writers and historians capable of presenting to the public and posterity a favourable record of their actions. One of Olivares' friends from Seville, Juan de Vera y Figueroa, the Count of La Roca, wrote a eulogistic biography,[91] while Jean de Silhon's *Le Ministre d'Etat*, first published in 1631, raised to the level of an exemplar the personal virtues of Richelieu, as tested and refined by the fire of experience. Of the crisis of 1629–30 Silhon wrote:

In this confusion of minds and business, the Cardinal never lost his constancy. His reason remained upright. His provisions for the relief of Casale were never interrupted, and he let it be seen that the wise man is above all passions, and that the just grief which he suffered as the result of his love for his great master still

[89] Brown and Elliott, *A Palace*, p. 162; J. H. Elliott, 'Quevedo and the Count–Duke of Olivares', in *Quevedo in Perspective*, ed. James Iffland (Newark, Delaware, 1982), pp. 227–50.

[90] Howard M. Solomon, *Public Welfare, Science and Propaganda in Seventeenth Century France. The Innovations of Théophraste Renaudot* (Princeton, 1972).

[91] His *Fragmentos históricos de la vida de D. Gaspar de Guzmán*, which, however, failed to find its way into print.

left him with sufficient strength and skill not to abandon the tiller, and to steer us to port in spite of the contrary winds.[92]

It was the image of the prudent statesman in the Stoic mould – that same image which Quevedo and his friends had appropriated for Olivares.[93]

Yet as the War of the Mantuan Succession was brought to an uneasy end by the Peace of Cherasco in the spring of 1631, the enemies of Richelieu and Olivares had good reason to question the prudence of their policies. The costs of intervention in Mantua had been horrifying for both France and Spain, and were made still heavier by the poor harvests and high food prices that afflicted both countries during the years 1629 to 1631.[94] In addition to the new fiscal demands created by the war, it also compelled a further postponement of long overdue reforms. In both countries *réputation* had won over reform.

For Spain the results were an unrelieved disaster. Its intervention in Mantua had antagonized European public opinion, driven the papacy into the arms of the French, strained Madrid's relations with Vienna almost to breaking-point, and wrecked Olivares' grand design for securing peace with the Dutch on terms rather better than those of 1609. Above all, the breathing-space that looked like being gained in 1627 had been recklessly thrown away. But France's future was mortgaged no less irrevocably than Spain's. With Marillac gone, there remained no one in a position of influence to contest the Cardinal's reading of events – a reading which made the defeat of the House of Austria the first priority. The *grand orage* had blown itself out in France and Spain alike; the two pilots were left grasping the tiller more firmly than ever; but the vessels they were steering were on collision course.

---

[92] Amsterdam, 1664 edn, p. 131.
[93] Cf. Quevedo's *Cómo ha de ser el privado*, and the Count of La Roca's *Fragmentos históricos*.
[94] Bonney, *King's Debts*, p. 143, for the subsistence crisis in France. For Castile, see Vicente Pérez Moreda, *Las crisis de mortalidad en la España interior, siglos XVI–XIX* (Madrid, 1980), pp. 299–300.

5

∞∞

War and *raison d'état*

The peace of Cherasco ended the War of the Mantuan Succession in April 1631. Four years later, in May 1635, France formally declared war on Spain. During those four years of cold war between the French and Spanish crowns – years which saw the installation of French garrisons in Lorraine and on the Rhine, the death of Gustavus Adolphus at Lützen, and the defeat of the Swedes at Nördlingen in September 1634 – the papacy made desperate attempts to bring about a reconciliation.[1] As part of Urban VIII's peace efforts, the nuncios in Paris and Madrid were instructed to work for a better understanding between Richelieu and Olivares, on the assumption that their personal hostility was a major impediment to the achievement of improved relations between their royal masters. As late as October 1635, five months after the outbreak of hostilities, Mazarin, at that time nuncio extraordinary in Paris, displayed a touching faith in the possibilities of summit diplomacy. 'Would to God', he wrote, 'that these two ministers could spend three days together, and every difficulty would be surmounted without the need for further efforts and without convening a congress.'[2]

What did Richelieu and Olivares really think of each other, and how far did personal antipathies influence their behaviour? The evidence, especially for Richelieu's attitude to Olivares, is unfortunately slight. There are very few references to him in the Cardinal's surviving correspondence, and yet it is hard to believe that he was not the subject of

---

[1] For a detailed but excessively benevolent view of papal diplomacy during these years, see Auguste Leman, *Urbain VIII et la rivalité de la France et de la Maison d'Autriche de 1631 à 1635* (Paris–Lille, 1920). A more critical view of the policies of Urban VIII is to be found in Quintín Aldea Vaquero, 'Iglesia y estado en la época barroca', *Historia de España Ramón Menéndez Pidal*, xxv (Madrid, 1982), pp. 605–31. The general international situation at the time of Nördlingen is discussed in A. Van der Essen, *Le Cardinal-Infant et la politique européenne de l'Espagne*, I (Brussels, 1944), ch. 1.

[2] Cited in Georges Dethan, *Mazarin: un homme de paix à l'âge baroque, 1602–1661* (Paris, 1981), p. 183.

endless discussion and speculation in the Palais Cardinal. De Morgues, who knew Richelieu intimately, speaks of the Cardinal's hatred for the Count–Duke.[3] Richelieu's journal for the early months of 1631 shows him receiving reports to the effect that Olivares held him responsible for all Spain's misfortunes and would shrink from no 'crime or artifice' to destroy him.[4] The intrigues of the Queen Mother and Gaston may well have helped confirm his suspicion that those reports were correct.

Olivares reacted indignantly to all such charges of malicious intent. When one of the Emperor Ferdinand II's councillors, the Prince of Eggenberg, offered his services as an intermediary, he replied that neither he nor the Cardinal had ever given each other any personal occasion for displeasure, and that he always spoke in laudatory terms of Richelieu's character and abilities.[5] This was not strictly true. Some months earlier, in a letter of August 1631 to the Marquis of Aytona, Spain's ambassador in Brussels, he wrote at some length of the situation in France, and of his attitude to Richelieu. After remarking on the benefit to Spain of France's internal divisions and on Richelieu's disgraceful behaviour in his dealings with Madrid, he commented that he feared a clever enemy more than a lucky one. But the Cardinal's run of luck was coming to an end, and his follies would destroy him. Rubens, continued the Count–Duke, had attempted to incite him against Richelieu and make their quarrel personal; but

although he tells me that [the Cardinal] is very hostile to me – and the pamphlets in which he ridicules me make this very clear – I can affirm that I am neither on bad nor on good terms with him, because either would prevent me from acting dispassionately . . . It would be a bad thing if, as the minister of France, and our sovereign's natural enemy, he were on good terms with us, just as it would be bad if I were on good terms with them. I am confident that God will punish any excesses, for his misdemeanours are directed against God, and against reason and justice, and he will not be permitted for long to stray beyond the bounds.[6]

Behind the bravura there are hints of bitterness, as if the Count–Duke could not quite understand the Cardinal's successes. He seems to have found it difficult to get the measure of Richelieu, whom he regarded, with some justice, as capable of every form of deceit and subterfuge. He

[3] 'Jugement sur la préface . . .' (1635), *Recueil*, p. 33.
[4] 'Journal', *Archives Curieuses*, v, p. 95.
[5] AGS, Estado, legajo 2333, consulta of Council of State, ? Feb. 1632.
[6] ADM, legajo 79, Olivares to Aytona, 23 Aug. 1631.

presumably depended for much of his information on the despatches of the Marquis of Mirabel, Spain's ambassador in Paris since 1620. Mirabel, who had his own network of agents, was notably hostile to the French, and at the same time anxious to keep on the right side of Olivares, to whom he was related by marriage.[7] He would also have received first-hand impressions from his cousin and confidant, the Marquis of Leganés. In 1628 Leganés accompanied Spínola on a visit to the French camp at La Rochelle,[8] and in December 1634 the Cardinal – carefully rehearsed by Mazarin – received him graciously when he stopped in Paris on his way back to Spain after the battle of Nördlingen.[9] With characteristic courtesy, Leganés later told Cardinal de La Valette that Richelieu's merits were without equal and that Olivares had a portrait of him hanging in his rooms.[10] No doubt it helped to study the enemy face to face.

Envoys on both sides presumably helped reinforce existing preconceptions by passing on to their principals what they imagined they would most like to hear. Bautru's despatches from Madrid in the winter of 1628–9 mock Olivares for the sound and fury of his interviews.[11] Commenting on Bautru's mission, Richelieu's memoirs in turn compare the Count–Duke's 'rodomontades insupportables' to the bombast of the Captain's speeches in the Commedia dell'Arte.[12] But along with the exaggerated images there was also a good deal of accurate, and confidential, information. Olivares was made privy to the secrets of the French court through the Marquis of Mirabel's contacts with Anne of Austria and her entourage, while there were occasions on which Richelieu was able to read transcripts of proceedings in the Spanish Council of State,[13] at least until Olivares succeeded in tightening security.[14]

A Spanish spy reported to Olivares in 1638 that the Cardinal 'knows everything, misses nothing, and is loved by nobody except the king and

---

[7] Devèze, *L'Espagne de Philippe IV*, I, pp. 130–3.

[8] Antonio Rodríguez Villa, *Ambrosio Spínola, primer marqués de los Balbases* (Madrid, 1904), p. 478.

[9] Dethan, *Mazarin*, p. 183.

[10] Avenel, VI, p. 490, note 1.

[11] AAE, Correspondance politique, Espagne, tome 15, fo. 288v, Bautru's account of his first meeting with Olivares, on 27 Nov. 1628, and his reference to the Count–Duke's 'discours pleins de fougues et de rodomontades'.

[12] *Mémoires*, IX, p. 4.

[13] For example, a consulta of the Council of State of early March 1632, enclosed by Barrault with his despatch of 15 March (AAE, Correspondance politique, Espagne, tome 16, fos. 362–9).

[14] Cf. the complaints of the Venetian ambassador to Madrid about the secrecy of discussions on foreign policy, in his despatch of 11 March 1634 (ASV, Spagna, filza 70).

his own creatures'.[15] Some ten years earlier Richelieu had been regaled with various choice items of gossip about the Spanish court, including the following: 'Olivares hated by the people, the grandees and everybody.'[16] His probable informant was one of the strangest characters in his entourage, Alphonse Lopez, allegedly an Aragonese Morisco. In 1610 Lopez, whose real origins were Jewish, settled in Paris, where he prospered as a diamond merchant. He ingratiated himself at court by advancing loans to members of the royal family and the high aristocracy, and in due course became financial agent to the Cardinal, who used him for much confidential business and made him responsible for financing the construction of his new town of Richelieu.[17] Lopez had useful connections with the international Portuguese Jewish community and it would be surprising if he were not in touch with the Portuguese financiers among the inner circle of Olivares' advisers. But whose game was Lopez playing? In 1638 he wrote privately to Olivares to say that he would like to return to Spain.[18] Was he an agent of Richelieu in Olivares' camp, or an agent of Olivares in Richelieu's camp; or perhaps both at once?[19]

Whatever the merits of their respective espionage services, the Cardinal and the Count–Duke were obviously watching each other like two cats. Personal distrust may well have made the task of reconciliation that much harder for papal diplomacy, but the pressures for war came primarily from a perceived conflict of interests in an international climate in which a 'natural enmity' between the crowns of France and Spain was traditionally assumed[20] and had been taken for granted by all parties since the fall of Marillac.

From 1631 both ministers saw the conflict coming, and laid their plans accordingly. Their principal concern was to make sure that, when war came, they should enter it under the most favourable conditions possible,

---

[15] AGS, Estado, legajo 3347, fo. 75, *Avisos*.
[16] *Maximes d'état*, p. 72.
[17] For Lopez, see Tallemant des Réaux, *Historiettes*, I, pp. 314–15, and the disappointingly thin study by Henri Baraude, *Lopez, agent financier et confident de Richelieu* (Paris, 1933). I am grateful to Prof. René Pillorget for locating for me a copy of this rare book, and also to M. Pierre Grillon for guidance on documentation relating to Lopez.
[18] AGS, Estado, legajo 3347, fo. 75, *Avisos*, and fo. 332, Don Juan Francisco to Olivares, 11 March 1638.
[19] For Richelieu's use of Lopez at the time of the riots in the Portuguese city of Evora in 1637–8, see I. S. Révah, *Le Cardinal de Richelieu et la restauration du Portugal* (Lisbon, 1950).
[20] For a contemporary analysis of this enmity, with many curious examples of alleged national characteristics, see Carlos García, *La oposición y conjunción de los dos grandes luminares de la tierra, o la antipatía de Franceses y Españoles* (1617) ed. Michael Bareau (Edmonton, 1979).

and neither was yet ready. The early 1630s therefore saw a race to mobilize resources and consolidate alliances in anticipation of the struggle.

The financial outlook in both countries was bleak.[21] In July 1632, on one of the many occasions when the Spanish Council of State discussed the desirability and feasibility of breaking with France, Olivares remarked that for Spain it would be 'the final ruin', but that it could hardly be anything less for the French.[22] In all these debates, which were held periodically right up to the outbreak of war in 1635, it is not easy to tell what the Count–Duke really wanted, in part at least because we cannot assume that he necessarily meant what he said. The British ambassador in Madrid reported that 'it is usually his manner of proceeding to deliver his opinion in public contrary to what he thinks and means shall take effect, because on either side he finds his justification, in the good success of the action by the success itself, in the bad by his voice'.[23] Richelieu resorted to the same stratagem. Marillac accuses him of inclining in the council towards peace at the time of the 1629 debate over the prolongation of the war in Italy, having already persuaded the king to decide in favour of war.[24] In 1633–4, on the other hand, we find Louis XIII straining at the leash for war, while Richelieu holds him back. When the decision to declare war was finally taken, the Cardinal took care to ensure that the decision was the king's, so that he could hold Louis to it later, if this became necessary.[25]

The Count–Duke, for all his sabre-rattling, was by temperament a cautious statesman, with a natural instinct to play for time. There were moments in the early 1630s when he was being urged by his colleagues to undertake a preemptive strike against the French, but somehow he always managed to pull back from the brink of the abyss. Then, some months later, in exasperation at some new manifestation of French hostility, he would be regretting his restraint.[26] But the impression left by his speeches and letters during this cold war period is of a man who would

[21] For France, Bonney, *King's Debts*, p. 164. For Spain, Domínguez Ortiz, *Política y hacienda*, pp. 44–8.

[22] AGS, Estado, K.1415, fo. 89, consulta, 11 July 1632.

[23] BL, Egerton Ms. 1820, fo. 266, Hopton to Lord Treasurer, 9 May 1633.

[24] Marillac, 'Apologie', quoted in Léon Desjonquères, *Le Garde des Sceaux Michel de Marillac et son oeuvre législative* (Paris, 1908), p. 79.

[25] Dickmann, 'Rechtsgedanke und Machtpolitik', pp. 317–18.

[26] ADM, legajo 79, Olivares to Aytona, 15 July 1632.

do everything possible, consonant with honour, to avoid an open break. He was understandably preoccupied with the struggle with the Dutch, and with the devastating impact of the Swedish intervention in Germany. In addition to this, his personal involvement in the annual negotiations with the crown's bankers may well have given him a more acute sense than Richelieu of the financial realities of war. Careful study had persuaded him, he told his colleagues in 1633, that war with France, apart from any general arguments against it, would prove the 'total ruin of Spain', whether it turned out badly or well.[27]

Behind the entirely understandable desire to avoid a conflict which he foresaw could well be disastrous for Spain, there also lurked a continuing hope that some sudden change of circumstance might yet make the resort to arms unnecessary. A renewal of civil war in France and the overthrow of Richelieu was always on the cards. Activists, like the Duke of Feria, the governor of Milan, wanted Madrid to take advantage of Gaston's flight to Lorraine in the spring of 1631 to promote discord in France, in order to create an opening for peace in the Netherlands and Italy.[28] But the Count–Duke was sceptical. Although contingency funds were made available for Gaston in Antwerp, Olivares insisted that they were not to be used for stirring up internal dissension.[29] He had a low opinion of the French malcontents, and he told Aytona in August 1631 that he simply did not see a sufficient body of solid support for Gaston, who would certainly be defeated if he attempted an invasion.[30]

Much as Olivares would have liked to believe in Gaston, he found it difficult to do so. He admitted in October that Gaston's schemes, 'if well managed', could be the most effective of all remedies;[31] and as relations with France deteriorated, he offered Gaston Spanish help. But even in August 1632, after Gaston had entered France with a small body of men and joined forces in Languedoc with the Duke of Montmorency, Olivares judged the enterprise 'very fragile'.[32] Montmorency's defeat and Gaston's reconciliation with the king and Richelieu showed how right he was. Yet he found the reconciliation of the royal brothers inexplicable, 'beyond all law and reason'. Surely Louis would never dare cut off

---

[27] AGS, Estado, K.1416, fo. 56, consulta of Council of State, 17 Sept. 1633.
[28] AGS, Estado, legajo 3336, fo. 189, Feria to King, 12 April 1631.
[29] ADM, legajo 79, Olivares to Aytona, 14 and 17 April 1631.
[30] The same, 23 Aug. 1631.
[31] The same, 28 Oct. 1631.
[32] AGS, Estado, K.1415, consulta, 12 Aug. 1632.

Montmorency's head as long as Gaston had a party in France. If he did, every prince in France would rise up in revolt.[33] Montmorency was executed just two weeks after these words were written. Obviously the Count–Duke had yet to appreciate the disunity of the Cardinal's opponents and the sheer ruthlessness of the man.

Olivares' half-hearted support for Gaston, which strained Madrid's relations with Paris while bringing Spain no obvious advantage, has to be set into the wider context of a foreign policy designed to contain what he saw as the aggressive ambitions of France. Richelieu had held on to Pinerolo by a trick after the Peace of Cherasco, and French forces had invaded Lorraine at the end of 1631. French troop movements in the Grisons threatened the passage of Spanish soldiers through the Valtelline, and early in 1632 Richelieu was only just dissuaded by the nuncio and Father Joseph from advancing on the Rhine and occupying Alsace.[34] In the circumstances, the Count–Duke naturally saw every French move as part of a grand design to destroy the House of Austria. At a meeting of the Council of State in September 1633 he spelled out the geo-political threat posed by the French. The King of France, he warned his colleagues, was plotting the Emperor's ruin. If, as seemed likely, he seized the Duchy of Lorraine, he would have destroyed the last links between Germany and Flanders, except by way of Cologne. Now that he had occupied Alsace and Breisgau, only the fortress of Breisach prevented him from cutting the road from Italy to Germany and becoming master of the mountain passes connecting France to Italy and Germany. He already blocked the route between Italy and Flanders.

France lies between Spain and Flanders, and, as a result, it is impossible to send help from Germany to Flanders or Italy, or to Italy from Flanders, or from Italy to Flanders, or to Spain from Flanders or vice versa, except by way of the Channel, with French ports on one side and English on the other, and the Channel itself swarming with the Dutch . . .[35]

Richelieu's obsession with the dangers of encirclement by Spain was therefore parallelled by Olivares' obsession with the French threat to the network of international communications on which Spanish power depended. What to France was a noose, was to Spain a life-line. To keep this life-line open, Spain needed allies. Historians have devoted much

---

[33] AGR, Sec. d'état et de guerre, Reg. 596, fo. 119v, Olivares to Abbot Scaglia, 13 Oct. 1632.
[34] O'Connell, *Richelieu*, pp. 260–2; Fagniez, *Père Joseph*, I, p. 586.
[35] AGS, Estado, K.1416, fo. 56, consulta, 17 Sept. 1633.

attention to Richelieu's patient attempts to construct a system of alliances as he prepared for war with Spain, but have not fully appreciated the extent to which Olivares was engaged in a similar undertaking. During the course of his career he invested an enormous amount of time and energy, as did Richelieu, in weaving the most complicated diplomatic webs.

The guiding principle of the Count–Duke's foreign policy was that Madrid and Vienna, the two branches of the House of Austria, 'must never, for any reason, be divided'.[36] The whole thrust of his diplomacy was therefore to bring about an offensive and defensive alliance between the King of Spain and the Emperor, in the conviction that the Emperor needed Spanish help to shore up his position in Germany, while Imperial assistance in turn was essential if France was to be held in check and the war against the Dutch brought to an honourable conclusion. But the quest for this alliance proved frustratingly elusive.[37] Spanish envoys were for ever being despatched to Vienna to persuade Ferdinand II of the vital importance of a treaty of alliance; but Vienna's priorities were never exactly the same as those of Madrid, and somehow the Emperor could never quite see his way to approving a formal and full-scale commitment.

On the death of Gustavus Adolphus at Lützen in November 1632 Olivares tried again. This was the moment, he told the Council of State, to 'finish off everything – to settle matters in the Empire . . ., get an honourable peace with the Dutch, reach a settlement in Italy, restore the Duke of Lorraine, and sow in France the discord it so handsomely deserves'.[38] All this was to be achieved by the formation of a grand alliance, to include Spain, the Emperor, the Princes of the Empire, and the Duke of Lorraine, together with Marie de Médicis and Gaston d'Orléans, whose reconciliation with Louis XIII after the defeat of Montmorency had lasted only a matter of days. On 12 May 1634 Gaston, in uneasy exile in Brussels, signed a secret treaty with Spain;[39] but the grand alliance, as Olivares had planned it, failed to materialize. Spanish

---

[36] AGS, Estado, legajo 2331, fo. 126, consulta, 10 Nov. 1630.
[37] See Heinrich Günter, *Die Habsburger-Liga, 1625–1635*, Historische Studien LXII, ed. E. Ebering (Berlin, 1908), and Straub, *Pax et Imperium*, esp. pp. 219–51 and ch. 10, which tells the story too much from the standpoint of Madrid. For the view from Vienna, see Robert Bireley, *Religion and Politics in the Age of the Counterreformation. Emperor Ferdinand II, William Lamormaini, S.J., and the Formation of Imperial Policy* (Chapel Hill, 1981).
[38] AGS, Estado, legajo 2151, 'voto del Conde Duque', 9 Jan. 1633.
[39] O'Connell, *Richelieu*, p. 288. In October, after Nördlingen, Gaston reached an accommodation with his brother and returned again to France.

and Imperial forces, however, making common cause, won such a decisive victory over the Swedes at Nördlingen in September 1634 that it was no longer possible for Richelieu to continue fighting his war by proxy. French intervention had become unavoidable.

All Richelieu's diplomatic efforts had been directed towards creating an anti-Spanish coalition as a counterbalance to the Habsburg coalition which Olivares was attempting to construct. The inclusion of Protestant powers in Richelieu's coalition – the Swedes and the Dutch and two German principalities – has conventionally been regarded as a landmark in European history. For example, Dieter Albrecht, in his study of Richelieu, Gustavus Adolphus and the Empire, writes of the negotiations with Gustavus Adolphus as marking the advent of a new age, distinguished by 'the triumph of *raison d'état* over confessional diplomacy'.[40]

This conventional view, at least in its most naked formulation, is difficult to sustain in the light of Richelieu scholarship over the past twenty years, which has added nuance to the traditional interpretation of the Cardinal's approach to foreign policy.[41] It is worth remarking, too, that the term *raison d'état*, although common enough in contemporary usage, appears very rarely in Richelieu's own writings. He is more likely to produce justifications in terms of 'necessity' than of 'reason of state'.[42] This by itself, however, can hardly be regarded as conclusive. Reason of state was still something that it was wiser to impute to one's opponents than claim for oneself.

It is not so much the phrase itself that is important, as the idea that lies behind it – that of an autonomous political morality, in which the interests of the state constitute the sole determinant of the legitimacy of its policies. There were indeed contemporary voices urging upon Richelieu just such an autonomous morality. Fancan, who fell from grace in 1627, begged him that same year to beware of the traps being laid for him by Spain and Rome, and 'show boldly that we know how to separate the interests of state from those of religion'.[43] Similarly, the Duke of Rohan's celebrated

---

[40] *Richelieu, Gustaf Adolf und das Reich* (Munich–Vienna, 1959), p. 52.

[41] See especially Dickmann, 'Rechtsgedanke und Machtpolitik', and Church, *Richelieu and Reason of State*.

[42] Gerhard, 'Richelieu', p. 96; Hassinger, 'Das politische Testament', p. 495. *Raison d'état* appears on pp. 234 and 345 of the *Testament Politique*.

[43] Fancan, 'Avis à Richelieu' (1627), reprinted in G. Fagniez, 'Fancan et Richelieu', *Revue Historique*, 108 (1911), p. 79.

book on the *Interest of Princes* (1634) advocated a foreign policy based purely on advantage and expediency. Rohan's work met with sufficient approval from Richelieu to achieve publication in the *Mercure français*, but this hardly warrants the kind of identification between Richelieu's ideas and those of Rohan which is made in Meinecke's study of the concept of reason of state.[44] Richelieu was quick to seize on any justification for his policies, whatever the source, as long as the endorsement was sufficiently fulsome.

The Cardinal's working papers and instructions for France's commissioners to a general peace conference illustrate his concern to ground his foreign policy on moral considerations and the extent to which his vision of the mutual relations of European states was set within a conventional framework determined by the presumed requirements of natural law, the just war and legitimate defence.[45] As he saw it, the peace of Christendom demanded a balance between the princes of Europe, 'so that, through their equality, the church can survive and maintain itself in all its functions and splendour'.[46] This balance, and with it the liberty of the church, had been undermined by the overweening ambitions of the House of Austria, which was busily promoting its own secular ends under the cloak of religion. It was the King of France's God-given obligation to ensure that the balance was preserved and a collective security system established under which the Pope and the lesser European powers could appeal to him with confidence in time of need. This in turn would reestablish his *réputation* in all its glory, and restore to him his traditional role as the guarantor of the Corpus Christianum.[47]

This overwhelming sense of the providential character of the King of France's mission ran through all Richelieu's thinking and was reinforced by each new success. The hand of God was to be seen at every turn in the Cardinal's account of the reign of Louis XIII, as he expounded it to the Parlement of Paris in January 1634.[48] Louis' achievements, he told his hearers, might seem to be the stuff of dreams, but they were indeed real,

---

[44] This point is made by Church, *Richelieu and Reason of State*, pp. 352–5. See Friedrich Meinecke, *Die Idee der Staatsräson in der neueren Geschichte* (2nd edn, Munich–Berlin, 1925), p. 209. (English trans., *Machiavellism* (London, 1957), p. 167.)

[45] Fritz Dickmann, 'Rechtsgedanke und Machtpolitik', and *Acta Pacis Westphalicae. Instruktionen*, I (Münster, 1962). See also Church, *Richelieu and Reason of State*, pp. 298–9.

[46] *Mémoires*, V, p. 293, quoted in Joseph Lecler, 'Politique nationale et idée chrétienne dans les temps modernes', *Etudes*, 214 (1933), p. 690.

[47] Wollenberg, *Richelieu*, pp. 65–70; Dickmann, 'Rechtsgedanke und Machtpolitik', p. 284.

[48] *Mercure français*, XX (Paris, 1637), pp. 5–24.

and were directly attributable to the virtues of a prince 'so manifestly blessed by God that even setbacks and reverses are converted into an occasion for glory'. As illustrations of this encouraging thesis he cited the English attack on the Ile de Ré and the consequent destruction of the Huguenot opposition, and the Mantuan affair, which allowed Louis to acquire a gateway into Italy, 'to be used for the benefit of Christendom'. The hand of providence was even to be seen in the recent faction struggles, which had allowed the king to stifle the sources of unrest, and left him free to work 'for the universal peace of Christendom that he so ardently desires'.

A man who interprets the course of history in such providentialist terms is unlikely to risk alienating a hitherto favourable deity by engaging in actions which will incur His disapproval. Louis, the Cardinal asserted, had 'never sought any advantage for this state by resorting to methods deserving of censure'. Any proposed course of action had therefore to be tested for its conformity with the mission conferred by God upon the king. As Richelieu saw it, this mission was cast in terms of a duty to protect the weak and the oppressed.[49]

This idea of protection, which was central to Richelieu's vision of France's role in Europe, was dramatically illustrated in *Europe*, a 'hero comedy' designed to be presented in the Palais Cardinal but which never went beyond the rehearsal stage because of the Cardinal's illness and death.[50] Richelieu himself provided the inspiration and the plot for this excruciatingly bad play, which tells how Ibère, having failed to win the love of Europe, attempts to ravish her, and how the noble Francion rushes to her aid. 'Europe', says Francion, 'it is better to perish than to be enslaved. Liberty must be bought with blood . . . I was born the guardian of all the young princes . . . and everywhere my allies implore my assistance . . . In sum, we must have war, and I am driven to it, not by ambition, but by necessity.'[51]

Already in 1629, in the Cardinal's famous *Avis* to the king, he had written of the need to secure gateways (*portes*) into the neighbouring states in order to be able to 'shelter them from Spanish oppression when the occasion arises'.[52] It is now generally conceded that his policy was

[49] See Hermann Weber, 'Richelieu et le Rhin', *Revue Historique*, 239 (1968), pp. 265–80.
[50] *Europe. Comédie héroique* (Paris, 1643); and see Lacour, *Richelieu dramaturge*, part III, ch. 4.
[51] Cited Lacour, *Richelieu dramaturge*, p. 155.
[52] Grillon, IV, pp. 25–7.

less one of 'natural frontiers' than of 'natural gateways', allowing French troops to move rapidly to the assistance of Italian or German princes threatened by a Habsburg attack.[53] By retaining Pinerolo in 1631 he secured his gateway into Italy, and the establishment of a French garrison at Philippsburg in 1632 gave him a gateway into Germany on the east bank of the Rhine.

In Spanish eyes, the French advance towards the Rhine testified to Richelieu's nakedly expansionist ambitions, but Richelieu himself formulated his policy in terms of legitimate intervention brought about by the need to 'arrest the course of Spain's progress'.[54] But to justify his policies to himself, his king and the world at large he set his experts to work to determine the precise circumstances in which intervention was permitted. Researchers were kept busy in the archives unearthing French claims to dominion over large parts of Europe reaching back to Charlemagne and even to the Gauls. The doctrine of the inalienability of royal demesne was also extracted from the purely domestic sphere and brought into play as a convenient instrument for the assertion of French rights against foreign princes.[55] The celebrated jurist Cardin Le Bret, who was sent by Richelieu in 1624 on a special mission to investigate the rights of the crown in Lorraine, enunciated the principle in his book on *Sovereignty* of 1632, which served as the juridical handbook of the Richelieu regime. The doctrine of an inalienable royal demesne, he asserted, was applicable to 'all the claims of our kings over the kingdom of Navarre, Naples, Portugal, Flanders, Milan, and a part of Savoy and Piedmont which, having formerly been acquired by the Crown of France, cannot at any time be alienated or voided'.[56]

It was one thing to assert these often fantastic claims, and quite another to enforce them; and Richelieu, as often as not, was content to hold them in reserve in case they should be needed. His primary task in the years before the declaration of war on Spain in 1635 was to lend credibility to his attempt to present Louis XIII as the natural protector and liberator of Christendom by constructing an effective anti-Habsburg coalition. This of necessity included alliances with Protestant powers –

[53] G. Zeller, 'La Politique des frontières au temps de la prépondérance espagnole', *Revue historique*, 193 (1942), pp. 97–110.
[54] Grillon, IV, p. 25 (*Avis* of 13 Jan. 1629); Dickmann, 'Rechtsgedanke und Machtpolitik', p. 279.
[55] Dickmann, Rechtsgedanke und Machtpolitik', p. 292.
[56] Quoted by Gilbert Picot, *Cardin Le Bret (1558–1655) et la doctrine de la souveraineté* (Nancy, 1948), p. 49.

the Dutch alliance, renewed in 1630, and the Treaty of Bärwalde with the Swedes in 1631 – which reawakened the controversy aroused in 1624 by his intervention in the Valtelline on behalf of the Protestant Grisons.[57] In negotiating these alliances he made strenuous attempts to secure the inclusion of clauses guaranteeing the rights of subject Catholic populations,[58] but these failed to silence his critics, who were inclined to regard them as no more than a charade. The Jesuit Father Caussin went to the heart of the issue in a personal letter to Richelieu in 1637: 'Innumerable people speak every day of your fortune. Allow me for once to speak of your conscience.'[59]

In the *Testament Politique* Richelieu defends Henry IV's alliance with the Dutch as an act of necessity grounded in natural law, arguing that no theologian would dispute the right of resorting to whatever help was at hand to save one's life, and that the prince enjoyed no less a right when seeking to avert the loss of his state.[60] A few pages later he defends in similar vein the justice of his own treaties with Gustavus Adolphus and German Protestant princes as being 'absolutely necessary for the salvation of the Duke of Mantua, who had been unjustly attacked, and for that of all Italy'.[61] A certain uneasiness is in fact apparent in the instructions given to Charnacé when he was sent to negotiate the treaty with the Swedes[62] – an uneasiness which the subsequent triumphs of Sweden over the Catholic forces in Germany amply justified. Richelieu seriously miscalculated when he gave encouragement and assistance to Gustavus Adolphus, and released on Germany a disruptive force that he was unable to contain.[63] But this did not shake his confidence in the essential justice of his anti-Habsburg policy and of the measures which he regarded as necessary for its successful pursuit. As he embarked on war with Spain in 1635 he did so with the clear understanding that – to use the words of the *Testament Politique* – 'there can be no successful war which is not just, because if it were not just, even if the outcome were good in the eyes of the world, it would still be necessary to render account of it before the tribunal of God'.[64]

[57] Cf. Church, *Richelieu and Reason of State*, pp. 103–72, and 291–2.
[58] Wollenberg, *Richelieu*, pp. 44 and 220.
[59] Quoted Lecler, 'Politique nationale', p. 552.
[60] *TP*, p. 109.
[61] *TP*, p. 118.
[62] Lecler, 'Politique nationale', p. 560.
[63] O'Connell, *Richelieu*, pp. 255–6.
[64] *TP*, p. 382.

Neither Richelieu nor his advisers lacked casuistical skills, and it was easy for the Cardinal's enemies to depict him as an arch-Machiavellian. Seeking to justify his own career in the *Nicandro* Olivares argued that, while he had not always been successful, at least – unlike his rival – he had not adopted measures that offended against God, religion and the high traditions of the House of Austria. Had he placed La Rochelle and the Huguenots under Spanish protection, 'favoured the German Protestants, allowed liberty of conscience in Flanders, permitted the Jews to settle in the Monarchy, and treated the Pope as the French treat him, then he would have saved millions, and avoided reverses'. How much better it was to be unsuccessful but right than victorious but wrong![65]

It pays, however, to scrutinize Olivares' record as well as his words. In 1625, when a confrontation with France appeared imminent, the Huguenots under Rohan rose in revolt in Languedoc and appealed to Spain for help. The Council of State considered the request favourably; a junta of theologians decided that assistance could legitimately be given; and although Olivares swore to the papal nuncio some months later that Madrid had not sent the Huguenots a subsidy,[66] all the indications point the other way.[67] A comparable situation arose in 1629 at the height of the Mantuan conflict. In February of that year, Olivares informed Don Gonzalo de Córdoba that he was sending him 200,000 ducats 'so that you may assist the party of the Duke of Rohan, which the theologians decided we can and must do on this occasion'.[68] The report of the junta of six theologians, who included the royal confessor and Olivares' own confessor, the Jesuit Hernando de Salazar, has fortunately come to light.[69] Their arguments in favour of assisting Rohan were, first of all, that France, in subsidizing the Dutch, was enabling them to wage war against Spain on land and sea, and 'sustain all the heresy and Judaism to be found in the world', and also that the French had returned to their age-old ambition of conquering Milan. Secondly, the only way to prevent the King of France from crossing into Italy was to encourage his heretical subjects to make war on him at home. Thirdly, all theologians agreed that

---

[65] *MC*, II, p. 268.
[66] AV, Spagna, 65, fo. 285, nuncio's despatch, 30 July 1625.
[67] For the discussions about aid for the Huguenots, see Ródenas Vilar, *La política europea*, pp. 32–7, and the modifications to his account in Straub, *Pax et Imperium*, p. 212, note 11, which includes a reference to the verdict of the theologians.
[68] AGS, Estado, legajo 2713, letter of 18 Feb. 1629.
[69] RAH, 9-71-8-6. 'Parecer de una Junta de teólogos . . .', 25 Jan. 1629.

a Catholic prince could legitimately call on the support of heretics when waging a just war, and the justice of Spain's war in Mantua on behalf of the Emperor had already been determined. The junta therefore concluded unanimously that it was not only licit for Philip IV to make use of heretical arms to launch a diversionary attack against the King of France, but also that he was morally obliged to do so. A formal compact between Spain and the Duke of Rohan was signed in May,[70] but Spanish help came too late to save the Huguenot revolt.

Ten years later, after tortured debate, Spain concluded what was in effect an alliance with the Protestant Grisons.[71] There is a curious irony in the fact that it should have been this same question of alliance with the Grisons which provoked the first of the great debates in France about the morality of Richelieu's policies. The complexities of the Valtelline question posed a similar challenge for both the Catholic powers; and both of them – France in 1624 and Spain in 1639 – succeeded in finding an appropriate formula for squaring necessities of state with the dictates of conscience.

It seems necessary, then, to discard any straightforward picture of a Spanish foreign policy dictated by purely confessional considerations, and a French foreign policy operating in conformity with the un-varnished requirements of *raison d'état*. Richelieu at least persuaded himself, even if he did not succeed in persuading everyone else, that his policies were based on traditional Catholic principles regulating the mutual conduct of states. Olivares, so far from letting religion dictate his policies at the expense of political advantage – an image that he himself was always careful to foster – sent assistance to the Huguenots on at least two occasions. It can, of course, be argued that Richelieu, by allying with two major Protestant powers, transformed an occasional practice into a system; and that, by his practice, if not by intent, he consequently ensured the triumph of *raison d'état*, and the replacement of Christen-dom by a Europe in which the alliances and rivalries of states were motivated solely by questions of interest. But if Olivares went no further down the same road, this may well be because of the lack of comparable

---

[70] J. Alden Clarke, *Huguenot Warrior: the Life and Times of Henri de Rohan, 1579–1630* (The Hague, 1966), p. 175, for the terms of the agreement. For Richelieu's attempts to distinguish between this 'black action' of the Spaniards and French support for the Dutch, see *TP*, pp. 108–10.

[71] The considerable documentation generated by this debate is to be found in AGS, Estado, legajos 3345, 3346, 3348 and 3349.

opportunities. There were not many Protestant princes in the world who could be regarded as natural allies of Philip IV. But the Count–Duke's anxiety to play down the confessional issues in Germany in order to create a pro-Habsburg coalition of Lutheran as well as Catholic princes,[72] and his persistent attempts to conclude an offensive and defensive alliance with Charles I of England,[73] show that he was no less capable than Richelieu of accommodating principle with interest.

This suggests that the traditional formulation of the foreign policy motivations of early-seventeenth-century statesmen in terms of confessionalism or *raison d'état* may itself be misconceived. Richelieu and Olivares were operating in a world in which there was indeed a fundamental conflict between those who can be described as *dévots*, and those who accorded absolute priority to interests of state. But, as genuinely devout men promoting the secular interests of pious royal masters, they could adhere to neither of these extreme positions. Instead they were forced to operate as best they could in a grey area of compromise, casuistry and equivocation, weighing political advantage against religious scruple and the dictates of conscience. Each regarded the other as deeply Machiavellian, but the evidence suggests that the consciences of both men were deeply troubled about some of the shifts to which they were sometimes compelled to resort. If the contrast between their words and actions prompts a certain cynicism, this does not necessarily imply that they themselves lacked sincerity in seeking to base their decisions on accepted principles grounded in the teachings of the church.

The nature of those principles was well illustrated in the pamphlet war that accompanied the formal break between the two crowns in May 1635. The two statesmen, well aware of the need to present their case before the bar of European public opinion, marshalled impressive teams of publicists to explain and justify the causes for which they fought.[74] Both

[72] Cf. Günter, *Die Habsburger-Liga*; O'Connell, *Richelieu*, p. 264.
[73] See J. H. Elliott, 'The Year of the Three Ambassadors', *History and Imagination. Essays in Honour of H. R. Trevor-Roper*, ed. Hugh Lloyd-Jones, Valerie Pearl and Blair Worden (London, 1981), pp. 165–81.
[74] For Spain, see José Ma. Jover, *1635. Historia de una polémica y semblanza de una generación* (Madrid, 1949). For the propaganda campaign mounted by Richelieu, see Church, *Richelieu and Reason of State*, part 4. Perhaps the most effective polemical piece produced by either side was the *Mars Gallicus* of Cornelius Jansen, which greatly troubled Richelieu and did much to increase his suspicions of the Jansenists (see Orcibal, *Origines du Jansénisme*, II, pp. 499–500, and Thuau, *Raison d'état*, p. 132).

countries inevitably depicted themselves as fighting a just and defensive war.[75] For Madrid, the French had been persistent violators of the *pax austriaca*, that beneficial ordering of Christendom guaranteed by the indissoluble alliance of Vienna and Madrid. They had broken the terms of the peace settlements of Vervins, Ratisbon and Cherasco. They had allied with heretics. The sole concern of Philip IV was to come to the defence of those who were unjustly attacked, and fight, not for the expansion of his own dominions, but for the conservation of a European order subverted by the machinations of the Machiavellian Cardinal. The French manifestoes contained identical arguments, with due allowances for wording.

However deeply convinced of the righteousness of their cause, the two ministers entered the war with trepidation, all too well aware of the new demands it would impose on their long-suffering peoples. It is not therefore surprising to find them putting out peace-feelers almost from the moment that the war began. The years after 1635 were to be characterized by a series of peace initiatives, launched by one minister or the other, in a vain attempt to secure a speedy settlement on satisfactory terms.[76] Both subscribed to the view enunciated in the *Testament Politique* that 'to negotiate without ceasing, openly or secretly, and everywhere, even if it yields no immediate fruit and the expected one is not yet apparent, is absolutely necessary for the well-being of states'.[77] Both would have liked peace. Neither could accept it on the other's terms. Failing to secure it, both professed confidence in the outcome of the war, and both saw the national character as crucial to success. 'The French are capable of everything', wrote Richelieu in the *Testament Politique*, 'provided that those who lead them are capable of teaching them well what they need to practise.'[78] 'In spite of the extravagant education of our youth', said Olivares in the Council of State, 'I place my trust in it and the nation.'[79] But would such confidence withstand the iron test of war?

---

[75] 'A defensive, holy and religious war', in the words of one of Olivares' publicists, Guillén de la Carrera. Cf. Jover, *1635*, p. 253.

[76] The story of these negotiations is followed in Auguste Leman, *Richelieu et Olivarès* (Lille, 1938), which is a purely diplomatic study.

[77] *TP*, p. 347.

[78] *TP*, p. 388.

[79] AGS, Estado, K.1644, fo. 11, 'El Conde Duque con ocasión del rompimiento de franceses en Flandes' (late May or early June of 1635).

4 Philippe de Champaigne, *Triple portrait of the head of Richelieu.*

'The essence of war can be reduced to four heads', wrote Olivares in 1637, namely 'men, money, order and obedience.'[80] During the 1630s, and especially after 1635, Richelieu and Olivares were transformed into full-time ministers of war, compelled to subordinate everything to the overwhelming requirement of sustaining the military effort of their respective countries. Problems of men, money, order and obedience absorbed their energies, as they struggled to mobilize the resources of societies which were simply not equipped, by temperament or organization, for the kind of sustained military and fiscal effort that was now being demanded of them.

Both ministers were deeply preoccupied by the lack of reliable men of calibre to assume the military and administrative leadership that war required. 'There are so few capable people', complained Richelieu in 1635, 'that one looks where one can for those whom one presumes

[80] *MC*, II, p. 154.

capable of serving . . .'[81] 'Leaders, sir, leaders (*cabezas*), that is what we lack', wrote Olivares to the Cardinal Infante a few months later.[82] The long line of great Spanish commanders was nearly extinguished, and the men who would bring lustre to French arms in the next two or three decades had still to make their names. The French in particular were hopelessly unprepared for a prolonged struggle, and Richelieu seems to have seriously underestimated the military strength that could still be deployed by the House of Austria.[83] A real French army and military system had yet to be created. This would be the achievement of Sublet de Noyers, who replaced Servien as secretary of state for war in 1636. Under Richelieu's supervision Sublet gave France for the first time an effective secretariat of war, and laid the foundations for French military successes in the reign of Louis XIV.[84]

Spain was administratively much better organized for war. The Council of War had been in existence for well over a century, and had an experienced corps of officials for the equipping of armies and fleets.[85] But this institutional superiority of Spain over France had its attendant disadvantages. To start from the beginning, building up as the occasion demanded a team of special temporary commissioners, like the *intendants* in France, may in some respects have been preferable to attempting to operate through a routine-bound bureaucracy. Richelieu, who in the nature of things was constantly having to improvise, was in effect compelled to create a new system, whereas Olivares was always trying to make an old system work. He found the machinery hopelessly slow moving, and was driven to despair by its prevarications and delays. In 1637, in an attempt to inject a new despatch and urgency into the direction of the war, he created what was in effect a war cabinet consisting of himself and a few chosen ministers, known as the Junta de Ejecución, which largely superseded the Council of State as the central policy-making body during his final years in power.[86]

---

[81] Avenel, v, p. 261 (Richelieu to Chavigny, 26 Sept. 1635).
[82] Bayerische Staatsbibliothek, Munich, Codex Monacensis, Hisp. 22, Olivares to Cardinal Infante, 25 May 1636.
[83] Fagniez, *Père Joseph*, II, p. 263.
[84] See Ranum, *Richelieu and the Councillors*, ch. 5, for Sublet de Noyers. For military organization and provisioning, see Douglas Clark Baxter, *Servants of the Sword. French Intendants of the Army, 1630–1670* (Urbana, 1976).
[85] See Thompson, *War and Government*. The antiquated study by J. P. A. Bazy, *Etat militaire de la Monarchie Espagnole sous le règne de Philippe IV* (Poitiers, 1864), attempts to compare the relative military strength of France and Spain.
[86] For the first appearance of the Junta de Ejecución, see *MC*, II, pp. 128–9, note 43.

But how could even a Junta de Ejecución get its orders obeyed? 'We are sinking because orders are not being executed', was Olivares' permanent refrain.[87] 'Those who work for the king', complained Richelieu, 'must remember that there is a great difference between simply ordering what needs to be done and getting the orders carried out. One must take care not to be satisfied with merely giving orders, for everything lies in the execution of them.'[88] Like the Count–Duke, he was perpetually wrestling with the insubordination of nobles appointed to high commands. Both ministers had to spend an inordinate amount of time attempting to reconcile commanders who had fallen out between themselves, often over trivial points of etiquette and precedence.[89] At other times they were faced with open defiance of their orders by nobles who despised them as their social inferiors and had no doubt that they knew best. The Count–Duke tried to deal with this kind of aristocratic insolence by establishing a special Junta for Obedience, which proved of doubtful value. The punishment meted out in 1634 to Don Fadrique de Toledo for refusing to command an expeditionary force to Brazil on the crown's terms was regarded by contemporaries as an act of vindictiveness, and merely widened the gulf between the high nobility and the Olivares regime.[90] In France, the Duke of La Valette, who was made the scapegoat for the failure in 1638 to capture Fuenterrabía, fled to England rather than risk the fate of Maréchal de Marillac, who had been executed in 1632. Condemned in his absence he was executed in effigy on a charge of *lèse-majesté*.[91]

Exemplary punishment might temporarily cow the nobility – although even this was problematic – but it was unlikely to transform them, as the Count–Duke and the Cardinal hoped, into unquestioning servants of the crown. What was really needed was a change of ethos and attitude. The conflict of values was nowhere better expressed than in Corneille's *Le*

---

[87] AGS, Estado, legajo 2658, 'El Conde Duque sobre lo que falta de executar lo resuelto', 28 March 1636.

[88] Quoted Hanotaux and La Force, *Richelieu*, IV, p. 433.

[89] For Richelieu, see for example Avenel, V, p. 48. For the feud between the Marquis of Torrecuso and the Count of Santa Coloma in Catalonia in 1639–40, which so preoccupied Olivares, see Elliott, *Catalans*, p. 396.

[90] For the treatment of Don Fadrique de Toledo, see Brown and Elliott, *A Palace*, pp. 172–3.

[91] For the La Valette affair, Church, *Richelieu and Reason of State*, pp. 324–8. The background to the affair is discussed in detail in the unpublished Ph.D. dissertation (Columbia University, 1972) of Nicholas B. Fessenden, 'Eperne and Guyenne: Provincial Politics under Louis XIII'.

Cid, first staged in Paris in the winter of 1636–7. Against the requirements of seventeenth-century monarchy as seen by Richelieu:

> . . . on doit ce respect au pouvoir absolu,
> De n'examiner rien quand un roi l'a voulu

must be set the words of Count Gomès, so symptomatic of the traditional attitudes of the aristocracy: 'Désobéir un peu n'est pas un si grand crime.'[92] Somehow, the nobility had to be taught that even a little disobedience was indeed a crime.

'We Spaniards', wrote Olivares, 'are very good when we are subjected to rigorous obedience, but when left to ourselves we are the worst people in the world.'[93] This is the voice of the disciplinarian, and Richelieu and Olivares were both supreme disciplinarians, attempting with a degree of desperation to inculcate the virtues of obedience into unruly pupils. 'In a word, gentlemen', said Louis XIII to the members of the Parlement of Paris in 1636 in a speech written for him by the Cardinal, 'I want to be obeyed.'[94] But how were discipline and obedience to be instilled? Ultimately, as the two ministers realized, a new form of education was needed.

Olivares had already made an attempt to improve the education of Spain's ruling class by turning the Colegio Imperial in Madrid into a royal foundation with a revised curriculum.[95] But by the early 1630s it was clear that the new foundation was a failure, and he addressed himself afresh to the question of educational reform. His new plan, first drafted in 1632 and revised in 1635, was for the creation of a number of academies or military seminaries, two in Madrid, and another six in the leading Iberian cities. Here young nobles would be instructed in military skills and the arts of government.[96] In 1636 Richelieu, likewise impressed by the educational possibilities of academies, proposed the founding of an academy for a thousand pupils, with instruction both in letters and arms.[97] But these ambitious plans for academies proved abortive on both sides of the Pyrenees, in part at least because of shortage of funds. Unwilling to accept defeat, the Cardinal tried again in 1640, but on a

---

[92] Act 1, scene 3, and Act 2, scene 1.
[93] *MC*, II, p. 76 (Olivares to Cardinal Infante, 27 Sept. 1632).
[94] Avenel, v, p. 393.
[95] José Simón-Diaz, *Historia del Colegio Imperial de Madrid*, I (Madrid, 1952).
[96] See *MC*, II, doc. XIIc.
[97] Avenel, v, doc. cdvi ('Académie pour mil gentilshommes').

more modest scale. This time he set up an academy in his own town of Richelieu, but once again his hopes were disappointed.[98]

Although their educational schemes came to nothing, the two ministers used every form of exhortation and example to promote those virtues of discipline and order which they considered essential in time of war. For Richelieu, faced with a congenitally insubordinate nobility, the task was even harder than it was for Olivares, who was faced with sullen resistance rather than open revolt. The Cardinal's attempt to change the established pattern of values was correspondingly more concentrated and more systematic. Somehow he had to establish in French society a new conception of virtue which would make obedience an instinctive response. His foundation in 1635 of the Académie Française was an explicit recognition of the power of language, of the superiority of eloquence and reason over naked force, and of the role of letters as 'instruments of virtue'.[99]

The kind of virtue he had in mind was essentially the heroic virtue of Rome at the height of its grandeur, and it is not surprising that, under Richelieu's direction, literature, the theatre and the arts in Paris should have dwelt extensively on Roman themes.[100] This was to be the new age of Augustus – a reign in which a stern and upright monarch ended the long period of civil discord and anarchy, and ushered in a glorious era of peace. Corneille's *Cinna*, performed in 1642 a few months before Richelieu's death, represents an Augustus of implacable sternness, insisting on absolute obedience, and yet capable at the climax of an act of clemency so overwhelming that his subjects will in future obey out of love, and not fear. In the concluding words of Livia, his people are represented as henceforth being willing to submit to his rule without complaint:

> Et les plus indomptés, renversant leurs projects,
> Mettront toute leur gloire à mourir vos sujets.[101]

[98] See Marcel Bataillon, 'L'Académie de Richelieu, Indre-et-Loire', in *Pédagogues et juristes. Congrès du Centre d'Etudes Supérieures de la Renaissance de Tours: été 1960* (Paris, 1963), pp. 255–70.
[99] See Sutcliffe, *Guez de Balzac*, pp. 244–5. Also A. Adam, 'La Culture et le pouvoir', in *Richelieu*, ch. 7.
[100] See the Introduction by Marc Fumaroli to the exhibition catalogue by Pierre Rosenberg, *France in the Golden Age: Seventeenth-Century French Paintings in American Collections*, The Metropolitan Museum of Art, exhibition catalogue (New York, 1982).
[101] Act V, scene 3.

But this was an ideal that, under the ruthless regime of Richelieu, was still a long way from attainment. It is the severe, not the magnanimous Augustus, whose voice we hear in those chilling words of the *Testament Politique*: 'In matters of crimes against the state, it is necessary to close the door to pity.'[102] In the Spain of Olivares, too, the door was sometimes closed to pity, as when Admiral Don Juan de Benavides was executed in 1634 for the loss of the treasure-fleet to Piet Heyn in 1628.[103] But as far as is known there is nothing in Spain to compare with the systematic repression exercised by Richelieu – the rigged trials, the preordained executions, the sinister police activities of the most obnoxious of his *créatures*, the notorious 'executioner' Isaac de Laffemas.[104] France in the 1630s was governed by a savage and pitiless regime.

The *Testament Politique* makes it clear that the Cardinal himself was well aware of the potential conflict between the Christian duty of forgiveness and the state's insistence on punishment; but although admitting that such maxims 'seem dangerous, and indeed are not entirely free of peril', he asserted that 'even if conscience can tolerate . . . a notable crime going unpunished, reason of state cannot allow it'.[105] There was, then, or so it would seem, one morality for the state, and another for the private individual. But, as Richelieu saw it, 'what is done for the state is done for God, Who is the basis and foundation of it'.[106] For him the state, firmly established in natural law, was the corrective to the egotistical passions and instincts of individuals, which led only to disorder and ruin; and its natural superiority endowed it with superior rights. This doctrine, too, found its place in *Cinna*:

> Tout ces crimes d'Etat qu'on fait pour la couronne
> Le ciel nous en absout alors qu'il nous la donne.[107]

Where the interests of the state are concerned, God absolves actions which, if privately committed, would be a crime.

During the 1630s the jurists around Richelieu developed a legal

---

[102] *TP*, p. 342.

[103] Antonio Domínguez Ortiz, 'El suplicio de Don Juan de Benavides', *Archivo Hispalense*, 2nd series, 76 (1956), pp. 1–13.

[104] See Georges Mongrédien, *Le Bourreau du Cardinal de Richelieu. Isaac de Laffemas, 1584–1657* (Paris, 1929).

[105] *TP*, pp. 344 and 345; and see Hassinger, 'Das politische Testament', p. 495, and Albertini, *Politische Denken*, p. 180.

[106] *TP*, p. 201, and Hassinger, 'Das politische Testament', p. 496.

[107] Act V, scene 2.

doctrine to accommodate the state's alleged need for recourse to repressive acts. This was the doctrine of *lèse-majesté*, already redefined in the Assembly of Notables of 1626–7 to embrace a wide variety of crimes against the state, including the publication of unlicensed writings. In Richelieu's hands, *lèse-majesté* became a conveniently flexible instrument for dealing not only with noble conspiracies, but also with acts of insubordination and attacks on his government.[108] Recent investigations have shown that succeeding editions of Cardin Le Bret's book on sovereignty took into account the growing tendency of Richelieu's government to resort to prosecution on a charge of *lèse-majesté* – a device which allowed it to bypass traditional legal procedures and entrust cases to extraordinary commissions rather than to the ordinary officers of justice.[109] By the end of the 1630s this had become a regime of extraordinary commissions and summary justice.

Le Bret's justification for such a deployment of the sovereign power lay in what he called 'le repos et l'utilité publique'.[110] 'Necessity', he argued, had 'the privilege of rendering just and legitimate actions which in other circumstances would be unjust.'[111] This age-old doctrine of the overriding power of necessity – a word with fewer pejorative connotations than reason of state – was a decisive weapon in the hands of both the Richelieu and Olivares regimes, although in Spain it does not seem to have prompted recourse to the kind of extraordinary tribunals favoured in France. In 1634 Olivares' lawyer, José González, now a minister of the crown, used arguments that echo those of Cardin Le Bret. In a debate on possible ways of increasing revenue, he argued that it was for the king and his leading ministers to decide what constituted necessity, 'because it is not for vassals to inquire into Your Majesty's resolutions in time of war'. The exact degree of necessity depended on how far an alternative approach ('morally speaking') was available. From here González went on to argue that the other kingdoms of the Spanish Monarchy should follow Castile's example in accepting extraordinary forms of taxation, 'because in such extremities no laws or privileges can be allowed to stand in the way'.[112]

[108] Church, *Richelieu and Reason of State*, pp. 185–6.
[109] By Ralph Giesey and his students. I am grateful to Professor Giesey for allowing me to see an unpublished paper on 'Le Bret and Lese Majesty' which embodies some of the results of this work.
[110] Picot, *Cardin Le Bret*, p. 181.
[111] *Ibid.*, p. 186.
[112] AHN, Estado, libro 862, fos. 50v–54, consulta, 22 Sept. 1634.

Reading José González's words, it is difficult not to sympathize with Paul Scarron, a *conseiller* in the Parlement of Paris, who was unwise enough to assert in 1640 that the King of France could not be 'in necessity' because his armies were victorious throughout Europe – a remark for which he was arrested and exiled.[113] The Richelieu and Olivares regimes were both reserving to the crown vast discretionary powers which they justified by an emergency of their own defining. It was under these discretionary powers that Paris and Madrid brushed aside the constitutionalist objections of parliaments and corporate bodies, raising money by every device at their disposal and bringing the most intense pressures to bear on harassed populations. 'This fine pretext of necessities of state has been no more than an excuse for ruining the kingdom', complained the Tard-Avisés, whose anti-fiscal rebellion swept through the provinces of south-west France in 1636–7.[114] No section of society was immune, not even the privileged and the exempt. There were major clashes over taxation between crown and clergy in Spain in 1631–2 and in France in 1640, with the regalist policies of Olivares and Richelieu involving them in bitter conflict with the papacy.[115]

The two ministers, however, had not the slightest doubt that the necessity was real. Royal bankruptcy was never far away in the France and Spain of the 1630s,[116] and resources were heavily mortgaged to the bankers. Richelieu might blithely confess to his ignorance of financial matters,[117] and leave the hard work to Bullion, but the consequences of the crown's penury met him at every turn. The same was true of Olivares, who threw himself with his customary energy into the business of negotiating loans and raising money, but complained with justifiable bitterness that he could not make bread from stones.[118] The desperate needs of the state, and the intense fiscalism to which they gave rise, had an overwhelming social and political impact on France and Spain during this most terrible of decades, imposing strains on the systems of both societies from which it would take them generations to recover.

Inevitably the first casualties in both countries were the programmes

---

[113] Cited by Bonney, *Political Change in France*, p. 116.
[114] Cited by Yves-Marie Bercé, *Histoire des croquants* (Geneva, 1974), I, p. 392.
[115] Aldea, *Iglesia y Estado en la España del siglo XVII*; O'Connell, *Richelieu*, pp. 397–8; Aimé-Georges Martimort, *Le Gallicanisme de Bossuet* (Paris, 1953), pp. 121–5.
[116] Bonney, *King's Debts*, p. 170; Domínguez Ortiz, *Política y hacienda*, pp. 102–3.
[117] Avenel, IV, p. 728 (to Bullion, 23 April 1635).
[118] ADM, legajo 79, Olivares to Aytona, 31 March 1632.

of reform. Richelieu had warned the king of this at the time of the Pinerolo decision in 1629, when he said that it would be necessary to abandon all thought of tranquillity, economies and reorganization at home.[119] The regret that he felt at the abandonment of his programme is implicit in the *Testament Politique*, with its refrain of what could be achieved if only there were peace;[120] but he was enough of a realist to reconcile himself to the inevitable. For Olivares this may have been harder, although a foreign observer in Madrid noted as early as 1632 that the demands of foreign policy now dominated to the exclusion of everything else.[121] In a long state paper of 1637, however, all the Count–Duke's frustrations over the sacrifice of reform to the demands of war rose to the surface.[122] 'The principal source of our misfortunes', he wrote, 'consists in our saying: "this is not the time; we'll do it when peace returns".' It was essential to revive those great projects of the 1620s – the schemes for repopulation and internal navigation, for the abolition of customs barriers and the employment of the poor – that were designed to restore prosperity to Castile. 'War', he continued, 'will hinder some of these projects, but does not make all of them impossible . . . I see no reason that is not contrary to all reason of state to lose confidence in them.' Even if they came to nothing, he argued, it was worth taking some action to show the people that the government had their interests at heart.[123]

The Count–Duke's plea seems to have had little effect, although new inquiries were undertaken into the feasibility of making the Tagus navigable along its entire length from Toledo to Lisbon.[124] For financial reasons the project came to nothing. The same was true of most of the internal navigation schemes in which Richelieu took such an interest, although work began seriously in 1638–9 on the Canal de Briare between the Loing and the Loire, and the canal was actually completed in 1642.[125] This itself was a rare accomplishment, and its very uniqueness only serves to emphasize the difficulty of combining war and reform.

It is tempting to see in Olivares' continuing commitment to his reform

[119] Above, p. 106.
[120] See, for example, *TP*, p. 252.
[121] ASF, Mediceo, filza 4959, Bernardo Monanni (secretary to the Tuscan embassy), 6 Nov. 1632.
[122] *MC*, II, doc. XIV.
[123] *Ibid.*, pp. 166–7.
[124] See *MC*, II, pp. 174–5, note 12.
[125] Hauser, *Pensée et action*, pp. 168–9.

programme a lack of that political realism with which Richelieu was so abundantly endowed. A comment made by the English ambassador, Sir Arthur Hopton, in 1638 implies an inability to react pragmatically to new situations: ' The Conde is indeed a very provident servant, in which, and in his secretaryship, I conceive consist his greatest abilities, for in matters of state he tieth himself so obstinately to certain grounds he hath laid as he will hazard all rather than leave them.'[126] Was he, then, too inflexible, too committed to grandiose projects for which resources were lacking and the time was not right?

His refusal to listen to arguments about the incompatibility of war and reform might seem to lend weight to this criticism; but in practice, however much he might inveigh against it, force of circumstance compelled him to jettison a large part of his reform programme as decisively as Richelieu. In reality, both men were driven by events into becoming selective reformers, concentrating only on those areas like military organization and fiscal reforms which were directly related to winning the war. Even here there were many occasions on which they were forced to acknowledge defeat and change their tactics.

In the early 1630s, for instance, Olivares still hoped to achieve his ambition, frustrated in the 1620s, of abolishing the *millones* and introducing a single consolidated tax. In 1631 the crown decreed the cessation of the *millones*, and their replacement by a universal salt tax on the lines of the French *gabelle*. The reform provoked violent opposition, especially in the province of Vizcaya, where revolt broke out in 1632.[127] Olivares handled this revolt with considerable skill, successfully reasserting the royal authority without resort to armed force, but executing the ringleaders. But in the process the salt tax, which anyhow had produced a disappointing yield, had to be abandoned. Whether this is called flexibility or retreat under pressure, it certainly suggests that the Count–Duke was not incapable of recognizing unpleasant realities.

The Vizcayan revolt of 1632–3 may be compared with the revolt of the Nu-Pieds in Lower Normandy in 1639 – another privileged province whose tax-exemptions were under attack. Richelieu, like Olivares, had not abandoned his hopes of fiscal reform, which, as in Spain, became all the more necessary under the accumulating pressures of war. In 1639, for instance, he seems to have turned again to his plans of 1626–7 for the

[126] PRO, SP 94.40, fo. 160, Hopton to Windebank, 26 July/5 Aug. 1638.
[127] See Elliott, 'El programa de Olivares', pp. 427–36.

abolition of the *taille*, which he hoped to replace by a 5% sales tax. This tax was fiercely resisted, and proved a failure well before it was eventually abandoned a few weeks after Richelieu's death.[128] In Normandy in 1634 the crown unilaterally set aside certain restrictions on the collection of the *taille*, and went on to impose a number of special levies which elicited bitter protests from the Estates when they were finally summoned in 1638.[129] But as in Vizcaya it was a tax on salt which finally led to revolt. The 1639 insurrection of the Nu-Pieds was provoked by the attempt to extend the *gabelle* to a previously exempt region. Richelieu reacted as Olivares had reacted, by having the royal order revoked – another example of flexibility, or retreat under pressure. But, unlike Olivares, he followed up his retreat by resorting to exceptionally harsh repressive measures. These included exemplary punishments meted out by Chancellor Séguier under the warrant of a special commission, together with the use of troops to crush the rebels and terrorize the population. 'No exemplary punishment can be heavy enough on this occasion', wrote Richelieu, who was determined to use Normandy as a warning to the rest.[130]

The harshness, and indeed vindictiveness, of the Cardinal's response to the revolt of the Nu-Pieds stands in marked contrast to Olivares' kid-glove handling of the Vizcayan uprising. As we look back on the events of the 1630s, it may indeed seem that the Count–Duke was not ruthless and repressive enough. In Catalonia and Vizcaya in 1632, and in Portugal at the time of the Evora riots of 1637, he sought to reassert the royal authority by indirect means, rather than suppress the rebels by force. Did prudence lie, as he appeared to believe, in biding one's time, and keeping armed intervention as a last resort, or did it lie in striking quickly and striking hard – a response which Richelieu seems to have preferred? But there was also the question of feasibility. Although there were garrison troops in Spain, it was not until the institutionalization of border warfare with France in the later 1630s that there was anything like a royal army serving at home. In France, on the other hand, royal armies had been active during the 1620s in the war against the Huguenots, and even those destined for service abroad could be directed without excessive difficulty to domestic trouble spots. This meant that Richelieu could

[128] Bonney, *Political Change in France*, pp. 183–5.
[129] Madeleine Foisil, *La Révolte des nu-pieds et les révoltes normandes de 1639* (Paris, 1970), pp. 62–3.
[130] *Ibid.*, p. 285.

deploy troops much more easily than Olivares to overawe and terrorize the local population, and could resort at an earlier stage than the Count–Duke to the use of force.

In both countries, however, similar processes were at work. The demands of war provoked an intensive fiscalism, which itself often had strong reformist characteristics because it extended taxation, whether direct or indirect, to regions and social groups which had hitherto been shielded by customary privileges. In the process it set up intense resentments, which in France in particular led year after year to major tax revolts. Every time they were faced with organized protest, Olivares and Richelieu had to make an assessment of the degree and seriousness of the resistance, and the desirability and feasibility of resorting to force to achieve their ends. It was a nerve-racking business, which left both of them physically and emotionally exhausted. Yet both held tenaciously to their long-term aims: the demands of war were paramount.

By the late 1630s it was an open question as to which country, France or Spain, would be the first to break. In the event, it was Spain. After major successes in the opening years of the war with France, the enormous military effort involved in fighting simultaneously against the French and the Dutch began to tell. The pressures of defeat – the loss of Breisach in 1638, the naval disaster at the Downs in 1639 – increased still further the strain on Spanish resources, and forced Olivares into ever more desperate expedients. His project for a Union of Arms to mobilize the resources of the peripheral provinces of the Iberian peninsula looked by the late 1630s even more necessary than at the time of its original drafting in 1625. It is obvious that, in attempting to involve Catalonia and Portugal more fully in the Castilian war effort, Olivares was playing with fire. Richelieu, on the other hand, was notably cautious about attempting to turn *pays d'états* into *pays d'élections*.[131] Should not Olivares have been equally cautious with his own equivalent of the *pays d'états*? Or did he have no alternative by 1640 but to take the risk and press ahead?

The decision to do so was, in the event, a disaster, although it is hard to judge whether he would have fared any better in the long run if he had left Catalonia and Portugal to their own devices. But there is no doubt that his intervention in those two sensitive regions of the peninsula precipitated catastrophe, whereas every month of disaster averted was

---

[131] Bonney, *King's Debts*, p. 145.

another month in which Richelieu might still trip and fall. Contemporaries were quick to recognize the decisive impact of the Catalan and Portuguese revolutions of 1640 on the European balance of power.[132] The Cardinal could now scent victory, but he was not yet out of danger. His enemies were rallying, and as the next two years would show, not even he was totally invulnerable to his own doctrine of necessity.

[132] See Elliott, *Catalans*, pp. 510 and 523.

6

∽◇∽

Failure and success

When war broke out between France and Spain in 1635, both Richelieu
and Olivares hoped, and indeed expected, that it would soon be won.
That spring Richelieu wrote to Bullion, the superintendant of finance,
telling him that this was a year in which a little exertion ('un peu de
peine') would be necessary in order to achieve 'un grand repos'
thereafter.[1] Early in the summer, Olivares drew up a grand plan of
campaign for a three-pronged attack on France from Flanders, Germany
and the Pyrenees, designed to let Spain 'win and finish the war with
supreme brevity'.[2] Neither country was prepared, physically or psychologically, for a prolonged struggle; and yet, as the months passed into
years with no decisive victory, the war became increasingly a war of
attrition. Both ministers had good cause to fear a long drawn-out
conflict, although it is probable that Spain, which had been at war
continuously since 1621, had even more to lose from such a conflict than
France. Richelieu was confident – perhaps too confident – that the
dispersed character of Spanish power would work to France's advantage.
In 1632 he had written to his envoy in Madrid: 'Nowhere is Spain in a
position to resist a concentrated power such as France over a long period,
and in the final analysis the outcome of a general war must necessarily be
calamitous for our Iberian neighbour.'[3] Olivares may have sensed this
when he accompanied his 1635 master-plan with the remark that, if it did
not indeed end the war with supreme brevity then it would be the end of
the Spanish Monarchy itself. In this he was too pessimistic, just as
Richelieu was too optimistic. The Spanish crown, in spite of everything,
still remained capable of mobilizing massive resources for war; and the
war itself would continue for another sixteen years after Olivares' fall
from power.

[1] Avenel, IV, p. 728 (23 April 1635).
[2] Cited Elliott, *Catalans*, p. 309 (14 June 1635).
[3] Burckhardt, *Richelieu and his Age*, III, p. 110.

To finance their war effort, both countries resorted to a combination of extraordinary taxes, massive borrowing, and adjustments of the coinage, although in this respect the French financial ministers managed better than the Spanish. In 1636 the Spanish crown had to renege on its promise never to tamper again with the *vellón* currency, and called in the better quality *vellón* for restamping at three times its current value.[4] Olivares admitted privately to the Cardinal-Infante that this was 'the worst of methods', but justified it as the only way to ensure firm payments for the armies.[5] The same year, the French devalued the *livre tournois*, with the object of stemming the drain of gold and silver from the country. The devaluation was followed in 1640–1 by a general recoinage, which helped restore stability to the French currency and played an important part in winning the war for France.[6] Olivares and his ministers, on the other hand, never succeeded in bringing Castile's currency under control. In 1641 they responded with new inflationary measures to the revolts of Catalonia and Portugal, and then had to reverse the process with a drastic deflation in 1642.[7]

The misery provoked on both sides of the Pyrenees by the attempts of two beleaguered governments to sustain an apparently interminable war very soon became a major element in determining the outcome of the war itself. As the chances faded of either country achieving an early victory, so the importance of the domestic front increased. By the end of the 1630s social and political resentments, a universal hatred of the two principal ministers, and sheer war-weariness were beginning to corrode the impressive but precarious edifices of royal authority that Richelieu and Olivares had so tenaciously sought to construct. Each was uneasily aware of this in relation to his own country, and each saw the possibilities when it came to exploiting his opponent's weaknesses. As early as 1634 Father Joseph wrote to the French ambassador in Madrid: 'It is important to see if one can make use of the discontents of the Catalans and the Portuguese.'[8] Richelieu kept his eyes on Catalonia and Portugal; he was prompt in 1640 to respond to Catalan appeals for help; and the conspirators in Lisbon may have received French funds – perhaps

[4] Hamilton, *American Treasure*, p. 84.
[5] Bayerische Staatsbibliothek, Munich, Codex Monacensis, Hisp. 22, Olivares to Cardinal Infante, 14 March 1636.
[6] Bonney, *King's Debts*, p. 170.
[7] Hamilton, *American Treasure*, pp. 85–6.
[8] BNP, Fonds français, 10,759, fo. 199, Father Joseph to the Comte de Barrault, 16 Oct. 1634.

channelled to them through the indispensable Alphonse Lopez – before the Portuguese *coup d'état* of 1 December 1640.[9]

The discontents in the peripheral regions of the Iberian peninsula played into the Cardinal's hands, and all he had to do was to come forward with offers of help at the appropriate moment. But Castile was a different proposition. Although Olivares was intensely hated, the Castilian opposition was fragmented and incoherent, and lacked a forum for the expression of its views. In the later 1630s a few disgruntled opponents of the Count–Duke used to meet in the Duke of Medinaceli's house in Madrid to air their grievances, and debate such issues as whether kings should have favourites or command their armies in person.[10] Medinaceli and his friends were still hopeful that, if they could only persuade Philip to imitate his brother-in-law and go on campaign, he would see for himself the disastrous consequences for Spain of the Count–Duke's government. It is not known whether anything more serious was discussed at these meetings, but in December 1639 Francisco de Quevedo, who had defected from the ranks of Olivares' supporters, was arrested in Medinaceli's house and carried off to imprisonment. The reasons for Quevedo's arrest have never been fully determined; but there is some evidence to suggest that he was taken into custody not only because of his vitriolic satires against the regime, but also because he was in contact with the French.[11]

It would certainly not be surprising to find Richelieu's agents in touch with opposition groups, but the aristocratic opposition in Castile seems to have done little more than talk, or at most express its dislike of Olivares by refusing to attend court functions – a gesture also adopted by the French grandees, who now rarely attended on Louis XIII.[12] The only indication of anything more serious came in August 1641, when the Duke of Medina Sidonia was charged with planning a secessionist conspiracy in Andalusia.[13] The Duke is alleged to have prepared a manifesto accusing the Count–Duke of ruining Spain with high taxation,[14] and there are some signs that he had foreign contacts and was planning his

[9] Révah, *Richelieu et la restauration*, p. 39.

[10] Elliott, 'Quevedo and the Count–Duke', pp. 248–9; and see *Le Dialogue 'Hospital das Letras' de Don Francisco Manuel de Melo*, ed. Jean Colomès (Paris, 1970), p. 53.

[11] Elliott, 'Quevedo and the Count–Duke', pp. 247–8, and *MC*, II, doc. XV.

[12] Ranum, 'Richelieu and the Great Nobility', p. 202.

[13] Elliott, 'El programa de Olivares', p. 495.

[14] A. Domínguez Ortiz, *Crisis y decadencia de la España de los Austrias* (Madrid, 1969), p. 127.

insurrection to coincide with the seizure of Cadiz by a Dutch fleet. But the conspiracy, although deeply wounding to Olivares as an act of treason by an illustrious member of his own house of Guzmán, was a poorly planned affair which seems to have enlisted very little support.

The aristocratic opposition to Richelieu, on the other hand, remained formidable, in spite of his successes against it in the early 1630s. Even if Gaston d'Orléans was superficially reconciled, there were many members of the upper nobility who were not, and each new high-handed action by the Cardinal added to the number of his enemies and swelled the ranks of the exiles. When the Count of Soissons took refuge in Sedan in 1637, the news was welcomed by Olivares in Madrid as enhancing the possibilities of achieving what 'good reason of state' counselled – the weakening of France by the encouragement of its internal divisions.[15] As the balance of forces began to tilt against Spain in 1639–40, so Olivares' hopes came to turn more and more on the possibility of a great domestic upheaval in France. These hopes, although fragile, were not entirely misplaced. Richelieu's enemies saw the perpetuation of the war as a Machiavellian device on his part for keeping himself in power; and in identifying themselves as the party of peace they were espousing a cause which commanded wide support.[16]

Recalling the disasters of Philip II's intervention in France in the 1590s,[17] the Count–Duke was careful to refrain from pushing the so-called 'Princes de la Paix'[18] too hard. But the Soissons conspiracy of 1641, which was wrecked by the death of Soissons at the moment of victory on the battlefield of La Marfée, was actively assisted by Spain, and provided a pattern for Spanish involvement in the last great anti-Richelieu conspiracy of the reign of Louis XIII, the affair of Cinq-Mars in 1642.

In the Cinq-Mars conspiracy all the elements conducive to the overthrow of the Cardinal looked as if they were about to coalesce at last – aristocratic opposition, subversion by Spain, war-weariness, and palace intrigue. France in the opening months of 1642 was close to organized aristocratic rebellion, with the complicity both of Gaston and the queen.

---

[15] AGS, Estado, legajo 2052, consulta of Council of State, 22 Jan. 1637.

[16] For discussions among Richelieu's opponents comparable to those held by Olivares' opponents in the Duke of Medinaceli's house, see the 'Trois entretiens' of 1641, reproduced in *Mémoires de Henri de Campion*, ed. Marc Fumaroli (Paris, 1967), pp. 231–82.

[17] AGS, Estado, legajo 2056, paper by Olivares, 14 June 1641.

[18] Philippe Erlanger, *Cinq-Mars ou la passion et la fatalité* (Paris, 1962), p. 136.

In March the conspirators negotiated a secret treaty with Olivares, under which they offered their assistance to a Spanish invading army in return for Spanish help with money and men. The object of the conspiracy was the elimination of Richelieu as the necessary prelude to the conclusion of a peace treaty between the two crowns, based on the mutual restitution of all conquests and France's abandonment of its Protestant allies.[19]

The conspiracy posed an especially acute danger for Richelieu because of the ambiguous behaviour of Louis. Barring assassination, the Cardinal's survival depended, like that of Olivares, on the continuing and unwavering support of the king. During the 1630s king and minister had worked together in close partnership, and Louis' letters contain nothing but approbation of the Cardinal's actions. But it was hard for a man of Louis' temperament to be continually beholden to another, and there were times when some passing remark hinted at the intensity of the resentment that lurked beneath the surface. The strain of war, too, was beginning to take its toll. Louis was increasingly subject to bouts of melancholy; the risks and the miseries of war were preying on his mind; and, like so many of his subjects, he had begun to yearn for peace.[20]

The king's disillusionment came at a time of growing infatuation with the young Cinq-Mars, the first of his favourites since the beginning of Richelieu's ministry to have genuine political ambitions of his own. Cinq-Mars made the most of Louis' discontents. He disparaged Richelieu in the king's presence, and went so far as to sing the praises of his Spanish rival.[21] He played, too, on the king's paternal feelings for his long-suffering people, apparently condemned by the iron will of the Cardinal to a perpetual war with Spain. There are indications that in the earlier 1630s, before the formal declaration of war, Louis had made private efforts to reach an understanding with Spain without the Cardinal's knowledge. Now, in the early months of 1642, under the intense pressures of the moment, he seems to have done the same thing again.[22]

While the queen was kept informed of the plot that was being hatched to overthrow the minister, and Gaston d'Orléans was, as usual, deeply

---

[19] Dethan, *Gaston*, pp. 267–8.
[20] See the account of Louis' conversation with the Venetian ambassador in August 1640 in Chevallier, *Louis XIII*, pp. 585–6.
[21] 'Procez de MM. de Cinq-Mars et De Thou', in *Archives Curieuses*, v, p. 284.
[22] Orcibal, 'Richelieu, homme d'église', p. 96.

involved,[23] the king himself may have had no more than faint suspicions that something was afoot. His immediate concern was to explore the possibilities for peace. After the discovery of the plot, Richelieu personally interrogated Cinq-Mars' confidant, François-Auguste de Thou, who told him that it was the king who had ordered him to make contact with Madrid.[24] Once a royal authorization of this kind was secured, the conspirators could make use of it for their own purposes, leaving the king in ignorance until their objectives were achieved.

Yet Louis' decision – assuming that de Thou's confession was true – pointed to the same ultimate conclusion as the actions of Cinq-Mars and his friends. If, as is not implausible, his sense of his royal duty had convinced him that the time had come to make peace with Spain, this same sense of duty would presumably have induced him to dispense with the services of a minister who had come to seem the principal obstacle to the ending of the war. The Cardinal's lessons in statecraft had not been lost on Louis, and he was perfectly capable of sacrificing his minister to necessities of state. As it was, the discovery of the Cinq-Mars conspiracy allowed Richelieu to turn the tables on the king. In his eyes, Louis, by putting his private inclinations for Cinq-Mars before his public duty, had placed the state in jeopardy, for *raison d'état* demanded that peace should not be concluded until Spain accepted the conditions outlined by Louis himself in a memorandum at the beginning of the year.[25]

Cinq-Mars and de Thou went to the scaffold in September 1642, but the Cardinal still had to confront a deeply embittered and resentful king. Under threat of resignation he finally induced the king to remove Cinq-Mars' remaining associates from court, and in effect to promise that he would never again allow his favourites to meddle in affairs of state.[26] He also secured an acknowledgement that it was not his own obstinacy but the unreasonable demands of Spain which constituted the principal obstacle to peace between the crowns.[27] By extracting this acknowledgement, even at the cost of humiliating Louis, the dying Richelieu made his final, and successful, bid to ensure that his work should outlast his life.

When the Cardinal won his final battle for the mind, if not the heart, of

[23] Chevallier, *Louis XIII*, pp. 589–90, and 596.
[24] 'Procez', *Archives Curieuses*, v, pp. 308–9.
[25] Dickmann, *Acta Pacis Westphalicae. Instruktionen*, I, pp. 21–3.
[26] Avenel, vii, doc. xcvi (*Mémoire du Cardinal*, 27 Oct. 1642); O'Connell, *Richelieu*, pp. 429–30.
[27] Avenel, vii, p. 176 (*Mémoire*, 13 or 14 Nov. 1642), and see Dickmann, 'Rechtsgedanke und Machtpolitik', p. 318.

a king who had assured him only six months earlier that ' I love you more than ever, and we have been together too long for us ever to be separated',[28] he had less than three weeks to live. In May 1642 he had fallen gravely ill at Narbonne on his way to Perpignan where Louis had insisted on joining the French besieging army. On 23 May, from his sickbed in Narbonne, he drafted his last will and testament, but was unable to sign it because of the abcess on his arm.[29] He had an enormous fortune to bequeath – 22.5 million *livres*, less 6.5 million in debts.[30] His great-nephew was made heir to the titles and estates of Richelieu and Fronsac, and the will included a number of special provisions and bequests. The ready cash which he left at the time of his death was to be spent on unspecified 'works of piety useful to the public', which he had already discussed with his niece, the Duchess of Aiguillon. He made detailed provisions for the preservation of his magnificent library, but the provisions were flouted by the Parlement of Paris, and the library was incorporated in 1660 into that of the Sorbonne.[31] To the king he bequeathed the Palais Cardinal, along with some of its furnishings, and 1,500,000 *livres* in cash. He had amassed this money for emergency state expenses, and the king was to keep it by him for the same purpose. He asked Louis to look after his relatives as a mark of royal esteem for a *créature* who had only sought to serve him; and he protested that in serving the king 'assez heureusement' in poor health and difficult times, in good fortune and in bad, he had never defaulted on his obligations to the Queen Mother, whatever was said to the contrary. The charge of ingratitude to Marie de Médicis, the patron he had abandoned, clearly troubled his conscience.

By a curious quirk of fate, on 16 May 1642, just a week before Richelieu, Olivares also drew up his last will and testament.[32] Like Richelieu's will, it shows a deep preoccupation with the perpetuation of the entail and the ducal title. These were to go, in default of legitimate offspring, to an alleged natural son of the Count–Duke, who, amidst

---

[28] Comte de Beauchamp, *Louis XIII d'après sa correspondance avec le Cardinal de Richelieu* (Paris, 1902), letter 580 (3 June 1642).

[29] The will is printed in Aubery, *Histoire*, pp. 619–25, and also in *Archives Curieuses*, v, pp. 361–87.

[30] Labatut, *Les Ducs et pairs*, p. 262.

[31] For the fate of Richelieu's library, see Wollenberg, *Richelieu*, p. 115, and Madeleine Laurain-Portemer, *Etudes Mazarines*, I (Paris, 1981), p. 516.

[32] Archivo Histórico de Protocolos, Madrid, 6233, fos. 717–68; and see Marañón, *Olivares*, pp. 172–3, and appendix xxxii.

general astonishment, had recently turned up at court and been legitimized. Like Richelieu, he made special provision for the preservation in perpetuity of his beloved library – and, as with Richelieu, the provision was ignored, in this instance by his widow, who began disposing of the books in order to pay for masses for his soul.[33] Since he ordered fifty thousand of these, she may have found herself under some constraint. To the king he left a piece of the true cross which he had always worn close to the heart; and, like Richelieu, he recommended his family to the king, and expressed at length his gratitude for the honour of having served him. 'I have always put first, after religion, the honour, authority, reputation and success of His Majesty.'

The Count–Duke's will – more prolix, as might have been expected, than the Cardinal's – dwells at some length on his sinfulness, where Richelieu was content with a brief request for divine forgiveness. While Richelieu asked for intercession by the Virgin and all the saints in general, Olivares named fifteen of them individually, including Saint Teresa of Avila, whose heart encrusted with diamonds he bequeathed to the Queen. After the disposition of the entail, Olivares turned to the allocation of specific revenues, expressing a particular interest in repopulation schemes and the fleet. His executors were to establish a Hieronymite convent, eight *montes de piedad* to be used for relieving the poor and repopulating deserted villages, a college in the University of Salamanca, three pilgrim hostels in Santiago, Loreto and Jerusalem respectively, and one hospice and two hospitals for retired soldiers. They were also to spend 100,000 ducats on rebuilding and repopulating the town of Algeciras and maintaining a squadron of galleons for the defence of the Straits of Gibraltar.

War might delay, but even death could not terminate, the implementing of his cherished programme of reform. Or so at least the Count–Duke seems to have hoped. But where Richelieu left a fortune, he left an estate encumbered with debts, and his ambitious institutional bequests seem curiously unrelated to his financial circumstances as far as they are known. His confessor later remarked that it would cost ten million ducats to put them into effect, and that 'the gentleman who made this will governed the Monarchy for nineteen years in the same style as he bequeathed his inheritance'.[34]

[33] Marañón, *Olivares*, p. 433.
[34] Cited *ibid.*, p. 479. Unfortunately no inventory has yet been found which would make it possible to calculate the Count–Duke's assets and commitments at the time of his death.

5 Diego de Velázquez, *Count–Duke of Olivares.*

In his psychological biography of Olivares, Dr Marañón adduces this will of 1642 as evidence of its author's mental abnormality.[35] If the Count–Duke was indeed beginning to show incipient signs of mental unbalance by 1642, this would hardly be surprising. The years since 1639 had brought nothing but disaster. Where for Richelieu everything had a

[35] Marañón, *Olivares*, p. 173.

way of coming out right in the end, all that Olivares touched somehow managed to turn to ashes in his hands. He was painfully aware of this, and sometimes he could not contain his agony. Why, he asked his colleagues on the Council of State when the first news of the Portuguese revolt reached Madrid in December 1640, should he take the blame for everything that went wrong? His hands were clean, his disinterest notorious. It was not he who was responsible for Spain's wars – indeed, he loved peace so dearly that he would throw himself at the feet of anyone who could secure it. Never once had he voted in favour of war, and the record was clear for all to see.[36]

The rambling, hysterical outburst suggests a man at the end of his tether, and yet paradoxically he not only managed to hold on to power for another two years, but even temporarily strengthened his position. In the short term the revolts of Catalonia and Portugal enhanced his dominance, because he seemed the only man capable of repairing the damage. In spite of his exhaustion he still threw himself with enormous energy into raising men and money for the recovery of Catalonia, while simultaneously struggling to sustain the war effort against the French and the Dutch and pursuing with tenacity every faint prospect of peace. His performance under pressure elicited admiration mingled with pity from those who watched him at close quarters. 'I must admit', wrote a Flemish official in Madrid in a secret letter of February 1641 to a colleague in Brussels, 'that I am losing heart when I see what is happening. Only God can save us. Here it is all a matter of demands for money, from which nobody is exempted, and our needs grow at the same time as our resources dwindle . . . I feel pity as I watch His Excellency, although he displays great spirit and prudence in everything.'[37]

The Count–Duke was desperately holding on, hoping against hope for the overthrow of Richelieu which he saw as the only chance for peace. In spite of all the adversities, the king seemed unwavering in his support, and as long as this continued, the Count–Duke's enemies among the nobility and in the administration were held frustratingly at bay. As always, they saw their best hope in persuading the king to leave Madrid and go on campaign. This time they succeeded. Philip left for Aragon in April 1642 to take command of his army for the reconquest of Catalonia, apparently

[36] AGS, Guerra Antigua, legajo 1331, Junta de Ejecución, 23(?) Dec. 1640.
[37] AGR, Conseil Privé Espagnol, Reg. 1506, fos. 212–13, Jacques de Brecht to Pierre Roose, 20 Feb. 1641.

overruling the Count–Duke's objections.[38] Olivares himself stayed on a little longer in Madrid, and retired for two days to the privacy of his residence at the Buen Retiro to write his will,[39] before leaving to join the king on campaign.

The Catalan campaign of 1642 achieved nothing, and its failure sealed the Count–Duke's fate. When he returned to Madrid in December, his carriage took a roundabout route to the palace to avoid the risk of popular demonstrations.[40] His own relatives among the high nobility, who saw the shipwreck coming and were anxious to avoid going down with the captain, were now working frantically behind the scenes to persuade Philip to part with his minister. Yet outwardly everything seemed unchanged, and the Count–Duke remained very much in charge.

On 4 December, two days before the Count–Duke's clandestine return to Madrid, Richelieu died in Paris. In his usual style the Count–Duke, on receiving from Brussels the report of his rival's death and his replacement by Mazarin, settled down to write a memorandum assessing the importance of the news.[41] It seems to have been his last state paper. In it he wrote:

The circumstance of the death of the *ministro inmediato* of France [the minister closest to the king], so absolute and independent as we have seen from the innumerable number of people who have perished at his command, compels His Majesty's ministers to consider the acute situation in which we find ourselves, so as to miss no opportunity afforded by this event to secure by any possible means a treaty of peace, which is all that can possibly restore our fortunes at this present juncture.

He went on to say that even an unworthy treaty might yet turn out well, and he thought that if Mazarin tried to prolong the war he would be faced with a general uprising. To smooth the way for negotiations he proposed that he should be offered a large bribe by some crafty Italian intermediary. And then, towards the end of his memorandum, the bitterness overflowed. Spain must never forget what had happened, and once peace had been signed, it must foment such divisions inside France that it would never be able to do the same thing again.

[38] Elliott, 'El programa de Olivares', p. 501.
[39] ASF, Mediceo, filza 4966, despatch from Tuscan ambassador, 21 May 1642.
[40] Elliott, 'El programa de Olivares', p. 502.
[41] AGS, Estado, legajo 3860, undated paper of Olivares with consulta of 10 Jan. 1643.

For we have seen how, without our wanting war or offering the least pretext for it
. . . France against all right and reason has attacked us on every front, and has
stripped Your Majesty of entire kingdoms in Spain by resorting to hideous
treachery, and has provoked such a universal convulsion that the possibility of
salvaging even a portion has generally been considered very slight . . .

These were the words of a defeated man. A few days later the
Count–Duke's faithful secretary, Antonio Carnero, wrote in confidence:
'My master is utterly exhausted and shattered, although, even with the
water over him, he still keeps swimming.'[42] On the following day, 17
January 1643, Philip gave his minister leave to retire. During the
preceding weeks he had been under intense pressure to dispense with the
Count–Duke's services. The campaign within the palace and the
administration was orchestrated by one of Olivares' relatives, the Count
of Castrillo, who owed his ministerial career to him. It developed against
a background of growing popular clamour provoked by the general
misery and the latest manipulation of the coinage, and it came at a time
when Philip, back from the campaign in Aragon, had seen for himself the
extent of the disaster. In future, he announced, he would rule by himself,
without a favourite. The Count–Duke was banished into the country,
where, with the help of his advisers, he replied to the accusations being
circulated against him with the *Nicandro*, a spirited tract in defence of his
record.[43] He died at Toro on 22 July 1645 – and the war still went on.

With the death of Richelieu in December 1642 and the fall of Olivares in
January 1643 this parallel investigation of the careers of two contempora-
neous statesmen approaches its end. A story, it would seem, of brilliant
success on the one hand, and of catastrophic failure on the other. How, in
the light both of contemporary assessments and of later inquiry, are their
very different records to be explained?

For Olivares himself the explanation was simple. The hostile pamphlet
which his *Nicandro* was designed to refute contained what he called a
'parallel' between himself and Richelieu, 'praising the one to discredit
the other'. To this the Count–Duke replied: 'I admit that Cardinal
Richelieu was fortunate in many things, but his means of achieving them
were detestable.'[44] The idea that Richelieu was a lucky man was one that

[42] AGR, Conseil Privé Espagnol, Reg. 1504, fo. 238v, Carnero to Roose, 16 Jan. 1643.
[43] *MC*, II, doc. XX.
[44] *MC*, II, p. 268.

Olivares had expounded in the past,[45] and it contrasted with a widely held perception that the Count–Duke was not. In the eyes of the British ambassador in Madrid in 1639, 'there wants nothing but fortune to make him the worthiest Favourite that any king hath had, but this hath not been propitious hitherto, nor I fear is likely to be'.[46] But what do we mean by fortune or luck when we speak of its contribution to a statesman's success? The death of Gustavus Adolphus in 1632 came at a highly opportune moment for Richelieu, just as the incompatibility of France's alliances with Sweden and Bavaria had brought his foreign policy to the point of collapse. This is a good example of the kind of unpredictable event which sometimes comes to a statesman's aid. But should we place in the same category the fall of La Rochelle in 1628, just in time for the Cardinal to move the king's army into Italy before Casale could be captured by the Spaniards? This would seem rather to have been a matter of exploiting an opportunity with remarkable speed and determination, and this would scarcely have been possible without careful long-range thinking and planning. On this Richelieu lets fall a revealing remark in a memorandum to the king written in 1627: 'Experience shows that, if one foresees from far away the designs to be undertaken, one can act with speed when the moment comes to execute them.'[47] It was this keen sense of anticipation, combined with decisiveness at the moment of execution, which enabled him on so many occasions to get his timing right.

Richelieu's gift for timing elicited the admiration of his contemporaries. 'The choice of time', wrote Jean de Silhon in his *Le Ministre d'Estat* of 1631, 'is perhaps the greatest secret in the handling of public affairs, and the most potent means of achieving success.'[48] In that same year Guez de Balzac wrote in *Le Prince* of the importance not only of using time but of knowing how to choose. For him the army's crossing of the Alps so soon after the capture of La Rochelle was a fine example of pressing hard upon Fortune, and allowing her no respite.[49] Against this can be set Olivares' failure on the same occasion. The Duke of Mantua's death in 1627 without a male heir had long been anticipated, and indeed

[45] See above, p. 114.
[46] PRO, SP. 94.41, fo. 211, Hopton to Cottington, 21/31 Oct. 1639.
[47] Grillon, II, p. 392 (*Mémoire*, 15 Aug. 1627).
[48] Silhon, *Le Ministre d'Estat*, p. 360.
[49] *Oeuvres*, I, pp. 91 and 102.

the eventuality had been discussed by ministers as early as 1623 at a meeting attended by Olivares.[50] When it came, the Count–Duke could either have disclaimed any Spanish interest in contesting the succession of Nevers, or have given immediate orders to the army of Milan to move into Montferrat, having previously cleared this move with the Emperor, and ensured that Don Gonzalo de Córdoba's forces were prepared for immediate action. But he had taken none of these preliminary steps.[51] As a result, the chance of surprise was thrown away, precious weeks were lost, and the Count–Duke managed to make the worst of every world, embarking late and with inadequate preparation on a legally dubious enterprise.

Although the Mantuan fiasco was probably the worst, and certainly the most avoidable, blunder of his twenty-two years of power, it points to a possibly significant weakness when his skills are compared with those of Richelieu. There is no doubt that he possessed, like the Cardinal, a great capacity for thinking ahead, and for assessing the varying implications of different lines of action. This gift for the long view was in many ways a strength. He had determined in his early years in office the long-term goals which he wished to pursue – the restoration of the King of Spain's reputation, the unification of his territories, the economic revival of Castile – and he never lost sight of them in spite of temporary setbacks. ' I have always understood ', he once wrote in a note to a ministerial colleague, ' that one should never be discouraged if a desirable outcome is delayed, or things seem to go wrong, because everything depends on a variety of accidents, and these change by the day and the hour.'[52] This attitude gave a remarkable consistency to his policies – a consistency which is often equated with inflexibility.

But the charge of inflexibility appears misconceived. No one was more inflexible than Richelieu in his determination to fight Spain to the finish, and this determination is generally taken as a sign of his statesmanship. Although the Cardinal's alleged pragmatism has won him much praise, Carl Burckhardt argues persuasively that ' continuity in the realization of his general aims was his foremost concern '.[53] In this respect, there is not much to choose between the Cardinal and the Count–Duke, who could also combine long-term strategic thinking with tactical shifts and retreats

---

[50] AHN, Estado, libro 869, fo. 48, undated consulta, November or December 1623.
[51] Cf. Fernández Alvarez, *Don Gonzalo de Córdoba*, pp. 56–7.
[52] AGS, Estado, legajo 2329, note to Don Juan de Villela, 20 March 1629.
[53] *Richelieu and his Age*, II, p. 54.

when these seemed necessary. But in Olivares the long-term view was accompanied by a dangerous tendency to assume that time itself was on his side. 'The wisest counsel', he wrote in 1634 on the question of whether or not to go to war with France, 'is to take time and try to hold things without risking everything', although – he characteristically hastened to add – this was not an infallible doctrine, and sometimes a short sharp dose of medicine was the most effective cure.[54] But somehow the short, sharp dose was something he found it very difficult to apply. At the moment of decision he appears indecisive, less willing than Richelieu to take the dramatic risk. Instead, his tendency was always to play for time, and choose what he called the 'middle course'. Richelieu, too, had a liking for the 'middle course',[55] but unlike his rival he does not seem to have used it as an alternative to action. All too often the Count–Duke gives the impression of being a man who cannot bring himself to act. He desperately wanted peace with the Dutch, but the terms were never quite right, and he always held on until too late in the vain hope of getting better ones. In 1635, at a time when the sending of an army into Catalonia was being canvassed in Madrid as a means of suppressing Catalan liberties, he resisted the suggestion on various grounds, one of them being that the behaviour of the Catalans themselves was not yet sufficient to justify such drastic action.[56] He may well have been right in his assessment that the disadvantages of using force in Catalonia outweighed the advantages, but, by never renouncing in his own mind this particular option, he eventually manoeuvred himself into a position in which it became necessary to adopt it, but in even more adverse circumstances than those of 1635.

There is every reason to believe that Richelieu went through the same kind of agony as Olivares in reaching his decisions, but that when he made them they came out clean, sharp and ruthless. The Cardinal's was at all times a high-risk policy, once his general objective was determined. Starting from a position of inferiority in his relationship with Spain, this was perhaps the most effective approach to adopt. But having once begun to play the game, Richelieu played it with growing confidence, since each risk successfully taken seemed to warrant the taking of another. Inevitably there were times of deep discouragement. The year of Corbie,

---

[54] AHN, Estado, libro 864, fo. 129v ('El Conde Duque sobre la materia de romper o no con Francia', 26 Jan. 1634).

[55] Wollenberg, *Richelieu*, p. 239.

[56] Elliott, *Catalans*, p. 315 (paper by Olivares, 12 December 1635).

1636, was a terrible year, and as the Cardinal-Infante's army advanced on Paris, only the counsel and chiding of Father Joseph prevented him from succumbing to despair.[57] There would be failures and defeats in the years ahead, like the loss of the Valtelline in 1637, and the failure of French arms at Fuenterrabía in 1638. But the turn of the tide at Corbie helped to fortify an already well-developed providentialist view of the course of events, and this came to his rescue at moments of adversity.

Here the contrast with the mental attitude of Olivares is striking. The Count–Duke's fortitude in adversity is undoubted, and was widely admired. Indeed, it was an essential characteristic of the neo-Stoic philosophy he had adopted as his own. When good news came from Italy in 1639, he refrained from excessive rejoicing, recalling, as he said, 'how unstable is everything in this life, and how important it is to remember bad times during good ones. In my view the clearest sign of a mean spirit is to be exultant in times of prosperity, when one should in fact be just the opposite.'[58] Like Richelieu, he too was imbued with the idea of Providence, and, like Richelieu, had embarked on his political career in the belief that his monarch was uniquely destined for greatness. But by the later 1620s he was having to make sense of setbacks and defeats. Up to a point it was possible to argue that God's ways were inscrutable and that there were bound to be reverses as well as victories in the course of any reign. His defenders used this argument at the end of the decade,[59] and it appears again in the *Nicandro*, which observes that the saintliest kings have sometimes been those most severely punished by God, 'either as a greater test of faith, or for secret purposes that we cannot understand'.[60] But as the cumulative run of misfortunes began to weigh on the king and Olivares, they both became increasingly persuaded that their own personal conduct was calling forth divine retribution. In the 1630s the Count–Duke acquired a morbid obsession with his private responsibility for public disaster. In his own mind he became a latter-day Jonah. All the misfortunes of the year, he wrote to the Cardinal-Infante in 1637, 'are my fault, and once I am thrown into the sea the storm will cease, and success and good fortune follow'.[61]

[57] Fagniez, *Père Joseph*, II, pp. 309–10.
[58] AGS, Estado, K.1419, fo. 81, Olivares to King, 14 May 1639.
[59] Quevedo, *Obras completas*, I (6th edn, Madrid, 1966), p. 817 ('El Chitón de las Tarabillas').
[60] *MC*, II, p. 269.
[61] Bayerische Staatsbibliothek, Munich, Codex Monacensis, Hisp. 22, Olivares to Cardinal-Infante, 29 Nov. 1637.

It is natural to wonder whether Olivares' self-fulfilling prophecies of disaster may not have affected his political skills, making him perhaps more cautious at moments when boldness was most required. Where Richelieu's religion was a religion of reassurance, which buoyed him up in times of trial, that of Olivares seems to have been essentially fatalistic, inculcating fortitude and Christian resignation in the face of the inscrutable ways of God. But does this reflect differences of temperament, or differences of circumstance? Would Richelieu have reacted like Olivares, if faced by a comparable run of disasters? Or do their differing responses reflect the differing moods of two very different Counter-Reformation societies?

It is instructive to compare two comments from sympathetic sources on the French and Spanish scenes at roughly the same point in the ministerial careers of Richelieu and Olivares. In the *Prince* Guez de Balzac writes that in the past six years – the first six years of the Richelieu ministry – France had ceased to be the France of yesterday, 'so sick and decrepit . . . Beneath the same faces I see different men, and in the same kingdom, another state. The outward appearance remains, but the interior has been renewed. There has been a moral revolution (*une révolution morale*), a transformation of spirit . . .'[62] Against this may be set the comment of one of Olivares' ministerial colleagues at more or less the same moment: 'It is true that we are approaching our end, but in other hands we would have perished sooner.'[63] Selective quotations no doubt, but they provoke reflection. Was a pervasive fatalism corroding Spanish confidence? Was there indeed a new spirit abroad in France, in spite of the miseries of the times? And, if so, is this perhaps to be linked to the upsurge of French Counter-Reformation spirituality in the opening decades of the century, at a moment when the original impetus of the Catholic revival in Spain was largely spent?

In considering the contrasting *mentalités* of our two statesmen, we have moved from two individuals to two societies, whose characteristics they may or may not have reflected with a fair degree of accuracy. This is surely necessary for a just appreciation of their failings and their merits as statesmen. For the craft of politics is not practised, and should not be studied, in a vacuum. The mood and morale of a society, its institutions,

---

[62] *Oeuvres*, I, p. 81.
[63] *Discursos de Don Antonio de Mendoza*, ed. Marqués de Alcedo (Madrid, 1911), p. 93.

capacity and resources, all help to create the context in which statecraft is conducted, and impinge at innumerable points on the process of decision-making. Indeed, many would argue that they are the supreme determinants, and that the statesman remains the prisoner of circumstance, and the creature of *conjoncture*. If Richelieu's political skills were indeed superior to those of Olivares, as this study of their careers in parallel has tended to suggest, did this tilt the balance in the confrontation between France and Spain? Or was France bound in any event to emerge victorious in such a confrontation? To put the question at its starkest, did the characters and policies of the rival statesmen make any real difference to the eventual outcome?

Olivares referred on one occasion to 'the soil of France being so rich, and ours so dry and rugged'.[64] With a population of sixteen million, more than twice that of the Iberian peninsula, it also possessed a decisive demographic superiority. But in the circumstances of the early seventeenth century a larger population and greater natural wealth were not in themselves a guarantee of superior power. Philip IV claimed in the 1620s to have nearly 300,000 paid men under arms;[65] Louis XIII in the 1630s had about half this number, or less.[66] Everything turned on the ability to mobilize resources – to tap without interruption reserves of money and manpower which could just as well originate from outside as from inside national boundaries. For example, the retention by Richelieu of Bernard of Saxe-Weimar's army on his death in 1639 played an important part in France's subsequent successes.[67] The fact that this was achieved through the good offices of Barthélemy Herwarth, a French Protestant banker in Saxe-Weimar's service, was testimony to the persuasive skills of the Cardinal, just as the involvement of Portuguese businessmen in the Spanish royal finances bore witness to those of Olivares. A seventeenth-century statesman had to find his men, his money and his professional expertise where he could. Olivares reacted indignantly to complaints that he had appointed foreigners to the Councils of War and Finance. Had not

[64] ADM, legajo 79, Olivares to Aytona, 12 Oct. 1632.
[65] *MC*, I, p. 244 ('Felipe IV al Consejo de Castilla', 1627).
[66] See Geoffrey Parker, 'Warfare', in *The New Cambridge Modern History*, XIII (Cambridge, 1979), p. 205, for a table showing the size of the armies of six European states in this period, and Bonney, *King's Debts*, p. 173 for contemporary estimates of the number of men in France's armies in 1634–6.
[67] G. B. Depping, 'Un Banquier protestant en France au XVIIe siècle. Barthélemy Herwarth', *Revue Historique*, 10 (1879), pp. 285–338, and 11, pp. 63–80.

the French, he argued in the *Nicandro*, 'appointed Mazarino, an Italian and a vassal of Your Majesty, to the post of prime minister which Richelieu held; and was not this because he was a person of talent', who had served the King of France well?[68]

Richelieu and Olivares were both skilled talent-spotters, as they had to be if they were to build up a team of ministers, officials and diplomats who could be relied upon to advance the service of the king. Men like Sublet de Noyers in France or José González in Spain owed their rapid ascent to being hand-picked by the principal minister, who groomed them for high office. Sublet de Noyers, like Villanueva in Spain, did not long survive the change of regime; but many of the 'creatures' of Richelieu and Olivares managed to hold to office, providing continuity of policy and a professional skill and dedication to royal service which proved indispensable during the difficult middle decades of the century.

But if there were certain obvious resemblances in the methods by which the two ministers sought to advance the royal authority, there were also, as they were well aware, profound differences in the requirements for governing France and Spain. In the *Decision of Apollo*, an imaginary Spanish dialogue between a Castilian jurist and Bodin, it was argued on behalf of the Count–Duke that 'it is very easy for the minister in France to govern with success because that kingdom is united and depends solely on itself'. The minister who governed Spain, on the other hand, had to 'preserve in peace, security and union so many kingdoms divided by land and sea . . . and see to their defence against invasions difficult to forestall'.[69]

In the sixteenth century the superior administrative organization of the Spanish Monarchy, the vitality of Castile and the resources of America had enabled it to turn to advantage what was potentially its greatest liability – its vast expanse and the diversity of its component elements. By the time of Olivares, the liabilities had come to outweigh the assets. The administrative system was becoming fossilized; the vitality of Castile had been sapped; and the resources of America were dwindling. It was because he perceived all this so clearly that the Count–Duke threw himself with such energy and dedication into

---

[68] *MC*, II, p. 254.
[69] Royal Library, Copenhagen, Gl.Kgl.S.590,2, 'Decisión de Apolo en la pretensión de mayor alabanza entre los dos validos de los mayores potencias de Europa', in a manuscript volume of the Count of La Roca's *Fragmentos históricos*, fos. 141–141v.

renovating an antiquated structure in the hope of giving it a new lease of life. Unity became for him the necessary precondition for survival, because the expense of protecting a constellation of territories which contributed unequally and often inadequately to the costs of imperial defence was now exceeding the benefits that empire was supposed to offer. But to construct this new unity he had to banish ancient prejudices, break the hold of ancient custom, and breathe new life into institutions too content with ancient ways.

The force of inertia was impressive in the Spanish Monarchy, and the Count–Duke was aware that the cost of challenging it would be high. But was it not better, as he said on one occasion, to 'die doing something'?[70] Or should he have followed from the beginning the sage counsel given by Guez de Balzac in a letter of 1638 to a friend: 'When our young friend has lived as long as we have, he will have no better opinion than us of those who wish to reform the world. Let him read the histories of every century, and he will see that this zeal for reformation has always given birth to new disorders, instead of ending the old ones.'[71]

Olivares' 'zeal for reformation' proved in the end to be his undoing. He could not leave well alone. But if he *had* left well alone and abandoned his attempts to mobilize the resources of the peripheral provinces of the Iberian peninsula through a Union of Arms, could he have managed to keep going even as long as he did? It was not unreasonable to think that a few more men, a little more money, might tip the scales. In 1636 Paris was close to falling, and Richelieu close to flight. Either event could have transformed Olivares' prospects. Both he and Richelieu were acutely aware that nothing in life was as unpredictable as war.

The challenge facing Olivares was therefore to reform and revitalize the Spanish Monarchy without letting it fall to pieces in his hands. In this he finally failed. The challenge facing his rival, on the other hand, was to weld together again a country which had fallen apart. Religious disunity and aristocratic factionalism, the legacy of forty years of civil war, made the immediate tasks of government much harder in France than in Spain. Yet at the same time by encouraging a natural reaction in favour of discipline and order, they may have strengthened the long-term chances of a tenacious minister determined to restore and strengthen the authority of the crown. The potential for that authority

---

[70] AGS, Estado, K.1416, fo. 56, consulta of Council of State, 17 Sept. 1633.
[71] Quoted Albertini, *Politische Denken*, p. 208.

was great in France – certainly greater than in Spain, outside Castile. In France the right of consent to taxation had in practice long since been abolished outside the *pays d'états*;[72] and the variety of competing authorities even within the *pays d'états* created opportunities for royal intervention in the guise of mediation which do not seem to have existed on a similar scale in Portugal and the Crown of Aragon. In addition, the doctrine of undivided sovereignty that had developed in France during the confusion of the civil wars made it difficult for parlements and provincial Estates to sustain a plea for active participation in affairs of state against the wishes of the crown; and the crown had an army at its disposal to give its will the force of law.

While in both countries there was a natural predisposition in society towards fragmentation, the forces working in favour of the concentration of power seem therefore at this moment to have been stronger in France than in Spain. Richelieu possessed the determination and the skill to mobilize these counteracting forces in pursuit of his aims. But did he also have the institutional resources to bring them to fulfilment? Here the effective loss of control by the French crown over its own bureaucracy through the systematic sale of office would seem at first sight to have been a crippling disadvantage. But in practice this forced upon him a creative improvisation, which led to the development of a corps of officials dependent solely on the crown and dismissible at will.[73] In Spain on the other hand the crown still retained at least nominal control over the selection and removal of its higher office-holders; and to have super-imposed upon these a new layer of officials would have created more problems than it solved.

By helping to collect taxes and suppress the revolts to which his own activities gave rise, the *intendant* did much – although at a heavy price – to bring about France's victory in its war with Spain.[74] But it was the war itself which did most to justify the use of the *intendant* and transformed him from an incidental into a regular agent of the royal administration. Here it was because of war, not in spite of it, that reform was introduced. Richelieu's achievement in effect was to create – however precariously – a state victorious in war, using war itself to advance the state-creating process.

---

[72] Cf. Bonney, *Political Change in France*, p. 443.

[73] *Ibid.*, p. 442.

[74] *Ibid.*, p. 443.

Olivares, if he had been victorious, would have done the same thing. But he was not victorious, and the consequences of his failure were self-multiplying for Spain. His nephew and successor, Don Luis de Haro, would continue the war in the hope of recovering some of Spain's losses, but the efforts to reform and transform the Spanish Monarchy were abandoned after 1643, as if by universal consent. The Count–Duke became a non-person, and the reforming legacy was consigned with the rest of his works to oblivion, to be convincingly resurrected only in the succeeding century, and under a new dynasty. In France, on the other hand, Richelieu in his triumph had created what looked like a formula for success, and in so doing had transformed the contours of the political debate. His name might be reviled, but there was no escaping the magnitude of his achievement, even if the upheavals of the Fronde within a few years of his death exposed the dangerous fragility of the structure he had built. Mazarin appropriated all that he safely could of the legacy, and a generation later Louis XIV would sardonically turn to Colbert at meetings of the Council with the words 'Here is M. Colbert who is going to tell us: "Sire, the great Cardinal would have done this or that . . ."'[75] Richelieu from beyond the grave still dictated the lines of policy and action.

Richelieu's state, as depicted by many historians, was the state of the future: centralized, compact, and firmly grounded on the principle of national identity. Indeed, in this reading, Richelieu becomes a symbol of the future and Olivares of the past. 'The aims of Richelieu', writes Golo Mann, 'were more up-to-date than those of Ferdinand II and Olivares; more modest, more capable of realization.'[76] Michel Devèze, in his study of the Spain of Philip IV (1970) is characteristically chauvinistic: 'It is undeniable that the French mentality was in advance of the Spanish mentality – or at least more representative of the future.'[77] For him, as for Golo Mann, Olivares was the victim of an anachronistic dream, the representative of a society which thought in terms of universal empire at a time of dawning nationhood; of the unity of Christendom at a time of growing religious diversity; of 'the cohesion of Catholic Europe

---

[75] Cited by Hauser, *Pensée et action*, p. 7. I am grateful to Prof. René Pillorget for drawing this citation to my attention.
[76] *Propyläen Weltgeschichte*, VII (Berlin 1964), ed. Golo Mann and August Nitschke, p. 174.
[77] *L'Espagne de Philippe IV*, I, p. 170.

threatened by the progress – in the seventeenth century primarily economic and maritime – of the Protestants '.[78]

The implication of this reading of early-seventeenth-century history is that Spain was condemned to defeat from the start. But this judgement smacks too much of simplistic determinism. France and Spain were faced with different kinds of problems – Spain with the problem of economic and spiritual renewal, France with that of recovering a sense of national purpose and cohesion. It is indeed possible that French society in this period had more creative energy than that of Spain, where the very weight of past achievements imposed its own restrictive mould. But the creative energies of French society had somehow to be harnessed if they were not to run to waste, and this is what Richelieu attempted by means of war with Spain. The risk was high; it is doubtful whether anyone else could have made the country stay the course; and until the Spanish debacle of 1639–40 the war swayed in the balance. Even then, it would take another twenty years of warfare, and a series of setbacks which placed the Cardinal's whole policy in doubt, before his successors could reap the rewards of his work.

If Richelieu achieved his triumph by a hair's breadth, the margin by which Olivares was defeated was correspondingly close. Was it Richelieu's superior political genius that defeated him, or the strength of the odds against success in the very difficult enterprise on which he had set his heart, or a little of both? I have here attempted to portray an Olivares who is more subtle and complex than he is generally depicted. He emerges as a man who was not only alive to the economic and maritime progress of the Protestants, but who also had no inhibitions about attempting to borrow from his enemies, and imitate the methods that had brought them success. Although believing profoundly in the unity of the Spanish and Austrian Habsburgs as essential for the salvation of his church and his faith, he was still realist enough to know that the restoration of the old Christendom was an idle dream, that it was necessary to do business with the Protestants, and that the United Provinces, in one form or another, had come to stay. He emerges, too, as a man who realized that the requirements of seventeenth-century warfare and the realities of seventeenth-century power demanded a radical reassessment of the traditional relationships between the kings of Spain

[78] *Ibid.*, pp. 161–2.

and their vassals. This reassessment meant a reordering of the supranational organization known as the Spanish Monarchy which would combine the universalist advantages of supranationality with the more practical advantages of concentrated power associated with the compact nation-state. In this he would fail, but the Austrian branch of the Habsburgs would achieve something very comparable in the second half of the century.[79] The French model of political organization was not the only one to emerge from those turbulent decades of warfare and disruption.

When seen in this light, Olivares, while attempting to grapple with a multitude of inherited problems from the dead weight of the past, is not perhaps quite such an anachronistic figure as he is sometimes represented. Nor, it may be added, was Richelieu quite so forward-looking as his defenders would imply. A man deeply imbued, like his rival, with the traditional ideal of 'reputation'; a man who, again like his rival, sacrificed reform to war; a man who, so far from being the exponent of a nineteenth-century style of *Realpolitik*, saw himself as a Christian statesman and devoted much time and energy to grounding his policies on Christian principles. In these respects, as in so many others, Richelieu belonged to his times.

All this suggests that Richelieu and Olivares are best taken on their own terms, and placed where they belong, in the context of the international rivalry and economic recession that characterized the Europe of the 1620s and 1630s. Both attempted to set right the long-standing disorders of the state; both sought to raise their monarchs to new heights of internal authority and international prestige; both attempted, through discipline and persuasion, to shape societies that would be more obedient, more deferential, more brilliant in peace, more effective in war. In both instances the sheer arrogance of their ambition is what most impresses. Both were ultimately attempting to mould a world to their image.

We can, of course, say that the times produced the men. But might one not also say, with no less truth, that the men produced the times? Both of them hewed with a tenacity bordering on obsessiveness to the line of policy they had chosen, trampling down in their relentless forward march anyone presumptuous enough to stand in their way. What was it that

---

[79] See Evans, *The Making of the Habsburg Monarchy*.

made them so convinced that they alone were right? The determination to dominate, to bend everything to their will, clearly sprang from a conviction not only that it *was* possible to transform the world, but also that they had a solemn obligation to undertake this task on behalf of monarchs who had been called by God to a special destiny. Mentally they lived in a world of absolute royal authority, which itself depended directly on the authority of God.

To some extent their activism as statesmen may be regarded as a natural reaction to the pervasive drift which characterized the rule of their immediate predecessors. But it may also reflect a change of mental attitudes in the world from which they sprang. The conviction seems to have been growing in those opening decades of the seventeenth century that man, if he made full use of his powers of reason, could – in spite of everything – exercise some control over events. There was no doubt an organic process of growth and decline, and a cyclical movement determining the rise and fall of states. But, even in Spain where the process of decline seemed in the eyes of many contemporaries to be already well advanced, the whole *arbitrista* movement of the early seventeenth century, with its proposals for reform and economic management, was postulated on the assumption that something could be done.[80]

One of the most intelligent of those *arbitristas*, Sancho de Moncada, in his treatise of 1619 on the *Political Restoration of Spain*, rejected the arguments of those who denied that there was any such thing as a 'science of government'. There was indeed such a science, as Plato, Aristotle and other great Republicans had shown. The reasons for this were obvious.

Government, or reason of state, is the method of founding, conserving or expanding a kingdom; . . . and just as there are certain principles and infallible rules which teach how to cure the sickness of bodies, and of souls, and the injuries which men do to each other, so there are infallible remedies for curing the ills which can afflict any kingdom. Secondly, men normally err, and so divine Providence arranged that there should be a fixed and infallible rule, standard and yardstick to guide and direct men along the right and certain path, and this standard is the science of government . . .[81]

Richelieu and Olivares were both beneficiaries of this growing contemporary conviction that men, by mastering the rules, could control

---

[80] See Elliott, 'Self-Perception and Decline'.
[81] *Restauración política de España*, ed. Jean Vilar (Madrid, 1974), pp. 229–30 (Discurso IX, cap. 1).

events and maximize their powers. There was a science of rhetoric, which taught one how to sway men's minds and win their hearts; a science of warfare, which took 'discipline' as its watchword; and a science of government, which expressed itself in 'prudence'. The basic principles of these different forms of science had all been laid down in classical antiquity. But it was not enough simply to imbibe them from Tacitus and the other great masters and apply them mechanically. Instead, they had to be tried, tested and refined in the light of history and experience. Once this was done – once the statesman or the commander had made them his own – then he had the world at his feet.

Buoyed up by this conviction, it is not surprising if these statesmen of the 1620s were more alive to the possibilities than to the limitations of power. With prudence and foresight, and by applying all their knowledge and skills, they could steer their course amidst the storms and still bring the ship to port. At one end of the gallery in the Palais Cardinal, Richelieu had a painting of *Prévoyance* – Foresight – seated on the clouds, resting her elbow on a globe, and holding in her right hand a tiller and her left hand a club.[82] It was his prudence – his mastery of the science of government – which had enabled him to steer with success the ship of state across the stormy seas.

At the other end of the gallery was another figure, dressed in white and looking over her shoulder. This figure was History. Both Richelieu and Olivares, as their careers proceeded, became increasingly preoccupied with the verdict of history. 'In truth', said Olivares in 1634, 'there are many things which we are neglecting, and not the least of them is history.'[83] In calling Virgilio Malvezzi to Madrid to serve as the official historian of the reign of Philip IV,[84] and in commissioning for the palace of the Buen Retiro paintings to commemorate the major victories of his armies, accompanied by scenes from the life of Hercules, he was appealing, beyond a contemporary audience, to posterity.[85] Richelieu, with the same two audiences in mind, also turned to the historians and the painters. In 1635 Hay de Chastelet published his massive *Recueil de diverses pièces pour servir à l'Histoire*, and a team was set to work to draft

---

[82] Labatut, *Les Ducs et pairs*, p. 304.
[83] *MC*, II, p. 185 (consulta of 27 Oct. 1634).
[84] See the introduction by D.L. Shaw to his edition of Malvezzi, *Historia de los primeros años del reinado de Felipe IV* (London, 1968).
[85] Brown and Elliott, *A Palace*, ch. 7.

the Cardinal's memoirs.[86] In the great gallery of his château at Richelieu, which he never saw, his achievements were depicted in parallel with those of the heroes of antiquity, so that the passage of the French army into Italy in 1629 recalled Hannibal's crossing of the Alps.[87]

Both ministers, by placing their achievements in the context of time, were in effect bidding for eternal renown, against the calumnies of their contemporaries. Reputation, for themselves and their masters, was what they had always sought. But of what did this reputation, or glory, consist? In the first place it meant the conventional glory earned by victory in war. But both ministers were also deeply conscious that glory was won through peace as well as war, and both sought to magnify their monarchs through patronage of the arts. A life of Maecenas, published in 1626, was dedicated to Olivares as the minister 'if not of the Emperor Augustus, then of a more august emperor, to whom peace owes greater successes, and war more glorious triumphs'.[88] Richelieu for his part commissioned from the artist Jacques Stella around 1637 a rendering of the Liberality of Titus, in which Louis XIII as Titus tossed wooden balls to his subjects, to be redeemed for gifts of food and clothing, while the Cardinal stood in a toga at his side (fig. 6).[89]

For both men, the urge to appear as the champion of peace became more pressing with every year of war. 'The sole desire of my heart', wrote Olivares in 1636, 'is for the tranquillity of peace, keeping nothing that belongs to anyone else, but only what God gave Your Majesty – a peace so free of anxiety that Your Majesty can enrich your great realms and vassals, and let them flourish in justice, piety and ease.'[90] The court of Philip IV at the Buen Retiro suggested a determination to cultivate the pleasures of peace even amidst the horrors of war. Richelieu, too, with his promise of a new Augustan age in France, developed with increasing urgency the theme of peace during his final years of power. But, as he told the negotiators for the peace conference of 1637, it had to be 'a peace which is not subject in the future to any alteration',[91] and this inevitably

[86] Deloche, *Autour de la plume*, pp. 500 and 504.
[87] Labatut, *Les Ducs et pairs*, p. 303.
[88] Juan Pablo Martír Rizo, *Historia de la vida de Mecenas* (Madrid, 1626), dedication.
[89] *France in the Golden Age*, ed. Rosenberg, catalogue no. 100. The scene is described by Cassius Dio, LXVI, 25. Its identification, here presented for the first time, is due to Avraham Ronen and Umberto Laffi, whose response to my appeal for help is most gratefully acknowledged.
[90] AGS, Estado, legajo 2657, 'El Conde Duque sobre las proposiciones del capitán Marco Antonio Gandolfo', 1 Dec. 1636.
[91] Dickmann, *Acta Pacis Westphalicae. Instruktionen*, I, p. 50.

6 Jacques Stella, *The liberality of Titus* (detail).

meant a peace on France's terms. In his allegorical play, *Europe*, he depicted Europe rejecting the false charms of Ibère, with its spurious offers of peace. Francion, who comes to Europe's salvation, denounces these offers. Ibère, says Francion, 'knows how to speak of peace, but I know how to make it'.[92]

But France did not know, any more than Spain, how to bring peace to Europe. Throughout the nearly two decades in which Richelieu and Olivares held high office, the drums of war were never silent, and they would continue to sound for almost another two decades, during the ministerial careers of their successors, Mazarin and Haro. In the name of what Richelieu once called 'peace with honour',[93] both men waged unremitting war with a relentlessness that made them both hated and feared. It is enough to look at the 1640s to see the terrible legacy of their years in office. 'Italy, Spain, Germany, the Netherlands, Lorraine, Burgundy, but above all France', wrote Richelieu's perennial critic, de Morgues, in an epitaph, 'will not recover in a century from the ruin which the short passage of his fortune has made.'[94] A harsh and unjust verdict, no doubt, but as one reads the long list of the Cardinal's victims – of those executed, imprisoned, and banished[95] – it is hard not to consider, along with the achievements, the terrible price that he exacted in order to impose his vision of the state. The France he left behind him was, like the Spain of Olivares, a country seething with revolt; a country crushed by high taxation and reduced to misery; a country in the hands of tax-collectors and war-profiteers, and of officials who filled their own pockets as they preached the virtues of obedience in the name of that mystical entity, the royal authority. The Fronde, as much as the France of Louis XIV, was the legacy of Richelieu.

With such a record, and such a legacy, 'failure' and 'success' become almost meaningless terms as criteria for judgement. Was not the Cardinal's 'success' from one perspective, his 'failure' from another? Was he right, or was he wrong, as against Marillac, when he opted for war over reform? Was the Count–Duke correct in his judgement that peace with the Dutch on the terms of 1609 was too high a price for Spain to pay,

---

[92] Quoted Thuau, *Raison d'état*, p. 304.
[93] Grillon, III, p. 205 ('Avis au roi', c. 20 April 1628). For Olivares' use of a similar phrase, see above, p. 87.
[94] 'Abrégé de la vie du Cardinal de Richelieu', *Recueil*, p. 13.
[95] 'Liste des noms de ceux qui ont esté esloignez, emprisonnez, condamnez et suppliciez', *Archives Curieuses*, V, pp. 109–30.

or that as long as Richelieu survived there could be no tranquillity in Europe? As he brooded on the past in his exile at Toro, Olivares summarized in a letter to his secretary what he had learned from life.

It is no good speculating, Señor Antonio Carnero, or turning things over in one's mind, for this is the world, and so it always was; and there were we trying to achieve miracles and reduce the world to what it cannot be, when it is certain that the one certain thing about it is its instability and inconstancy and lack of gratitude. We entirely forgot God and placed our faith in men, and the more we turn this over in our minds, the madder we become.[96]

[96] *MC*, II, p. 279 (letter of 8 Aug. 1644).

Bibliography

Albertini, Rudolf von. *Das politische Denken in Frankreich zur Zeit Richelieus* (Marburg, 1951).

Albrecht, Dieter. *Richelieu, Gustaf Adolf und das Reich* (Munich–Vienna, 1959).

Alcalá-Zamora y Queipo de Llano, José, *España, Flandes y el Mar del Norte, 1618–1639* (Barcelona, 1975).

Alcedo, Marqués de, ed. *Discursos de Don Antonio de Mendoza* (Madrid, 1911).

Aldea Vaquero, Quintín. *Iglesia y Estado en la España del siglo XVII* (Comillas, 1961).

'Iglesia y estado en la época barroca', *Historia de España Ramón Menéndez Pidal*, xxv (Madrid, 1982), pp. 525–633.

Almansa y Mendoza, Andrés. *Cartas, 1621–1626* (Madrid, 1886).

Andrés, Gregorio de. 'Historia de la biblioteca del Conde–Duque de Olivares y descripción de sus códices', *Cuadernos Bibliográficos*, 28 (1972).

Archives Curieuses de l'Histoire de France, ed. F. Danjou, 2nd series, v (Paris, 1838).

Aubery, A. *Histoire du Cardinal Duc de Richelieu* (Paris, 1660).

Balzac, Jean-Louis Guez de. *Oeuvres*, 2 vols. (Paris, 1854 edn).

Baraude, Henri. *Lopez, agent financier et confident de Richelieu* (Paris, 1933).

Barozzi, Nicolò, and Berchet, Guglielmo. *Relazioni degli stati europei. Serie 1. Spagna*, 2 vols. (Venice, 1856).

Bataillon, Marcel. *Erasme et l'Espagne* (Paris, 1937; revised Spanish edn, *Erasmo y España* (Mexico, 1950).

'L'Académie de Richelieu, Indre-et-Loire', in *Pédagogues et juristes. Congrès du Centre d'Etudes Supérieures de la Renaissance de Tours: été 1960* (Paris, 1963), pp. 255–70.

Batiffol, Louis. *Richelieu et le roi Louis XIII* (Paris, 1934).

Autour de Richelieu (Paris, 1937).

Baxter, Douglas Clark. *Servants of the Sword. French Intendants of the Army, 1630–1670* (Urbana, 1976).

Bazy, J.P.A. *Etat militaire de la Monarchie Espagnole sous le règne de Philippe IV* (Poitiers, 1864).

Beauchamp, Comte de. *Louis XIII d'après sa correspondance avec le Cardinal de Richelieu* (Paris, 1902).

Bercé, Yves-Marie. *Histoire des croquants*, 2 vols. (Geneva, 1974).

Bertaud, Madeleine. 'Le Conseiller du prince, d'après les mémoires de Richelieu et son testament politique', in *Les Valeurs chez les mémorialistes français du XVIIe siècle avant la Fronde*, ed. N. Hepp and J. Hennequin (Paris, 1979), pp. 111–29.

Bireley, Robert. *Religion and Politics in the Age of the Counterreformation. Emperor Ferdinand II, William Lamormaini, S.J., and the Formation of Imperial Policy* (Chapel Hill, 1981).

Boissonnade, P. *Histoire de Poitou* (Paris, 1915).

Boiteux, L.-A. *Richelieu 'grand maître de la navigation et du commerce de France'* (Paris, 1955).

Bonney, Richard. *Political Change in France under Richelieu and Mazarin, 1624–1661* (Oxford, 1978).

The King's Debts. Finance and Politics in France, 1589–1661 (Oxford, 1981).

Bourgeois, Emile, and André, Louis. *Les Sources de l'histoire de France. Le XVIIe siècle, 1610–1715*, IV (Paris, 1924).

Boyajian, James C. *Portuguese Bankers at the Court of Spain, 1626–1650* (New Brunswick, 1983).

Briggs, Robin. *Early Modern France, 1560–1715* (Oxford, 1977).

Brightwell, P. J. 'The Spanish System and the Twelve Years' Truce', *English Historical Review*, 89 (1974), pp. 270–92.

'The Spanish Origins of the Thirty Years' War', *European Studies Review*, 9 (1979), pp. 409–31.

'Spain and Bohemia: the Decision to Intervene, 1619', *European Studies Review*, 12 (1982), pp. 117–41.

'Spain, Bohemia and Europe, 1619–1621', *European Studies Review*, 12 (1982), pp. 371–99.

Bronner, Fred. 'La unión de las armas en el Perú', *Anuario de Estudios Americanos*, 24 (1967), pp. 1133–77.

Brown, Jonathan, and Elliott, J. H. *A Palace for a King. The Buen Retiro and the Court of Philip IV* (New Haven–London, 1980).

Burckhardt, Carl J. *Richelieu*, 4 vols. (Munich, 1933–67); Eng. trans., *Richelieu and his Age*, 3 vols. (London, 1940–71).

Cabrera de Córdoba, Luis. *Relaciones de las cosas sucedidas en la corte de España desde 1599 hasta 1614* (Madrid, 1857).

Cánovas del Castillo, Antonio. *Estudios del reinado de Felipe IV*, 2 vols. (Madrid, 1888; 2nd edn, 1927).

Caro Baroja, Julio. *Inquisición, brujería y criptojudaísmo* (Madrid, 1970).

Carré, Henri. *La Jeunesse et la marche au pouvoir de Richelieu, 1585–1624* (Paris, 1944).

Casey, James. *The Kingdom of Valencia in the Seventeenth Century* (Cambridge, 1979).

Charron, Pierre. *La Sagesse* (Paris, 1671 edn).

Chevallier, Pierre. *Louis XIII* (Paris, 1979).

Church, William F. 'Cardinal Richelieu and the Social Estates of the Realm', *Album Helen Maud Cam*, II (Louvain–Paris, 1961), pp. 261–70.

Bibliography

'Publications on Cardinal Richelieu since 1945. A Bibliographical Study', *Journal of Modern History*, 37 (1965), pp. 421–44.

Richelieu and Reason of State (Princeton, 1972).

Clarke, J. Alden. *Huguenot Warrior: the Life and Times of Henri de Rohan, 1579–1630* (The Hague, 1966).

Colomès, Jean, ed. *Le Dialogue ' Hospital das Letras' de Don Francisco Manuel de Melo* (Paris, 1970).

Crozet, René. *La Vie artistique en France au XVIIe siècle* (Paris, 1954).

Deloche, Maximin. *La Maison du Cardinal de Richelieu* (Paris, 1912).

Autour de la plume du Cardinal de Richelieu (Paris, 1920).

Denis, Dom Paul. *Le Cardinal de Richelieu et la réforme des monastères bénédictins* (Paris, 1913).

Depping, G.B. 'Un Banquier protestant en France au XVIIe siècle. Barthélemy Herwarth', *Revue Historique*, 10 (1879), pp. 285–338, and 11, pp. 63–80.

Desjonquères, Léon. *Le Garde des Sceaux Michel de Marillac et son oeuvre législative* (Paris, 1908).

Dethan, Georges. *Gaston d'Orléans. Conspirateur et prince charmant* (Paris, 1959).

The Young Mazarin (London, 1977).

Mazarin: un homme de paix à l'âge baroque, 1602–1661 (Paris, 1981).

Devèze, Michel. *L'Espagne de Philippe IV*, 2 vols. (Paris, 1970–1).

Deyon, Pierre. 'A propos des rapports entre la noblesse française et la monarchie absolue pendant la première moitié du XVIIe siècle', *Revue Historique*, 231 (1964), pp. 341–56.

Dickmann, Fritz. 'Rechtsgedanke und Machtpolitik bei Richelieu', *Historische Zeitschrift*, 196 (1963), pp. 265–319.

Acta Pacis Westphalicae. Instruktionen, 1 (Münster, 1962).

Disney, A.R. *Twilight of the Pepper Empire* (Cambridge, Mass., 1978).

Domínguez Ortiz, Antonio. 'El Almirantazgo de los países septentrionales y la política económica de Felipe IV', *Hispania*, 7 (1947), pp. 272–90.

'El suplicio de Don Juan de Benavides', *Archivo Hispalense*, 2nd series, 76 (1956), pp. 1–13.

Política y hacienda de Felipe IV (Madrid, 1960).

La sociedad española en el siglo XVII, 2 vols. (Madrid, 1963–70).

Crisis y decadencia de la España de los Austrias (Madrid, 1969).

Dorival, Bernard. 'Art et politique en France au XVIIe siècle: la galerie des hommes illustres du palais cardinal', *Bulletin de la Société de l'Histoire de l'Art Français* (1973), pp. 43–60.

Elliott, J.H. *The Revolt of the Catalans* (Cambridge, 1963, reprinted 1984).

'El programa de Olivares y los movimientos de 1640', *Historia de España Ramón Menéndez Pidal*, xxv (Madrid, 1982), pp. 333–523.

'Self-Perception and Decline in Early Seventeenth-Century Spain', *Past and Present*, 74 (1977), pp. 41–61.

'Quevedo and the Count–Duke of Olivares', in *Quevedo in Perspective*, ed. James Iffland (Newark, Delaware, 1982), pp. 227–50.

'The Year of the Three Ambassadors', *History and Imagination. Essays in Honour of H.R. Trevor-Roper*, ed. Hugh Lloyd-Jones, Valerie Pearl and Blair Worden (London, 1981), pp. 165–81.

and Brown, Jonathan. *A Palace for a King*. See under Brown and Elliott.

and Peña, José F. de la. *Memoriales y Cartas del Conde Duque de Olivares*, 2 vols. (Madrid, 1978–80).

Erlanger, Philippe. *Cinq-Mars ou la passion et la fatalité* (Paris, 1962).

Evans, R.J.W. *The Making of the Habsburg Monarchy, 1550–1700* (Oxford, 1979).

Everat, Edouard. *Michel de Marillac. Sa vie, ses oeuvres* (Riom, 1894).

Fagniez, Gustave. *Le Père Joseph et Richelieu*, 2 vols. (Paris, 1891–4).

'L'Opinion publique et la presse politique sous Louis XIII, 1624–1626', *Revue d'Histoire Diplomatique*, 14 (1900), pp. 352–401.

'Fancan et Richelieu', *Revue Historique*, 107 (1911), pp. 59–78, and 310–22; 108 (1911), pp. 75–87.

Fayard, Janine. 'José González (1583?–1668), "créature" du comte-duc d'Olivares et conseiller de Philippe IV', in *Hommage à Roland Mousnier* (Paris, 1980), pp. 351–67.

Les Membres du Conseil de Castille à l'époque moderne, 1621–1746 (Geneva, 1979).

Fernández Alvarez, Manuel. 'El fracaso de la hegemonía española en Europa', *Historia de España Ramón Menéndez Pidal*, xxv (Madrid, 1982), pp. 635–789.

Don Gonzalo Fernández de Córdoba y la guerra de sucesión de Mantua y del Monferrato, 1627–1629 (Madrid, 1955).

Fernández Duro, Cesáreo. *Armada española, desde la unión de los reinos de Castilla y Aragón*, 9 vols. (Madrid, 1895–1903).

Fernández-Santamaría, J.A. *Reason of State and Statecraft in Spanish Political Thought, 1595–1640* (Lanham, 1983).

Fessenden, Nicholas B. 'Eperne and Guyenne: Provincial Politics under Louis XIII' (Dissertation, Columbia University, 1972).

Foisil, Madeleine. *La Révolte des nu-pieds et les révoltes normandes de 1639* (Paris, 1970).

Fumaroli, Marc. *L'Age de l'éloquence* (Geneva, 1980).

ed. *Mémoires de Henri de Campion* (Paris, 1967).

García, Carlos. *La oposición y conjunción de los dos grandes luminares de la tierra, o la antipatía de Franceses y Españoles* (1617), ed. Michael Bareau (Edmonton, 1979).

Gerhard, Dietrich. 'Richelieu', in *The Responsibility of Power*, ed. Leonard Krieger and Fritz Stern (New York, 1969), pp. 91–114.

González Palencia, Angel. *La Junta de Reformación* (Valladolid, 1932).

'Quevedo, Tirso y las comedias ante la Junta de Reformación', *Boletín de la Real Academia Española*, 25 (1946), pp. 43–84.

Günter, Heinrich. *Die Habsburger-Liga, 1625–1635*, Historische Studien LXII, ed. E. Ebering (Berlin, 1908).

Bibliography

Hamilton, Earl J. *American Treasure and the Price Revolution in Spain, 1501–1650* (Cambridge, Mass., 1934).

——— 'Spanish Banking Schemes before 1700', *Journal of Political Economy*, 57 (1949), pp. 134–56.

Hanotaux, Gabriel, and La Force, Duc de. *Histoire du Cardinal de Richelieu*, 6 vols. (Paris, 1893–1947).

Harding, Robert R. *Anatomy of a Power Elite. The Provincial Governors in Early Modern France* (New Haven–London, 1978).

Hassinger, Erich. 'Das politische Testament Richelieus', *Historische Zeitschrift*, 173 (1952), pp. 485–503.

Hauser, Henri. *La Pensée et l'action économiques du Cardinal de Richelieu* (Paris, 1944).

Hayden, J. Michael. *France and the Estates General of 1614* (Cambridge, 1974).

Henrard, P. *Marie de Médicis dans les Pays-Bas, 1631–1638*, Annales de l'Académie d'Archéologie de Belgique XXXI (Antwerp, 1875).

Herr, Richard. 'Honor versus Absolutism: Richelieu's Fight against Duelling', *Journal of Modern History*, 27 (1955), pp. 281–5.

Historia de España Ramón Menéndez Pidal, ed. José María Jover Zamora, XXV (*La España de Felipe IV*), (Madrid, 1982).

Houssaye, M. *Le Cardinal de Bérulle et le Cardinal de Richelieu, 1625–1629* (Paris, 1875).

Humbert, Jacques. *Une Grande Entreprise oubliée. Les Français en Savoie sous Louis XIII* (Paris, 1960).

Israel, Jonathan I. *The Dutch Republic and the Hispanic World, 1606–1661* (Oxford, 1982).

Jago, Charles. 'Habsburg Absolutism and the Cortes of Castile', *American Historical Review*, 86 (1981), pp. 307–26.

Jansen, Cornelius. *Le Mars françois* (French trans. of the *Mars Gallicus*, without place of publication, 1637).

Jover, José M. *1635. Historia de una polémica y semblanza de una generación* (Madrid, 1949).

Kagan, Richard L. *Students and Society in Early Modern Spain* (Baltimore, 1974).

Keohane, Nannerl O. *Philosophy and the State in France* (Princeton, 1980).

Kretschmer, Ernst. *Physique and Character* (2nd edn, New York, 1970).

Labatut, Jean-Pierre. *Les Ducs et pairs de France au XVIIe siècle* (Paris, 1972).

Lacour, Léopold. *Richelieu dramaturge et ses collaborateurs* (Paris, 1925).

Laurain-Portemer, Madeleine. *Etudes Mazarines*, I (Paris, 1981).

La Vaissière, Pierre de. *Un Grand Procès sous Richelieu. L'affaire du Maréchal de Marillac, 1630–1632* (Paris, 1924).

Lecler, Joseph. 'Politique nationale et idée chrétienne dans les temps modernes', *Etudes*, 214 (1933), pp. 385–405, 546–64, 683–702.

Lee, Sidney, ed. *The Autobiography of Edward, Lord Herbert of Cherbury* (London, 1886).

Lekai, Louis J. *The Rise of the Cistercian Strict Observance in Seventeenth*

Century France (Washington, 1968).

Leman, Auguste. *Urbain VIII et la rivalité de la France et de la Maison d'Autriche de 1631 à 1635* (Paris–Lille, 1920).

Richelieu et Olivarès (Lille, 1938).

Lloyd, Howell A. *The State, France and the Sixteenth Century* (London, 1983).

Lublinskaya, A.D. *French Absolutism: the Crucial Phase, 1620–1629* (Cambridge, 1968).

Lutz, Georg. *Kardinal Giovanni Francesco Guidi di Bagno* (Tübingen, 1971).

Magendie, M. *La Politesse mondaine et les théories de l'honnêteté, en France, au XVIIe siècle, de 1600 à 1660*, 1 (Paris, 1925).

Major, J. Russell. *Representative Government in Early Modern France* (New Haven–London, 1980).

Malvezzi, Virgilio. *Historia de los primeros años del reinado de Felipe IV*, ed. D.L. Shaw (London, 1968).

Mann, Golo, and Nitschke, August, eds. *Propyläen Weltgeschichte*, VII (Berlin, 1964).

Manzoni, Alessandro. *The Betrothed*, trans. Bruce Penman (Harmondsworth, 1972).

Marañón, Gregorio. *El Conde–Duque de Olivares. La pasión de mandar* (Madrid, 1936; 3rd, revised, edn, 1952).

Maravall, José Antonio. *Estudios de historia del pensamiento español. Siglo XVII* (Madrid, 1975).

Martimort, Aimé-Georges. *Le Gallicanisme de Bossuet* (Paris, 1953).

Martin, Henri-Jean. *Livre, pouvoirs et société à Paris au XVIIe siècle, 1598–1701*, 2 vols. (Geneva, 1969).

Marvick, Elizabeth Wirth. *The Young Richelieu. A Psychoanalytic Approach to Leadership* (Chicago, 1983).

Meinecke, Friedrich. *Die Idee der Staatsräson in der neueren Geschichte* (2nd edn, Munich–Berlin, 1925), Eng. trans., *Machiavellism* (London, 1957).

Melo, Francisco Manuel de. *Epanáforas de vária historia portuguesa*, ed. Edgar Prestage (Coimbra, 1931).

Le Mercure français (Paris).

Meuvret, Jean. *Etudes d'histoire économique: recueil d'articles* (Paris, 1971).

Moncada, Sancho de. *Restauración política de España*, ed. Jean Vilar (Madrid, 1974).

Mongrédien, Georges. *Le Bourreau du Cardinal de Richelieu. Isaac de Laffemas, 1584–1657* (Paris, 1929).

10 novembre 1630. La Journée des Dupes (Paris, 1961).

Moote, A. Lloyd. *The Revolt of the Judges. The Parlement of Paris and the Fronde, 1643–1652* (Princeton, 1971).

Morgues, Mathieu de. *Recueil de pièces pour la defense de la Reyne Mère* (Antwerp, 1643).

Mousnier, Roland. *La Vénalité des offices sous Henri IV et Louis XIII* (Rouen, 1945; 2nd edn Paris, 1971).

'Le Conseil du Roi de la mort de Henri IV au gouvernement personnel de

Bibliography

Louis XIV', *Etudes d'Histoire Moderne et Contemporaine*, 1 (1947), pp. 29–67.

'Le Testament Politique de Richelieu', *Revue Historique*, 201 (1949), pp. 55–71.

Fureurs paysannes (Paris, 1967).

Les Institutions de la France sous la monarchie absolue, 1 (Paris, 1974).

ed. *Lettres et mémoires adressés au Chancelier Séguier*, 2 vols. (Paris, 1964).

Novoa, Matías de. *Historia de Felipe IV, Rey de España*, Colección de documentos inéditos para la historia de España LXIX (Madrid, 1878).

O'Connell, D.P. *Richelieu* (London, 1968).

'A *Cause Célèbre* in the History of Treaty-Making: the Refusal to Ratify the Peace Treaty of Regensberg in 1630', *The British Year Book of International Law*, 42 (1967), pp. 71–90.

Oestreich, Gerhard. *Neostoicism and the Early Modern State* (Cambridge, 1982).

Orcibal, Jean. *Les Origines du Jansénisme*, II, *Jean Duvergier de Hauranne, Abbé de Saint-Cyran et son temps, 1581–1638* (Paris, 1947).

'Richelieu, homme d'église, homme d'état', *Revue d'Histoire de l'église de France*, 34 (1948), pp. 94–101.

Pagès, Georges. *La Monarchie d'ancien régime en France* (Paris, 1952).

La Guerre de Trente Ans, 1618–1648 (Paris, 1949).

'Autour du "grand orage". Richelieu et Marillac: deux politiques', *Revue Historique*, 179 (1937), pp. 63–97.

Parker, David. *La Rochelle and the French Monarchy* (London, 1980).

Parker, Geoffrey. *The Army of Flanders and the Spanish Road, 1567–1659* (Cambridge, 1972).

'Warfare', in *The New Cambridge Modern History*, XIII (Cambridge, 1979), ch. 5.

Pérez Moreda, Vicente. *Las crisis de mortalidad en la España interior, siglos XVI–XIX* (Madrid, 1980).

Petit, Jeanne. *L'Assemblée des Notables de 1626–1627* (Paris, 1936).

Picot, Gilbert. *Cardin Le Bret (1558–1655) et la doctrine de la souveraineté* (Nancy, 1948).

Pierret, Marc. *Richelieu ou la déraison d'état* (Paris, 1972).

Pillorget, René. *Les Mouvements insurrectionnels de Provence entre 1596 et 1715* (Paris, 1975).

Pintard, René. *Le Libertinage érudit dans la première moitié du XVIIe siècle* (Paris, 1943).

Pithon, Rémy. 'Les Débuts difficiles du ministère de Richelieu et la crise de Valteline, 1621–1627', *Revue d'Histoire Diplomatique*, 74 (1969), pp. 289–322.

Porchnev, Boris. *Les Soulèvements populaires en France de 1623 à 1648* (Paris, 1963).

Prestwich, Menna. 'The Making of Absolute Monarchy (1559–1683)', *France: Government and Society*, ed. J. M. Wallace-Hadrill and J. McManners (2nd edn, London, 1970).

Quevedo y Villegas, Francisco de. *Cómo ha de ser el privado*, in *Obras completas*, ed. Felicidad Buendía, II (6th edn, Madrid, 1967).

Ramírez, Alejandro. *Epistolario de Justo Lipsio y los Españoles, 1577–1606* (Madrid, 1966).

Ranum, Orest. *Richelieu and the Councillors of Louis XIII* (Oxford, 1963).

'Courtesy, Absolutism and the Rise of the French State, 1630–1660', *Journal of Modern History*, 52 (1980), pp. 426–51.

'Richelieu and the Great Nobility', *French Historical Studies*, 3 (1963), pp. 184–204.

Révah, I.S. *Le Cardinal de Richelieu et la restauration du Portugal* (Lisbon, 1950).

Richelieu, Collection Génies et Réalités, Hachette (Paris, 1972).

Richelieu, Armand du Plessis, Cardinal Duc de. *Lettres, instructions diplomatiques et papiers d'état du Cardinal de Richelieu*, ed. D.L.M. Avenel, 8 vols. (Paris, 1853–77).

Les Papiers de Richelieu. Section politique intérieure. Correspondance politique et papiers d'état, ed. Pierre Grillon (Paris, 1975–).

Maximes d'état et fragments politiques du Cardinal de Richelieu, ed. Gabriel Hanotaux (Paris, 1880).

Mémoires du Cardinal de Richelieu, ed. Société de l'Histoire de France, 10 vols. (Paris, 1907–31).

Testament Politique, ed. Louis André (Paris, 1947).

Instruction du chrestien (Poitiers, 1621).

Europe. Comédie héroique (Paris, 1643).

Traité qui contient la méthode la plus facile . . . pour convertir ceux qui se sont séparéz de l'Eglise (Paris, 1651).

Roca, Conde de la. *Fragmentos históricos*, see Vera y Figueroa, Juan Antonio de.

Roca, Emile. *De Richelieu à Mazarin, 1642–1644* (Paris, 1908).

Ródenas Vilar, Rafael. *La política europea de España durante la guerra de treinta años, 1624–1630* (Madrid, 1967).

Rodríguez Villa, Antonio. *Ambrosio Spínola, primer marqués de los Balbases* (Madrid, 1904).

Rohan, Henri, Duc de. *De l'interest des princes et estats de la chrestienté* (Paris, 1639).

Rosenberg, Pierre. *France in the Golden Age: Seventeenth-Century French Paintings in American Collections*, The Metropolitan Museum of Art, exhibition catalogue (New York, 1982).

Rowen, Herbert H. *The King's State* (New Brunswick, 1980).

Ruiz Martín, Felipe. 'La banca en España hasta 1782', in *El banco de España: una historia económica* (Madrid, 1970).

Russell, Conrad S.R. 'Monarchies, Wars and Estates in England, France, and Spain, c. 1580–c. 1640', *Legislative Studies Quarterly*, 7 (1982), pp. 205–20.

Sanabre, José. *La acción de Francia en Cataluña en la pugna por la hegemonía de Europa, 1640–1659* (Barcelona, 1956).

Sánchez-Arce, Nellie E., ed. *La segunda de Don Alvaro* (Mexico, 1960).

Bibliography

Comedia famosa de Ruy López de Avalos (Mexico, 1965).

Santamaría, Juan de. *República y policía cristiana* (Lisbon, 1621 edn).

Silhon, Jean de. *Le Ministre d'Estat* (Amsterdam, 1664 edn).

Simón-Diaz, José. *Historia del Colegio Imperial de Madrid*, 1 (Madrid, 1952).

Solomon, Howard M. *Public Welfare, Science and Propaganda in Seventeenth Century France. The Innovations of Théophraste Renaudot* (Princeton, 1972).

Stradling, R. A. *Europe and the Decline of Spain* (London, 1981).

Straub, Eberhard. *Pax et Imperium. Spaniens Kampf um seine Friedensordnung in Europa zwischen 1617 und 1635* (Paderborn, 1980).

Suárez Fernández, Luis. *Notas a la política anti-española del Cardenal Richelieu* (Valladolid, 1950).

Sutcliffe, F. E. *Guez de Balzac et son temps* (Paris, 1959).

Tallemant des Réaux. *Historiettes*, 1 (Paris, 1960).

Tapié, Victor-L. *La Politique étrangère de la France et le début de la guerre de Trente Ans, 1616–1621* (Paris, 1934).

La France de Louis XIII et de Richelieu (Paris, 1967); Eng. trans., *France in the Age of Louis XIII and Richelieu*, trans. and ed. D. McN. Lockie (London, 1974).

Thompson, I. A. A. *War and Government in Habsburg Spain, 1560–1620* (London, 1976).

Thuau, Etienne. *Raison d'état et pensée politique à l'époque de Richelieu* (Paris, 1966).

Thuillier, Jacques. *Rubens' Life of Marie de Medici* (New York, 1967).

Tomás y Valiente, Francisco. *Los validos en la monarquía española del siglo XVII* (Madrid, 1963).

Trevor-Roper, H. R. 'Spain and Europe, 1598–1621', *The New Cambridge Modern History*, IV (Cambridge, 1970), ch. 9.

Ungerer, Gustav. *A Spaniard in Elizabethan England: The Correspondence of Antonio Pérez's Exile*, 2 vols. (London, 1974–6).

Valdory, Guillaume de. *Anecdotes du ministère du Cardinal de Richelieu et du règne de Louis XIII*, 2 vols. (Amsterdam, 1717).

Anecdotes du ministère du comte duc d'Olivarés, tirées et traduites de l'Italien de Mercurio Siry, par Monsieur de Valdory (Paris, 1722).

Van der Essen, A. *Le Cardinal-Infant et la politique européenne de l'Espagne*, 1 (Brussels, 1944).

Vera y Figueroa, Juan Antonio de (Conde de la Roca). *Fragmentos históricos de la vida de D. Gaspar de Guzmán*, in Antonio Valladares, *Semanario Erudito*, II (Madrid, 1787), pp. 145–296.

Vilar, Jean. 'Formes et tendances de l'opposition sous Olivares: Lisón y Viedma, defensor de la patria', *Mélanges de la Casa de Velázquez*, 7 (1971), pp. 263–94.

Waddington, A. *La République des Provinces-Unies*, 2 vols. (Paris, 1895–7).

Watter, Pierre. 'Jean Louis Guez de Balzac's *Le Prince*: a Revaluation', *Journal of the Warburg and Courtauld Institutes*, 20 (1957), pp. 215–47.

Weber, Hermann. 'Richelieu et le Rhin', *Revue Historique*, 239 (1968), pp. 265–80.

Wollenberg, Jörg. *Richelieu* (Bielefeld, 1977).

Zeller, Berthold. *Richelieu et les ministres de Louis XIII de 1621 à 1624* (Paris, 1880).

Zeller, G. 'La Politique des frontières au temps de la prépondérance espagnole', *Revue historique*, 193 (1942), pp. 97–110.

Index

Index